Hitler Youth
To
Church of England
Priest

My Autobiography

George Gebauer

GEORGE GEBAUER

GEORGE GEBAUER, HITLER YOUTH TO CHURCH OF ENGLAND PRIEST, MY AUTOBIOGRAPHY.

Printed by Createspace

ISBN -13:978-1496129246

ISBN-10:1496129245

I dedicate this book to

Gladys

My dear wife and companion

Of 60 years

And on behalf of all the

German Prisoners of War,

Who spent some time in

Great Britain or the U.S.A.,

To the people of those countries

For their kindness.

Acknowledgements

I need to acknowledge those who made this book possible.

It was John Youngman, a lecturer in basic skills and work based learning, who finally convinced me that I should write down the story of my life for posterity.

In no particular order, I begin with Roger Clear. Never having possessed a computer of any kind, he bravely lent me his Laptop and said play with it, see how you get on with it; you can do no damage. Looking back it was indeed a great help and has proved invaluable ever since.

Having invested in a Laptop of my own, I started recording my story but I needed more help. I required someone to proof read and correct my mistakes. Here my great and dear friend Margaret came to the rescue. She corrected all my spelling mistakes and faulty grammar.

For the help Mike Tanner gave me with my computer and getting to know some of the ways it works, I will be forever grateful. Also for helping me to get the story of my life into book form and for his assistance with getting it published it as well.

I give grateful thanks to Chris Levy of woodleynet.co.uk for supplying the images of Ganger Camp on the Front Cover and in Chapter 17.

All the aforementioned helped me in their own and special way in getting this book written and published.

Contents

Prologue

Lounging in a comfortable armchair on the balcony of the P&O ship ARCADIA, halfway across the Atlantic, very relaxed, the sea calm, with a glass of champagne in my hand, which came with the compliments of the ship's company. Opposite me Margaret my very good friend, equally happy and content, also feeling blessed to be able to cruise the seven seas. I could not help thinking how far I have come in this life from very humble beginnings and I wondered how far back I could go into my childhood sitting here relaxed and happy. Being in my eighty sixth year this could prove very interesting.

The seeds to write about my life were sown over a number of years. For reasons best known to themselves people, friends, neighbours and acquaintances alike, found my life very interesting. The suggestion to write a book became more numerous and more frequent since my ordination as a priest in the Church of England.

I dare say the question many people ask themselves:

"How can a chap born in East Berlin, grown up in Hitler's Germany, fighting Allied Troops in Normandy, become a priest in the Church of England?"

Well, I decided to tell them.

After some persuasion I eventually put pen to paper to write the account of my life as a thank you to the British people for the way they received us, German Prisoners of War, immediately after the Second World War. The way they welcomed us, treated us and befriended us was very humbling and made us feel like one of them. There will be some that had a different experience to mine, but most had the same sentiments about the British people as I have. So on behalf of most of us who had the good fortune to spend some time in Britain and experience your hospitality and warm heartedness, I extend our heartfelt thanks.

But let it be understood that, whatsoever is written in the following pages, is the account of my life and mine alone. It is how I remember the past. As I have lived most of my life in England, British culture and the British way of life contributed a great deal to shape my own character. The friends I have made and am surrounded by come from all over the United Kingdom. My personal thanks to you all. After all, if it were not for your help and encouragement, this book would never have been written or printed.

Chapter 1

My Earliest Memories

What are my earliest and clearest childhood memories? Born in East Berlin on 25th November 1925 the earliest memory I can recall is when I was about four years old. We were a close family. My aunts and uncles and cousins were part of my daily life. We lived in close vicinity of one another, all in walking distances. What I remember most and what I remember best are the birthdays. With twenty eight of them in the extended family there were a lot of birthdays to go to. Birthdays were made a lot of in the twenties. Germany had experienced a time of great inflation. The German Mark not worth tuppence, the First World War still to be paid for. The people were poor. Families meant a lot to us then and we needed to support one another. Times were hard. What made these birthday parties so memorable to me, a four year old boy was that sometime during the evening we sang the 'Birthday Song', better known to the English speaking world as 'The Bumps'. There was no way I was willing to go home before that song was sung to the birthday child and lifted up high. To me that was the highlight of the evening. It had to be the evening because it was not until five or six o'clock in the evening that the family was complete. Although women and children gathered in the afternoon at the V.I.P. of the day's home, it was not until the last member of the family had arrived from work that everybody was happy. How soon that was depended very much in which part of town the men were working. After everyone was accounted for we sat down and had our evening meal after which the ladies retreated into the kitchen to do the chores, whilst the men sat around the table putting the world to rights. The children went into a corner to play or into another room if there was one. That is as far as I can go back and paint a clear picture. What I find so remarkable now, looking back, we seldom, if ever squabbled.

Something else I can recall very clearly from around that time, money was in short supply. The world was in the midst of a depression. We all lived on a shoestring and a very tight budget. I remember well the occasions when by Thursday night the money had run out and the larder was empty and cupboards bare. To overcome this, the family decided to gather in one of the homes taking turns cooking the evening meal for the family, using the wage packet of whoever arrived first at the chosen home to get the provisions for the evening meal. Then it was a rush to get to the corner store in time and buy groceries and other items of food before they closed for the night. The amount was quite substantial as it included bread and butter for next day's breakfast as well. As the breadwinners arrive with their wage packets one by one the ladies sorted out the finances whilst the meal was cooking, the men chatted about the day's work and worldly matters. The children were unable to contribute to the family purse as we were all too young to go out to work, except my two brothers who had left school by then and were apprentices at that time. One a glazier the other an electrician, not their first choice it must be said. One wanted to be baker the other a butcher. As apprentices all they could expect was a Mark or two a week for pocket money from their employers. I know, when in later years we talked about our youth they felt very badly about it. They knew they were a liability to our parents.

Thankfully my father was always in full employment as a railwayman, able to provide his family with all the basic needs. It was his childhood dream to become an engine driver, sadly he failed his eye test when it was discovered he was colour blind. The railway company offered him a job as a white collar worker, but he declined as he could not see himself as a pen pusher. But he stayed with the railway working as a porter. Working at Friedrich Strasse station, that was used by most of the international diplomats and business people as the start or end of their journeys; he often made more on tips during the week than his wage packet amounted to. How much depended upon which shift he was on. His helpful and caring nature would have helped as well. He was also a man with great patience and good at creating things as well at D.I.Y.. My Father made all our toys, mainly out of wood. He made dolls houses for the girls, not only for my sisters, but also for nieces and girls of friends. At one Christmas he made a train for me consisting of an engine, tender, carriage and goods wagon. No track to run on of course, but that did not matter, with no restrictions, I could use the whole of the floor in the sitting room to run my train. To complete the set he also made a station for my train to pull in to. Throughout my youth I never knew my father to sit around not doing anything. I remember well, during the war, when things were in short supply and one needed either a ration book or coupons to buy anything, he taught himself how to make slippers. He bought himself an adjustable last, wax, pitch and a ball of good string as well as two needles suitable for sewing soles to uppers. Then he went scrounging for off cuts from a local tailor, whom he knew well, and the leather from a number of cobblers in our area. The idea of using wax and pitch was to make the string waterproof. He first waxed the string, than pitched it to make it lasting. What he did in fact, he turned the string into yarn which became almost indestructible. The first two or three pairs were for the family. Once he had the technique right he made slippers to order and they were sound, sturdy and lasting.

Holidays during that time were spent in the country. Luckily, our parents as well as most of our aunts and uncles had relatives in the provinces. Easter holidays were usually in the country with mum's cousins in Selisia, a village called Oberquelle, meaning 'Upper Spring.' The summer holidays were by the sea more often than not, on the isle of Ruegen in fact, where relatives of one of my Godmothers lived. These holidays were always something to look forward to as open spaces in our part of town were few and far between and on the small side. The reason we could travel to these places every year was because we had free railway passes, as our father was employed on the railways. I always enjoyed these holidays I must say, whether in the country or by the sea.

When staying with cousins in the country it was on a large estate. They lived in cottages, situated in the grounds of the Schloss, as these big houses are known by in Germany. The workers who lived there were all employed in the big house, if not as butlers or maids, then in work associated with the house, such as coachman or gardener. My folks were gardeners or coachmen except one cousin; he was the chief mechanic on the estate and mostly drove heavy farm machinery which was beginning to become more and more evident on large estates and farms just before the Second World War

Five or six kilometres from Oberquelle was a village that belonged to the estate. These places were known as Dominion. The entire place, lock, stock and barrel were part of the estate. Most of the farmworkers and their families lived in the village which was really a large farmyard as all the livestock was housed there, cows, pigs, poultry, also the draught horses and all the farm machinery. As far as I can recall I never saw any sheep in all the years I went there. The buildings, cow pens, pig sties, hen houses, stables, barns and other buildings, arranged in a square made up the farmyard. The cottages for the farm workers were just a short distance away Back in Oberquelle, the Schloss overlooked a large area of parkland. At the back of the house were the cottages for the families that worked in the big house. Nearby the other outbuildings such as stables for the coach horses, tack room, coach house as well as other useful buildings. Here a man by the name of Hartman, a distance relative, was in charge. He looked after everything including me when I was around. It was a lovely, tranquil, peaceful setting. I can see it even now. The open space between the house and the cottages and outbuildings was nicely landscaped. In the centre of this open space was a water feature, a landscaped pond, not really large enough to be called a lake. It was fed from a spring-well which was next to it. The water was taken from the spring through a pipe to a pump like structure. From there it flowed into the pond and it did so day and night twenty four hours a day, summer and winter. The spring supplied the house with fresh water as well as the cottages that were in the grounds of the home farm. In the early morning and in the still of the evening the sound of the running water, constantly flowing into the pond, sounded heavenly to me. It sounded like being part of a symphony of nature being played in a beautiful setting in the country. The water level of the pond remained constant because any surplus water was channelled into the main street of the village where it flowed merrily down the centre of the street and at the end of the street turned into a babbling brook. Hence the name of the village; Oberquelle – Upper Spring!

Whilst the grown-ups were out to work somewhere on the estate getting on with their daily task I spend most of the day with the coachman. He took me under his wing and taught me all sorts of useful and practical things. Wherever he went I followed, that meant an early start to the day. We were out and about by 6 o'clock in the morning, every morning, except on Sunday, when I spent the day with my cousin Ernst and his wife, who were the hosts during my stay in the country. The first job of the day was checking on the livestock. That meant looking in on the horses. It was in late March or April that I was visiting the family, coinciding with the time when the mares have their foals. An anxious time for all concerned, so our first call was to look in at the mares and foals to see that they were alright.

Being with the horses was great fun and a great experience especially when the foals were still young and with the mares. As all young livestock, they had the time of their lives running round and round chasing each other and kicking their heels. Satisfied that all was well we turned our attention to the rest of the animals. Feeding, watering and cleaning done, we went home and had breakfast and started again at nine o'clock and worked our way through the agenda of the morning. The jobs we tackled were wide ranging. In the tack room the harnesses that were required for the day were checked and got ready, cleaned and polished if necessary as well as any other equipment requested. Mr Hartman was also doing odd jobs in the 'Big House' from time to time. Occasionally I accompanied him and met the Baron and the Baroness as well as the Baron's mother. The Dowager Lady was a real darling to me. Sometimes, when the weather was nice, she would request the trap to be made ready to drive out to the village to see the workers and talk to them without the manager bring present. Usually she was taken round the estate by car with the manager in attendance.

Horse and trap ready we took it across to the house and waited for her Ladyship. When she came out, which was always on time, Mr Hartman assisted her to get into the trap whilst I was holding the horse. When she was settled I handed her the reins and off she went. Round about the time when we expected her back home we found ourselves a job near the house so that we could assist her Ladyship when enlightening. There was then just one more task before lunch, taking the horse back to the stables and that could prove quite tricky, that is why Mr Hartman took charge here. As everybody knows who ever handled horses, when they return home and find themselves in familiar surroundings, they are rather anxious to get to their stable and they become difficult to handle, so they need a firm hand from a person they can trust and whose voice they know.

On one occasion, when I was a little older and the mother of the Baron got to know me better, she invited me to take her out to the village. As you might well have guessed, I did not decline the offer. She handed me the reins and off we went. Imagine what a thrill that gave me, me, a ten year old, driving her Ladyship through the country side. It was also my first ever visit to the village. I had been nearby when we took lunch to Ernst, as occasionally he made a very early start, leaving home before anyone else was up and about. He left without his lunch box and we took it out to him later to the place on the estate where ever he happened to be working and that could be near the village of course. But here I was proudly holding the reins, the first time in charge of something. Some villagers may well have been surprised seeing a strange young boy driving her Ladyship round the estate. But it happened and it is true. On our return to the home farm Mr Hartman was waiting, rather anxiously I suspect, to hear how we got on and more worried about the horse than anything else, helped her Ladyship to enlighten, took the horse back to the stables, patted me on the back and said: "Well done!"

There was another occasion that is as clear in my mind today as on the day it happened. As it was a fine, sunny day, the Baron decided to take one of the hunters and ride out to the farm instead of taking the car. On his return he asked me if I would like to mount and ride back to the stable instead of leading the horse. Would I? Without thinking twice about it I nodded and said yes. The Baron and Mr Hartman then lifted me into the saddle and the fun began, for the two men that is! Never having been on a horse I was totally lost as what to do. The horse knew what to. It took off straight away before I took hold of the reins even, made its way across the courtyard, around the pond and then without hesitation made for the stables where I ducked just in time before we went through the door and into its stall, as horses seem to do when they get home. The Baron and Mr Hartman could see what was going on and laughed their heads off. Mr Hartman said I looked like a sack of potatoes on that horse. But all ended well with no damage done. Needless to say I have never been on a horse since.

These were happy and carefree Easter holidays for me back in the Nineteen Thirties, made largely possible because of my free railway pass. Each member of the family could have up to three a year. My uncle and aunt did not mind feeding an extra mouth, not having children of their own they were delighted to have a child around the house for a while. They produced much of the basic food themselves. Potatoes and other vegetables they grew in their garden or allotment. There was a henhouse at the bottom of the garden and plenty of space for a chicken run or two. The occasional rabbit came from friends out in the country who worked on the estate. The employees also had fresh milk every day as well as firewood supplied by the estate as part of their wages. Happy days indeed and Mr

Hartman made all the difference, kind, caring, helpful. Who can forget a man like that?

How different the Summer Holidays were. They were spent with one of my aunt's siblings who lived on the Isle of Ruegen in the Baltic Sea. This time it was for two weeks in towns instead in the country. The first week was in Bergen, the capital of the island, with my aunt's brother who was a butcher. What a time I had with them. Again there were no children in the marriage, so a child around the house for a while was very welcome. To get onto the island was quite complicated in the days before they built the bridge. This time we travelled north out of Berlin instead of east, so the scenery and place names were different, which made a welcome change. When we arrived at Stralsund, the town where we caught the ferry to get onto the island, the train was divided as only the carriages that continued the journey were taken aboard the ferry. That took quite a while but nonetheless interesting to watch as the carriages were unhooked one by one and then shunted onto the ferry to continue their journey all the way to Sweden.

When all the carriages that went to Sweden were aboard, the journey continued across the sound and, arriving on the island the train was put together again and on we travelled to our next stop, Bergen. There I was met and warmly greeted and taken to the house which was my home for the next week where a meal was waiting for me. It was late afternoon by now and having made a very early start, with just a sandwich or two on the train, I was ready for a big meal. Big in as much it may only have been a two or three course meal, but the portions were large, it was tasty and I was very hungry as one expects a young, growing lad to be. The meal over I was anxious to go out and see what if anything had changed since my last visit, either with the outbuildings, the yard, the slaughterhouse, stables or anything else, usually very little, if anything at all. Young, growing boys get tired and after a long, in many ways exciting day, it was an early night for me, looking forward to all the things there were to do in the next week. The tasks would be many and varied.

The uncle I stayed with was a master butcher running his own business which consisted of his own slaughterhouse on the premises, a shop attached to the house and a market stall on Saturdays in the town centre. Market day was the highlight of the week, all work that had gone before throughout the week bore fruit on market day in the town square. This is how the week usually worked out. Monday was scrubbing up day when everything that was used the previous week in the handling of meat and other foodstuff was thoroughly cleaned and scalded if necessary including the slaughterhouse and holding pens for the livestock. The process of buying the animals began on Tuesday when we went out into the country visiting farms looking for suitable cattle, pigs and sheep as well as poultry for the next weekend to be sold as meat or meat products in shop and market. If the right animals could not be found, there was always the next day to complete the search. Wednesday was collecting day when what was purchased the previous day was loaded into the van and taken back to town and securely penned as there was no more food given, only water was freely accessible. The pigs usually proved to be the most troublesome. Cattle and sheep sometimes came on foot, led by the farmer or one of his workers. They often stayed in town to do some other business. Pigs always had to be transported by cart and even then it did not always go as planned. To this day I remember clearly the time we had a particularly determinate pig on board. Right from the outset it was determined to jump off the cart, even though we had a thick, strong net to keep it safely on board. We had to stop several times on the way home to tighten the net, especially on corners where gaps had appeared. Try as we would, the pig would not settle down and in the end broke out, escaped and the chase was on. As everyone, who has any experience with pigs knows, a pig on the run is not easy to catch. They are quite crafty these creatures, as well as intelligent and very stubborn too. With the help of other people we eventually cornered it and got it back on the cart. Being tired and worn out it settled down and gave us no more trouble or anxiety for the rest of the journey. Back at the yard we got the pig into the sty without further problems, tired but thankful. We went indoors for our lunch which was rather later than planned but we did not care, we were happy to know, all the animals bought the day before were safely in their pens, sties or coops.

But the day did not end there. After a little rest, off to work we went again. Now we got everything ready for the next day. Thursday was slaughter day. Everything had to be ready and in place as an early start was needed to get through all the work that needed to be done. The boiler was lit, the knives sharpened, choppers, pens, bowls and dishes made ready and put in place so that everything was handy to grab when and where required. Satisfied that all was well, following a last look at the animals to see that they had settled, we then had the rest of the day to ourselves. I said we, although the only child in the house, there were other children about, mostly from the workers my uncle employed. They were my companions and playmates during my stay in Bergen.

Thursday dawned and up with the lark the long day began. That was for the grownups, the children got onto the act later in the day. First to be dealt with was the beef stock, usually only one animal. By the time we, the children, got to the scene the carcase was already quartered and hung up. We just helped to clear up and got the slaughterhouse ready for the sheep which were next. When the men were ready to proceed with their work, slaughtering the animals that is, we again amused ourselves playing somewhere in the yard or adjoining fields until we were required to help to get everything ready for the pig to be slaughtered. This time we stayed within shouting distance of the slaughterhouse because once the pig was killed we were required urgently. Why? Well, I will tell you. As soon as the pig is dead the blood is pumped out of the carcase into a bowl. This is achieved by using one of the forelegs as a leaver to pump the blood out of the body. This was done by one of the children, whilst at the same time another child was preventing the blood from congealing by putting one hand, with fingers spread wide open, into the bowl of blood, stirring it vigorously. That blood was used later in the day in the production of black pudding. Once all the blood was out of the pig the hard work really began. The carcase was put into a trough which then was filled with boiling water and the task of scraping all the hair and bristles off got under way. That I remember was quite hard work to me, but still, I got on with the job feeling quite grown up doing it. The women that came to help on that day usually busied themselves with the poultry, plucking and dressing them and generally getting the birds ready for market day.

As for the carcases, they were expertly dealt with by the hired help and sorted into various cuts that made up the joints for cooking. The offal and other offcuts were sorted quickly and cooked, where appropriate, to be made into sausages and other meat products later in the day or evening. Whilst all these activities were going on, the slaughterhouse was turned into a sausage factory as various kinds were manufactured. The first to be made were the kind that needed smoking for a while such as frankfurters, only we knew them then as Wiener Knack Wurst. That type of sausage had to be ready to be put into the smoking chamber before anyone could call it a day and go home. As I said, Thursdays were long, hard days. Fridays were taken up with the weekend trade in the shop, which my aunty looked after, and getting ready for the market the next day. Also on Friday, the meat that was yet to be used, was made into pate', pies and all kinds of sausages. All the work done, the cleaning and clearing up began. That task usually took us up to teatime or even early evening. Then I had my reward, something I was really happy to have been part of, which made the whole week and all the work I put into it worthwhile for me, which I considered to be my wages if you like, eating frankfurters straight from the smoking chamber. Eaten immediately whilst they are still warm they taste brilliantly. To this day I can still taste that delicious flavour. That naturally enough, gave me a liking for frankfurters. Even now I enjoy a certain make of them. If they are fresh and served with potato salad, preferably homemade, they make a wonderful snack or light lunch.

Saturday was market day and as on most other days it meant an early start to get to the market as soon as possible. Once there, the stall had to be erected, the meat and other products laid out and displayed to catch the early shoppers. After all, the early bird catches the worm. The market closed at 1 pm and after we loaded the unsold meat and meat products back into the van we made our way home. But before we could call it a day we first unloaded the van. Put the meat and other perishable goods into the refrigerators. By the time we done all that it was teatime again. But never mind we all had a good week. As always a wonderful meal was waiting for us back in the house and with it another week in Bergen came to an end. Next morning I caught the train to Sassnits and the week by the sea began.

That week was completely different from the one that had just come to an end, not only was it by the sea but it was also in a sea port. In some ways, understandably so, it lacked some of the excitement I had in Bergen. Not that there were any interesting things to do or to see. There is a lot going on in any port, be it sea or airport. The arrivals as well as departures of ferries are quite thrilling in a way, as they come perhaps from faraway places and some of the passengers on board may set foot on German soil for the very first time. For some people it may have been their first journey by sea or even their first time abroad, who can tell? A day at the docks was certainly included during my stay in Sassnits. When the weather was dry, warm and sunny we went down to the beach, where we looked forward bathing in the sea and with the Baltic Sea not being tidal, the water's edge was never far away. We often popped into the water and splashed about having great fun. If on the other hand it was cool, cloudy and windy we took a stroll along the shore, looking for pieces of amber of which we found quite a number over the years, none of any great value it must be said. But come what may, on one day during my stay, a visit to the "Koenigstul"; (The King's Throne) was a must. It is a beauty spot high up on the chalk cliff with a fabulous view out over the sea. To get to it we either walked along the shore or more often than not took the scenic route on top of the cliffs which led through woods and copse all the way. The return journey back to town usually was an inland route. Again, it took us mainly through forest and woodland. The attraction here was the wild berries. Both wild strawberries as well as blueberries were ripe or ripening. Needless to say we made frequent stops along the way and picked a handful or two of this sweet tasting fruit. It takes a lot to beat the flavour of ripe, wild berries, they are simply delicious. Almost out of this world one might say. Yes, they were happy, carefree days I must say. It may not come as a surprise then that I was not aware of Hitler creating a vast holiday complex on the island, as did many more of my generation. Even if I did, it would not have meant anything to me anyway. These were my annual holidays in the thirties and I still remember them well. In any case I had my last school summer holiday in July 1939. The outbreak of war in September that year changed everything.

With my cousin Dorchan

A.

Nr. ~~736~~

Berlin am 25. November 19 25

Vor dem unterzeichneten Standesbeamten erschien heute, der Persönlichkeit nach durch Heiratsschein ~~unbekannt~~ anerkannt,

Max Otto Gebauer, Gipsträger

wohnhaft in Berlin, Pfannschuppe 13,

und zeigte an, daß von der Johanne Margarete Gertrud Gebauer geborene Roesler, seiner Ehefrau,

wohnhaft bei ihm

zu Berlin abends

am ~~fünf und zwanzig~~ / ~~im~~ November des Jahres tausend neunhundert ~~fünf und~~ zwanzig ~~nachmittags~~ mittags

um ~~siebeneinviertel~~ Uhr ein ~~Knabe~~

geboren worden sei und daß das Kind ~~den~~ Vornamen

Gerhard

erhalten habe

Vorgelesen, genehmigt und ~~unterschrieben~~

Otto Gebauer

Der Standesbeamte.

Sorge[?]

27

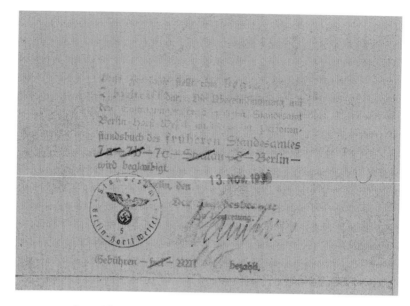

Certified Copy of my Birth Certificate

Chapter 2

Early School Days

I left school in March 1940 to start my apprenticeship as an electrician in one of the railway works in Berlin. Leaving school can be quite a wrench. You leave familiar surroundings which strangely enough gave you a sense of security and now you face an uncertain future and your mind goes back to your first day of school.

No child in Germany will ever forget the first day at school. It says good bye to mother quite happily knowing that just after two hours she will be back outside the school gate to greet you with a great 'Zuckertuete'; a cone shaped carton filled with all kinds chocolates, sweets and fruit. Good psychology I think. I am sure we are all afraid of the unknown to some extent, some more than others. For a child of 6, as it was in Germany in my time, here in the U.K. even earlier at 5 years of age, just think how that little heart must be pounding as it is being taken to the school gate, then expected to let go of the security it has felt and known ever since birth, now being asked to let go of mother's hand and to put its hand and trust into a hand of a stranger who then takes you to an unknown environment, meeting strange faces, unfamiliar smells, with unaccustomed voices speaking to you. That is enough to scare any child whatever the age. But a lot of this unknown fear and anxiety is taken away by the knowledge that two hours later, which may seem a lifetime to a child, your mum and may be other members of the family will be waiting for you at the school gate where earlier you let go of the person that guarded and protected you is there to welcome you back into her arms with that Zuckertuete, which might be larger than yourself. The fear that was there as the first day of school approached is gone, if not gone than greatly diminished by the hope, if not knowledge, that the new phase in your life is mapped out and secure. That pattern is with us throughout our life. From the beginning to the end, from birth to death, because most of us, if not all of us, fear the unknown and the final question; after death, what?

My Second cousins and their children on completion of their first day at school with their Zuckertuete

Not that this kind of question bothers a child of that age, nor the philosophy that goes with it. Knowing there is a reward after something that has to be endured makes most children look forward to their first day at school and even enjoying the whole experience. I took it in my stride, I know, and by and large enjoyed my school days. Looking back now and thinking about it makes me realise how lucky and how blessed I was having the support of my father as well as my two brothers, who had left school by then and started their respective apprenticeships, one to be a glazier, the other an electrician. My sister, being four years older than myself, was already at school when I started and like my mother was inclined to care more about my physical wellbeing. Truth were known, I enjoyed going to school, partly because learning came easily to me and I had no problems recalling things that were taught in class earlier. If I got stuck over something my father or my brothers would spend time with me until things clicked and I could understand the subject. So I trotted off to school happily every morning on my little own. My mother took me only one more time after the first day just to make sure her little boy knew the way, after that I went by myself. How differently it is today, when nearly as many grownups make the trek to school as children. It's a sad reflection of the times we live in when streets are not as safe as they used to be.

In the eight years I was at school I had only one change when in October 1934 we left the East End of Berlin and moved into the suburbs, the district of Lichtenberg. The reason being my mother was expecting another baby. With the two oldest children independent of the parental home, my father felt we could make the move and provide a better environment for the expected baby. As the area round the Posener Strasse and Ruedersdorfer Platz, where the four of us grew up as children, was quite a busy one. It was part of an artery that connected the main railway station in East Berlin,

Schlesinger Bahnhof in my days and later renamed Ost Bahnhof, to the main thoroughfare that took traffic out of the city to the east of Berlin and East Germany. With ever increasing traffic on the road it was becoming more dangerous by the day for children to grow up and play there. The accommodation too left much to be desired. It was a densely built up area of four story high apartment blocks. The ground floor was usually made into shops with the upper stories made into flats. There often was a tunnel that led from the street to a courtyard at the back of the building where in most cases there was yet another block or blocks of flats surrounding the courtyard. The buildings at the back were occupied either by hauliers for storage, sometimes by light engineering or manufacturing companies. There were places where yet another tunnel led to another backyard. In our case the buildings surrounding the yard at the back were dwellings. We lived in one of them on the first floor; in fact we occupied two adjoining flats. Most of these flats consisted of one or two rooms and a kitchen. The two flats we occupied, one was made up of one room and a kitchen, the other of two rooms and the kitchen. One of the kitchens was turned into a bedroom for one of the boys. That gave us four rooms and the kitchen at the end of the flats we used as the kitchen, as it was the bigger of the two. Behind our block of flats was another courtyard which was turned into a lovely garden area with two walnut trees, one at either end of the garden. The garden was kept tidy and planted by the tenants as I remember. My father often tended the flowers and shrubs in the spring and during the summer, but then he loved gardening. This type of area was not unique to Berlin between the two world wars I should imagine. Other big cities in Western Europe and in North America had similar areas and developments I would think.

There was another reason my parents felt we should move. As I said, it was a busy thoroughfare with trams running every few minutes all day long and just about a hundred yards away five roads converged, where in the late twenties and early thirties, when the political parties in Germany fought hard to gain supremacy over their rivals often met and came to blows. The three main contenders were the Liberals, Communists and Nationalists which later became known as the Nazis. In the run up to the elections in 1933 a lot of street fighting took place between the various factions especially so at weekends. On Saturday afternoons and/or any time on Sunday, marching columns coming, from different directions, converging at the big road junction, with brass bands leading them. As they met invariably fighting broke out. Usually it started off with fist fighting and then the party at the losing end drew fire arms and the shooting began. At that point any onlooker dived for cover or made for the nearest doorway and slammed the door fast and stayed there until after the police arrived and broke up the fighting, made several arrests and sent the parties back to where they came from. As a five year old I did not see any danger as I did not understand what was going on. War and bloodshed, fighting for power meant nothing to me. What drew me to these events were the marching bands and their music. When there was just one party coming down the road I tagged along with them marching in step with the music enjoying myself. Usually their demonstration ended near my auntie's flat, so I knew my way home quite well and never got lost. That fascination for brass bands and their music got me into trouble on May Day in 1934 but about that later.

Because the facilities where we lived in the Posener Strasse were very basic, was one more reason why my parents desired a move before the baby arrived. The flats were small; they consisted either of one room and a kitchen or two rooms and a kitchen. We occupied two adjoining ones and used the smaller kitchen as an extra bedroom. In the kitchen there was a cooking range, heated by solid fuel, two gas rings, a basin or sink and a cold water tap. Just imagine the time, effort and work there was for every member of the family to have a bath at the week end. To enable anyone to lift the bath tub to pour the water into the sink after the bath was quite laborious too. It meant a lot of water had first to be bailed out to make it light enough to be lifted. To make it easy for all concerned, whenever we could effort it we went to a public bath. My two brothers did so regularly as soon as they began to earn some money. On each landing there was just one toilet for the use off by the occupiers of the four flats. How many might need to use it at any given time one never knew, but we managed. After a while one gets used to it, after all, it's no good crying for the moon when you know you cannot get what you want. There was a small park area not far away where we could go to and play. It was meant for mothers and babies to come and enjoy some sunshine and fresh air and not ball games for growing, boisterous boys. Also it was a little way from home but on the way to school, so my mother was not worried that I might get lost on the way there and back. I had travelled that route practically every day since I was born. When still in the pram, my brothers being twelve years older often were asked by our mother, to take me with them when they went to the park to play. Partly to get me out into the air and partly so that she could get on more quickly with the house work. Now boys being boys, it did not come as a surprise to me when later at family gatherings, to learn, that after having a wonderful time playing ball games, they went off blissfully happy, goodness knows where to, forgetting all about their little brother Gerhart in the pram back at the park under some bush or other. When eventually they did get home, without me needless to say, my mother nearly died of shock thinking the worst, as mothers do. At the double my brothers returned to the park, now beginning to get worried too. As we know now, all turned out well in the end or I would not be here telling the story. They found me well, happy and unharmed at the spot they left me.

When we lived in Posener Strasse 13 we had a good sized garden at the eastern outskirts of the city, a place called Baumschulen Weg, which might be translated as a tree nursery or arboretum, a large area developed into allotments with plots large enough to have substantial summer houses on them. We often stayed there over night in the summer and at weekends as well as in the Easter and summer holidays. Sometimes aunts, uncles and cousins would be there as well, not all at once of course but a few at the time as the house had two large bedrooms and an enormous dining area with a kitchen at one end. On the land there were a variety of apple trees as well as plumb, pear and cherry trees of which some were near and around the house, others were surrounding the large lawn area and provided welcome shade on warm, sunny summer days. There were also fruit bushes of each and every kind as well as one corner, a quarter area of the whole plot I recall, set aside for the kitchen garden on which was also the strawberry plot. The only setback, for me anyway, that it was quite a distance to walk from the station. There were few cars about in the thirties and in any case the roads on the allotment area were unmade and could not have coped with the traffic if everybody had come by car. So it was by public transport that we made our way out into the fresh air. The only snag was that long walk from the station. It took fifteen minutes to walk to the allotments and at least another ten minutes or more, to get to our plot. Always heavy laden of course. On the way out with provender and on the way home with produce from the garden. Everybody, without exception, had to carry his or her share. But the situation of the garden and the joy of being out in the open in the fresh air and being able to play safely made up for any inconvenience. Even the long trek back to the station at the end of the day when everybody was tired and worn out did not spoil our day in the country. Yet we always had to keep one eye on the clock not to miss the train which we did more than once it has to be said. That meant we had to wait for half an hour for the next one and that is not funny on a cold, windy platform when you are tired.

As I said there was the plus side. It was in the open, it was in a wonderful location. It may have been half an hour's walk from the station, but it was only five minutes through the woods to the river and being near a river is always fascinating. Yes, we often popped across and enjoyed the ever changing river scene. In the summer there were the pleasure boats making their way up river with the day trippers looking forward to a day in the country. There were the rowing boats up and down the river as well as the canoes, paddle boats and other crafts. On a warm summer evening there was the joy and pleasure to see the lights flicker along the shore opposite and the pleasure boats returning all lit up with the music from the band on board drifting across the water and maybe a touch of envy not having been part of it. Yes they were happy, care free childhood days as I recall except for the one occasion when my mother certainly was frantically worried. First of May 1934 was May Day.

Ever since I can remember the First of May was a public holiday, Labour Day. In the days before Hitler came to power the various political parties staged their rallies all over town and people that had an affinity with them went along to these rallies to make their allegiance known and as I said, sooner or later during the day on which these marches took place the routes of rival parties would meet and fighting broke out. The police would arrive, separate them, maybe make one or two arrests and life returned to normal. All this changed after the rise to power by the Nationale Sociale Arbeiter Partei. From then on Hitler ruled O.K. Any political party opposing Hitler was banned. Germany had become a one party state. Hitler and his Nazi Party began to dictate the life of the German nation. The streets were quieter now; only the Brown Shirts were seen parading the streets. Flags and banners flying, bands playing they made their way to Templehof Airfield on May Day. The Trade Union movement was soon merged with the new ruling party and made the Nazis even more dominant than they were already.

There was now just one big gathering in Berlin. That was at the Tempelhofer field. Everybody over eighteen years of age had to be a member of a Trades Union and the union leaders saw to it that its members were present at the time and place where the May Day parade would start from. That could be outside the factory gate or it could be an open space or park area near offices or shops. These small groups would meet up with others to form larger columns and then with brass bands leading them made their way to Tempelhof where the big rally would take place. Big names from the Trade Unions and The Party would make speeches before Adolf Hitler arrived to give his May Day message to the party and the country.

Not everybody by a long way was enthusiastic about this annual event, certainly not in my family. May Day had been a public holiday for quite a time before Hitler came to power and people liked to spend May Day in their own way rather than wasting a good part of the day marching and standing listening to endless and boring speeches, getting tired doing nothing in the process. My two brothers certainly were not in favour of spending half the day in this boring way, nor were my uncles for that matter. My father was not affected by these rules. Working on the railways the chances were he would be working anyway, being on shift work, also helped. These workers were excused from turning out to support these rallies. Not surprisingly then many people found a way to drop out and get away as soon as they could. You were expected at the place where their march was scheduled to start to be seen and be struck off the list as present. Reporting sick was not an option as it proved too complicated and difficult to obtain a sick note overnight. To get out of this, workers reported their presence at the time and place from where they began their march. Then marched along with the group until one or two mergers had taken place and when the column had become too large for the union and party leaders to keep an eye on their own group, they slipped away at the first opportunity and spent the rest of the day their way. Anyone not getting away en route to Tempelhof certainly did so when they got there. Crowds were large and no one would miss you. The support for Hitler and his party was far from unanimous.

So it was that on the first day of May 1934, when the May Day parades marched along our street, I was caught up with their music and banners flying. As an eight year old I found all this very exciting. Being a public holiday there was no school either. What is more, I could also join the parade without fear of any fighting breaking out. It was a fine day, the band playing marching tunes, most of them I knew and they were familiar to me. So I tagged along caught up in it all forgetting about the time I had to be home. We were spending the day in the garden as my father went there straight from work and mother had to have the lunch ready. He planned to have a nice long afternoon working in the garden. As every gardener knows at that time of year you need an extra pair of hands to cope with all the work waiting to be done, so he would not be well pleased if I ruined his plans. Mother waited as long as she dare, but with few people having a private telephone, mum eventually decided to leave for the garden not waiting any longer for me, as not to be too late with the meal as all the family said they would be there. She informed the neighbours about her plight and how anxious she was about me, left some money for my train fare should I turn up and went on her way carrying all the provisions herself.

Here was I, following the band happily. Eventually it must have dawned on me that it was time to go home. I had no idea what time it was but felt I had better make my way home. Arriving back home the neighbour called out to me saying rather sternly what a naughty boy I was and how worried mother had been when she left. She gave me the train fare urging me to be careful and not to follow anymore bands on the way. Then she let me go and I went off quite confident which station to go to. I had a choice of two, from which to catch the train. Whenever we went by train I prided myself to know which station to go to, which platform we would go from, telling whether or not the incoming train was ours or not. I knew the train I needed had the name of the final destination in black on a green background on the front of the train, Gruenau, Green Meadow. I had bought tickets before, with one of my parents or brothers behind me to see that I got it right, doing so now came almost naturally. Arriving at the station I knew exactly what to do, where to go, which train to take. At the other end my confidence was equally as strong. Familiar sights, buildings, adverts and place names told me when to get off the train. I had my ticket ready to hand to the ticket collector, as I had done scores of time before. Outside the station I took the shortest route I knew to get to our garden.

When I got to our piece of land, cheerfully announcing my arrival, I was greeted by a very angry and furious mother. Heaven's I thought, what have I done? She was livid with me, grabbed the first stick she could lay her hand on and gave me a thorough beating. She wildly hit me not caring where the stick would land or what injury it inflicted upon me. When her grip loosened I made my escape and seeing my father I went straight to him for protection and comfort. He spoke to my mother, calming her down saying, we should all be thankful that no harm had come to me and that I had safely returned, which of course she was. It was sheer relief seeing me back, which made her act the way she did and felt sorry for it later no doubt. She even may have regretted her action I don't know, she never talked about it afterwards. Looking back now I cannot recall ever having been hit by my mother either before or after that particular incident nor by my father for that matter except on one occasion when my father must have felt a bit grumpy. He came home after his morning shift and had his meal, after which he often rested for a while before working on the project in hand. My father was quite creative with his mind and his hands. He certainly had lots of patience and made lots of things out of scraps and offcuts. Among them were all kinds of toys, dolls prams, dolls houses and many other things. He was also quite an expert in making slippers from scraps of material. These came from one or two tailors dad knew. In return he made slippers for them, which were hard to come by during the war. I cannot remember what he was working on at that time of this incident but I know he was very positive I should call him in an hour's time as he was anxious to get the job done, whatever it was, as the date he promised it would be ready was near. Dutifully I called him as the hour was up but he did not stir. A few minutes later I went to him and called him again reminding him of what he said to me: "In an hour call me without fail!" and still he made no move to get up. So what was I to do? A third time I went in to him urging him to get up when something must have snapped somewhere. He jumped up, got hold of me and gave me a beating I never knew my father was capable of. It was brief I am happy to say and he quickly regretted it. I could not run to my mother for help or comfort as she was not in the house at the time. Something must have irritated him or been on his mind that day, as I never seen him act in this way before or thereafter. In any case these were the only two occasions I had received corporal punishment from my parents. School of course is another matter.

After Hitler came to power life in Germany changed rapidly. With high unemployment not only in Germany at that time but also over all Europe and the western industrial world, Hitler's schemes to reduce the number of unemployed were very welcomed. One such scheme was building the Autobahn. A lesser known one was the creation of the Freiwilliger Arbeits Dienst; meaning voluntary workers service. Those who signed up for it had the guarantee of accommodation as well as three meals a day and a little weekly pay amounting to no more than pocket money really. At the end of a year's service there was the promise that a job would be found. This offer was for men only as the projects on which these workers were employed were all manual and in the open air. They were largely community projects such as land drainage and building dykes to improve the productivity of the land. Some men were helping farmers at harvest time too. How do I know all this? One of my brothers joined this service. After having served his apprenticeship and was a qualified glazier and on full wages he was no longer wanted by his boss and declared redundant and so joined the ever growing number of unemployed. He thought the best thing all round, for him and the family, would be to leave home and join the voluntary work force. That would ease the financial pressure certainly. My other brother, after having completed his apprenticeship was also made redundant and joined the dole queue. He took up another offer by the government. He enlisted in the army, when after a minimum of time of service he too would be found a job. He joined a foot regiment stationed in Potsdam, just a few kilometres west of Berlin. He came home every Saturday afternoon, brought home his dirty washing which mother lovingly washed, dried and ironed, ready for him when he returned to barracks on Sunday evening. He went off to see his girlfriend, whom he married in the summer of 1938, after he left the army to start his new job as head electrician in one of the four railway works in Berlin. He . told us after the war, when Hitler gave the order to cross the river Rhine to occupy the military free zone between the river and the French border, as laid down by the allied forces after the first world war. The troops that crossed the bridges, to a warm welcome from the local population, did not have a round of ammunition between them. That was Hitler's first bluff and he got away with it. Reinhold, that was his name, became a master of his trade by the time he was thirty and did very secret work on defence during the Second World War, which took him to every capital city in German occupied countries in Europe. He was much sought after by the East German Government after the Second World

War and under constant surveillance. That made any idea of escaping to the west impossible and we saw very little of him and the family until after he retired.

Werner, the name of my other brother, was quite happy with his decision to do a year's community work out in the country. He came home three or four times during that year, again bringing lots of clothing home to be washed and mended. He was offered a job as a clerk in an aircraft factory, which he accepted. He worked there until he was called up. Serving in an air defence regiment, he was wounded in one of the air raids on Hamburg. Happily it caused no lasting injury. He never returned to Berlin to live, settling in Frankfurt where he found a permanent job working for the Deutshe Bundes Bank until his retirement. He too got married and lived happily ever after.

My early school days

Chapter 3

Moving Flats

Moving out to Lichtenberg in October 1934 also meant moving school, as Elli, my sister, had only six months to go before leaving school, it was decided that she should stay at the school she had been attending. My father was able to get a free railway pass for her to travel on the train between the two destinations. Father also gave up our land in Baumschulenweg simply because it was difficult to get to it now. We would have to have gone by train and it would have meant at least two changes and be very time consuming. Anyhow, it was a leafy and quiet suburb and the flat we lived in was far superior to the one we had previously occupied. All rooms were in the front of the house, we had quite a large balcony as well, on which my father was able to display his much loved pot plants. Then of course there was the bathroom, what luxury, and a toilet just to ourselves! With only ten tenants in this block of flats compared with goodness knows how many in the Posener Strasse, it was much quieter too. The landlord owned a small dairy, situated in the back yard, consisting of half a dozen cows in milk which were replaced from time to time by freshly calved cows, so as to keep up the quantity of fresh milk needed to supply his customers. The landlord also owned two more sizeable plots, one next door which made an ideal safe play area for children. The other, even larger than the one next door, was opposite and had a small chicken farm on it supplying the neighbourhood daily with fresh free range eggs. Other shops too were close by. The butcher just two doors away to the left and three hundred meters further along on the corner of the street the baker's shop which supplied us from Monday to Saturday with freshly baked rolls before breakfast . Across the road was the tobacconist, much to father's delight. Not far to go to buy more cigars should he run out of them, which happened quite frequently as he was a very heavy smoker. To the right as you came out of the building, no more than two hundred meters to go, was the grocery store where you could buy just about everything you might need to run a home and look after a growing family. We lived on the fourth floor, the top floor; the only thing above us was the laundry room, so not far to take the weekly washing. Next to it was the drying floor where you hung the wet clothes for the next twenty four hours and it was amazing how effective this system worked. Clothes were certainly dry enough to iron. Best of all for me, the school was only three minutes' walk away. In fact one could see it through the windows on the landings at the back of the building where we lived.

It did not take us very long to settle in, enjoying all the things we did not have before and the move did not come too soon as the expected baby arrived on the 18th January 1935. It was a baby girl and my father liked the name of Hildegard, by which name she was registered and baptised but forever after known by and called Hilla! I must say I quite enjoyed having her around, for it was great fun watching her grow up. My two brothers, being twenty two years of age and earning, loved, adored and spoiled her. We all did really and mother always found a willing hand to help looking after her.

Apart from not having to walk so far to school, I enjoyed the change. The headmaster greeted us very warmly on my first day. I say us, because this time it was my father who came along with me, not because I might get lost, but to introduce me to the staff and to help me in getting familiar with the layout of the building. After completing the formalities of enrolling at the school I said good bye to my father and the Head took me to my classroom and introduced me to my form teacher. The timetable and hours per week when I went to school were totally different from what I know them to be in England today. In Northern Ireland, Scotland and in Wales they may vary, I don't know. In England a typical school day begins at 9 a.m. and finishes at 3 or 3.30 p.m. five days a week, compared to my school days in Berlin before the second world war, when a day could be as few as two hours or as many as six hours, depending on age and school year. The total hours of tuition you received over a period of six days in a week, yes, we went to school on Saturday, started from twelve hours in the first term to fifteen hours by the end of your first year, to thirty hours in a six day week in the last two years at school. The senior classes started at eight in the morning and went on to one or two p.m. The middle range, the eight to twelve year olds, started at eight or nine o'clock in the morning until twelve noon or one o'clock in the afternoon. On Saturday your start in the morning depended on how many hours there were left to make up your weeks total. The seniors started at 8 a.m. others at 9 a.m. to make up their total and the junior classes joined us at 10 o'clock. We all came out together at twelve noon. Lessons were of fifty minutes duration with a five minute break between lessons. The first big break came at 9.45 and lasted twenty minutes. The next long break was fifteen minutes at 11.50. The two longer breaks were spent in the open in an exercise area and conducted in an orderly fashion, walking round in a circle eating our sandwiches. When the teacher on duty thought everyone had finished, we were allowed to run about and have some exercise before returning to class. There were no school dinners in my time but we had free milk at the 10 o'clock break.

For the next six years I grew and developed into a teenager. I enjoyed my schooldays as I seemed to cope with the workload very well. Reading came easily to me, thanks to all the family, who never tired of helping and tutoring me in this subject. Geography I found very interesting and history quite fascinating. Basic arithmetic I was quite good at and still am, different though when it came to geometry and I realized rocket science definitely was not for me. When it came to sport, well, shall we say I was a little slow off the mark! I certainly was not a sprinter but enjoyed playing in team sports and was happy to do my best when chosen to play. What I was quite good at was swimming. When the time came for swimming to be included in our school activities I was quite excited as I desperately wanted to learn to swim. The reason for it I will explain later. During the year when swimming was included in the sporting syllabus our school was allocated Wednesday afternoons at the public bath. Even the prospect of having to walk twenty minutes to get there and twenty minutes back, did not curb my enthusiasm and I only missed one week during that year due to a heavy cold.

My mother felt it would be wise not to get into the water. I went along with the class and watched enviously as my class mates took to the water. There were two certificates we could obtain. The first was achieved by fifteen minutes breast stroke without holding on to the sides or resting at the shallow end of the pool. That was the test and it was verified not by a member of staff but an official of the national swimming association. I was in the first group that took the test and qualified first time. The second certificate we could go in for was a test of endurance. It meant swimming forty five minutes none stop using any or all strokes. That was quite a task but I made it. Needless to say not everyone went in for that certificate. It must be said though, when coming out of the water the legs felt quite weak, the knees shaky and the head dizzy. Proudly I presented that certificate to the family that evening. Exhausted but happy I went to bed not caring much what tomorrow would bring.

So the years at school came and went. I was never outstanding at any subject but kept up with what was expected of me. As all my school reports were lost during the war, I don't know what they said about my achievements. All I do know, my parents were never worried about my progress and I was never under any pressure to do extra homework except revision before examinations. Anyway, every year I moved on to the next grade. The worst subject was music. The reason being we never had a teacher that was good at it. During music lessons in my time, apart from the last five minutes or so, he talked about every subject under the sun except music. We thought it was fun and sometimes even hilarious at the time but in retrospect; no. I love music and certainly have a good ear for music. I have been told by organists and choir masters I have a good pitch, but a voice? No. Well you can't have everything can you. What might have helped me keep up with school work and not missing school because of colds and flu was undoubtedly my good health. Colds and flu never kept me away from school, I had the usual illnesses of course such as measles and mumps, but that was before my school days. It was an epidemic of diphtheria that struck the school that kept me away for nine weeks. The whole school was closed for four weeks and I had a wonderful time. The weather was good I remember. Although most of my school friends were either in hospital or convalescing at home there were one or two not from our school I could play with in the afternoons or at weekends and there were always my cousins of course. It was at the last weekend, just before the school reopened on Monday, that my symptoms of the illness appeared. There was nothing for it, my father took me to hospital where I spent the next four weeks in isolation with three other boys and one week at home before returning to school. I had a lot of catching up to do but I got there before the end of the academic year. The other time I missed school was not quite so devastating. It was only for a week due to a broken arm I received falling of my bike. I was chased by two other boys and was not looking where I was going, ran against a bolder, lost control and off I came. It was summer time and I had been playing on a building site. Over a period of time we had created quite a race track for our bikes and it was great fun chasing around there. Obviously playing all the afternoon I was dirty when the two strange boys came along and chased us off. Why they picked on me I haven't a clue. It was a Saturday evening and I was due to have a bath after playtime. Having played all day I sure needed one, but it was not to be. When I got home, pushing my bike of course, I went up to our flat leaving the bike down stairs in the hall way. My parents had one look at my arm, turned me round and off to a nearby clinic I went, dirty as I was. The clinic was less than ten minutes' walk away, so it was not too long after the accident that I received medical attention. It was a type of cottage hospital, run by a religious order of nuns. Luckily my father was at home and he could take me leaving mother free to look after my baby sister. They took one look at me realising the situation and the dilemma I was in. No matter, they gently undressed me, put me into a bath and cleaned me up and then took me to a doctor who put a temporary splint on and then they put me to bed. I had to wait till Monday morning before the arm was set and put in plaster. I stayed another night and then went home on Tuesday morning. I had the rest of the week off school. As it was only a broken arm I had no exemption from homework, lessons or other activities except sport and physical exercise as long as my arm was in plaster or in a sling. What did bother me though in the last two years at school was my form teacher. I must admit my writing was and still is very bad, but that teacher insisted that I could improve my writing and he would see to it that I did. He kept me in after class, gave me a hundred lines to write; 'I can write better if I tried!' time and again, but it did not work. Then he tried the last thing he could think of, the cane, not on my buttocks but on my hands. Now how that can improve anyone's handwriting I don't know, and that was almost daily in the last year. That same teacher, believe it or not, wanted me to take up teaching as a profession. He tried his hardest to persuade my parents to let me go to Grammar School and teacher training college, but my father was adamant I was to learn a trade as the other two boys, I did, I became an electro mechanic.

That was in the future of course. First I had to complete my basic education before thinking of a career. I had to grow up and learn about life, its ups and downs, its pit falls. I had to widen my horizon and learn there is life beyond school. Again, my brothers helped me a great deal. In common with other countries both in Europe and around the world there was a youth movement in Germany. In the United Kingdom it is known as the Scouts. In Germany before Hitler's time that movement was known as the Pathfinders. That changed to the Hitler Youth movement after the Nazis came to power of course, as did a lot of other things. As in the Scout Movement there were two sections, juniors and seniors, Volksjugent and Hitlerjugent. We met once a week for two hours and as before the change of name, were taught about citizenship, how to be helpful to those in need especially the elderly. The emphasis now was on how to be a good patriot that the Fatherland mattered more than anything else that the Third Reich would last forever. As it turned out, it only lasted just over twelve years compared with the one that went before, the Second Reich, which lasted over forty nine years. We played games and sports in a field close to our regular meeting hall

What I remember most during my time as a member of that movement were the meetings on Friday nights when we were taught map reading, orienteering, the sky at night and basic skills of survival, including first aid. This was put to the test during the monthly camping weekends throughout the year. During the summer months they took place under canvas. We assembled at 13.00 on Saturday, bearing in mind we did not leave school till midday it was a tight schedule for many, everything had to be ready and packed before setting out to school that morning. Mother had the provisions parcelled up; uniform laid out ready to jump into, a quick change and off to the meeting place you went. When all were present we marched in an orderly fashion to the appropriate station that would take us to our destination. The camping site more often than not was some distance from the station and involved a march to get there as no public transport was available in those rural districts. Remember we were eleven/twelve year olds, carried our own packs which included, apart from our personal belongings, our share of the food, some camping equipment and a sheet of canvas which was a section making a tent for tree when assembled. Assembling the tent was the first task after arriving on site except for the two boys assigned to gather wood and light the fire. After having something to eat and a drink sitting around the fire we laid out our sleeping bags, that done we reassembled round the fire and sang for the rest of the evening, enjoying folks songs, marching and patriotic songs as well as fire and camp site songs until bed time.

The real test came in the morning. First of all some physical exercises, next ablutions, then breakfast, after that out into the fields, meadows and woods to see how much we remembered from what we had been taught the previous three or four weeks. The morning went all too quickly before it was time for lunch, packing up camp, clearing the site and leaving it tidy for the group that came after us the following weekend. Once everything was checked and accounted for we began our march back to the station singing most of the time. On the train back to Berlin most of us went to sleep, worn out but happy. At home, mum had a lovely meal ready waiting for me as well as one of my favourite puddings either rice, semolina or jelly and custard. Neither of them needs much chewing. They remain favourites of mine to this day. During the winter months we did much the same only instead of being under canvas we slept in barns or stables which could be quite cosy on straw or in the hay. Water was handy so was firewood. The cooking was done under an open shelter away from anything that could become a fire risk.

There was one exception, the annual summer camp in July. That could be over two or three weeks. The pattern was this. You could either start your fortnight in camp or a week on route march. The route marches were quite interesting. Being summer time and during the school holidays an earlier start could be made and the destination much further away from Berlin. Given new surroundings as well as a feeling that this outing was more of a holiday, than just a weekend away from home. The route marches were well organised. As I said, it was an early start and usually a day's journey by rail, much further than the weekend outings. When we arrived at our destination we were billeted with local residents who were waiting at the station greeting us warmly. They collected our rucksacks and carried them for us, which made quite a change. At the house I was shown to my room where I was to sleep the night had a wash, a wonderful meal with the family and then at the appointed time went to the village green where we entertained our guests with fireside and camp side songs and games. After a good night sleep and a substantial breakfast our hosts took us to the assembly point where a lorry was waiting to take our rucksacks and to follow us as we made our way on foot to our next stop for our midday meal, again supplied by the villagers, and a rest before setting out for the place where we were to spent the next night. Marching all the while, singing as we went along. Anyone that got footsore or exhausted waited by the roadside for the lorry to pick them up. This pattern was repeated throughout the week until we arrived at the campsite. There the usual camp activities took over. Activities were such as map reading, orienteering, and judging of distances. Team building was another item on the week's agenda. The week over, after an early rising, we packed our bags, marched to the station, caught the train and home we went in the knowledge that most of us had a happy time. Those who chose to do the week in camp first did their route march in the second week. I enjoyed these annual camps, so much so, that in 1938 when my brother Reinhold got married, I preferred camping rather than stay home and go to the wedding. Being in a different part of the country each year made it even more exciting to go every year. It was during that time when I had a very bad habit of biting my fingernails. One of our leaders was determined to cure me of this. When we were together at weekends the time was much too short to do anything about it, so he decided that when we are at summer camp I would be sleeping in his tent next to him thus being in his sight 24 hours a day. Every time I lifted my hands to bite my fingernails he would either look at me sternly or shout to me to stop. I worked. By the end of the fortnight I was cured.

In the years before the war, after Hitler had become Chancellor of Germany, we in the Hitler Youth movement had to go on parade of course. Patriotic meetings or May Day rallies took place at some large sporting arena or other open venue in Berlin. Big names in the party would come to address the youth of the nation, paving the way for the Fuerer to give the final speech. After the Olympic Games in 1936 the Olympic Stadium was used for the annual May Day gathering of the youth in Berlin. We had to be in place by 9.30 a.m. and ready for rehearsal so that everything went according to plan when the national leaders arrived. Getting 50 to 60 thousand boys and girls to their right places was no easy task. As so often it meant an early start and a late lunch. But this time we could go by train instead of marching all the way. It was a long, long way from the eastern outskirts to the western outskirts where the Olympic Stadium was situated. We also turned out to line the streets when foreign dignitaries came on state visits. There was the Emperor of Japan, a number of royal Princes from the Balkan countries and more than once when Mussolini came to see Hitler. Another occasion when we lined the streets was when the troops returned from fighting in the Spanish Civil War. They were acclaimed heroes helping General Franco to win the civil war in Spain.

Chapter 4

Life under Hitler

Many of the people who voted for Hitler to become Chancellor of the German Republic could not have foreseen the disaster Germany and her people would end up in because of the ruthless actions committed by him and his party. Laws, rules and regulations that would make it easy for the country to become a one party state were soon introduced with the outcome that the Nazi party began to dictate the life of the German nation. It was not long after, that Hitler's portrait appeared in public buildings and offices and everyone realized who was in charge. As the annals of history tell us Hitler's campaign to suppress and persecute the Jews soon followed. It was then, I recall, the nation woke up to the fact that here was a ruthless regime ruling the country. As we know, it was too late, once a dictator gets into power, only a revolution will get rid of them. In the case of the Third Reich it took a long and bloody world war to dispose of them.

One of the questions that were being asked by younger generations both in Germany as well abroad is why Hitler was so popular and why vote for him to become Chancellor? One of the reasons, he was a smooth, persuasive and convincing talker. He could convince you of almost anything. So was Goebbels of course, Hitler's Minister of Propaganda. Although I was very young, I still can see him now addressing the youth of Berlin in the Olympic Stadium on May Day in the three years before the war. The other reason, the world was still in recession when Hitler started to make his bid for leadership. Maybe there were signs of recovery, but people remembered the hard and tough times after the First World War when in the twenties, high inflation caused the currency to drop by 50% over night. Workers were paid daily in those days and in the end took a suitcase to work to collect their daily pay and when they got home spent it immediately as the next day it might be worthless. It was a struggle to buy enough food for the day with father's daily pay, let alone meet other running expenses. That period was followed by the world wide depression with unemployment running into millions. Along comes Herr Adolf Hitler with his smooth talk, telling the nation he would shake off the shackles of the Treaty of Versailles, he would fight for justice. He blamed the Jews for all the troubles in the world. All this of course was to justify his party's actions at home and abroad. In Hitler's opinion the Jews were responsible for all Germany's woes. Depression, inflation, poverty, you name it, they were to blame. How did this effect family life? The younger generation accepted it very readily. After all, as in our family, the two oldest children were found jobs and were able to contribute to the family budget and pay tax to the state. My two brothers enjoyed their late teens and early twenties. They took part in a lot of sports. Both of them were long distance runners and I often went along to cheer them on their way. Werner, one of my brothers, was also keen on winter sports especially skiing, whilst Reinhold played handball in the winter, which was very popular before the Second World War in Germany, as well as mountaineering. I only saw him climbing once and that was on my first visit to the Alps during the

Easter holidays in 1939. It was very exciting as most first experiences are. To get the most out of the Easter break in the mountains, which are quite a long way away from Berlin, meant an overnight train journey to Munich where we changed trains. From there we took a local train into the mountains. We arrived at the terminal at about nine o'clock in the morning ready for a good breakfast before setting out on foot to our final destination, an Alpine hut high up in the mountains. The weather was dull in the village but the innkeeper assured us that it would brighten up later in the day. Certainly no rain was forecast over the holiday weekend. So with cheerful hearts we set out singing as we went along. When we reached higher altitudes it became quite misty with even dense fog for a little while and our spirits dropped. It was not quite how we interpreted the innkeeper's forecast. Imagine our joy then when we got through the clouds and warm sunshine greeted us. I was awe struck. For the first time in my life I saw mountain peaks covered with snow bathed in sunshine, what a view to behold. Not far away now we could see the house where we were to stay for the next few nights. It was all very basic then, including the food, compared what holiday makers expect now. It did not bother any of us in our party; we all grew up under basic conditions. Dormitories were basic as well, no single or double rooms here. When you got to the top of the stairs, there on the landing were two doors, one to the right the other to the left. Yes, you've got it, the sexes were segregated, one room for the ladies and one room for the men. I enjoyed my first visit to the mountains very much, seeing my brother climbing was quite a thrill, as was the warm sunshine every day and the beautiful walks too. You can see now why young folks could not care less at this early stage of Hitler's reign. Opinions changed rapidly when the younger generation was ask to do things such as serving compulsorily in what had now become the National Workers Service.

Not so with our parents and grandparents, they had seen it all before in one form or another. They no doubt were wary from the beginning, knowing what methods Hitler's troops, the Sturm Apteilung and Schutz Staffel, employed to gain power. These troops were known as S.A. and S.S., political thugs as it turned out. Our elders also knew that political opponents were arrested and put into prison. I am not so sure that they had any idea what these new camps that were being built would be used for. They might be more labour camps or for the military. It was not until rumours became more persistent that it became clear that these new establishments were for political prisoners including the Jews. Kristal Nacht, the night the Synagogues were vandalised, as well as other Jewish owned shops, businesses and other Jewish establishments, including big department stores, people were beginning to feel sorry for the Jews, just the opposite of Hitler's intention. The decree that all Jews must wear visibly the Star of David on their sleeve was about the last straw. It was very humiliating for the Jews and embarrassing for the Christian church in Germany. Anyone speaking out against these policies was arrested often publicly. That included not only eminent church leaders but also many comedians and other members of the entertainment world and obviously political opponents of Hitler's regime. Some, as we know now, were never heard of again.

So it was that Jewish members of the professions left Germany in droves including our own family doctor and I mean family doctor, he was the doctor to all the family, highly regarded by all. He was I kindly, caring man, gentle and understanding, especially with children. On his last visit to us when he brought the good news that my heart was sound and I was not suffering from angina he told us that he would be leaving Germany. To my parents that came not as a surprise. But I can see my mother now shedding a few tears. All this meant very little to me. I know people spoke about these things in private but never openly. During those days whenever the family came together and my rebellious uncles started to speak out about the latest inhuman acts and atrocities done in the name of the German people they were immediately told to be quiet as children were present. It was not unknown that children went out innocently talking to others what their father or uncle said about Hitler and his cronies. A zealous party member hearing this would report it to the police and the man or men were duly arrested and more often then went to prison to teach them a lesson. Worst of all their names went on the black list.

Politics meant nothing to me then, there was so much else that was going on at that time. We had the 700th celebration of the founding of Berlin. There were the Olympic Games of course and I was more interested in play with friends or riding my bike. All I know Hitler was acclaimed a hero by the younger generation every time he had his own way over the Western powers. All in all life was good, I enjoyed what I did, was in very good health, overcame all the childhood diseases, felt good within and without. I kept up with my swimming. In the summer I went to an outdoor bath by the Spree, close to our local power station. It had two pools, into one flowed the cooling water from the power station, which made the water pleasantly warm. The other formed part of the river, its temperature very much dependent on the weather. In the winter there was always the public bath to go to.

Berlin's foundation celebrations were an exciting time. As so many other places, Berlin had small beginnings. It started as a fishing village on the banks of the river Spree and became the capital city of Prussia and later of Germany of course. The schools played their part through local history lessons and fieldwork in Old Berlin. The Nicolai Quarter where it all began has been rebuilt and is very impressive even now. History was re-enacted in music and drama. There were parties and parades as well as carnival processions with tableaus showing the development of the city and of course fire work displays. City authorities created theme parks to entertain the thousands of visitors that were expected. My father took my sister Elli and me to see it and we spend a whole day there having a wonderful time.

Then of course there were the Olympic Games in 1936 when Berlin was once again in the headlines. The games came to Berlin I understand because of the civil war in Spain where they were scheduled to be held. How Hitler pulled that one off I have no idea. As in all other cities where these games are staged, Berlin was spruced up. Public transport extended their lines so that all venues could be easily reached, many of them without the need to change trains or trams. Certainly you could go to the Olympic Stadium from any part of town without changing, if you used the S Bahn. The return journey could prove more tricky, as you needed to know from which platform your train home would leave, there were so many of them. Again, the city laid on lots of entertainment for the visitors to enjoy. This time the whole country was invited to participate. I remember a huge area set aside near the stadium with several large marquees where regional food, traditionally cooked was offered and served in traditional costume as well as the region's products and produce. My father and I spent a wonderful day there looking and admiring it all. This time my sister was not with us as she already visited the site with some friends at an earlier date. Yes it was an exciting time.

The Olympic Games are all about sport yet I was never a great competitor in sport though I like to follow it on radio or television. Amazing how fanatic people do get about sport, but not me. I prefer to exercise in a more leisurely way, like messing around in a boat on the river which I did quite a lot in my last year or two at school. A good friend of mine had a canoe and we spent the day on the river whenever we could. That was not all that often. Friday evenings was Hitlerjugend night. There was the monthly weekend camping. In the summer of course we and other families of the tribe spent several weekends during the year with an uncle in Lehnitz, a lovely little place just north of Berlin. We started going there after we gave up our land in Baumschulenweg. His house with a very large garden was close to the river Havel, a mere hundred yards or so away. The river meandered through the country side flowing south-west. The Spree flowed into it just west of Berlin. The Havel continued south-west until it merged with the river Elbe. The Havel carried a lot of commercial boats and barges as well as pleasure craft. To shorten journey times, a canal system was devised that isolated some of the wandering sections of the river. Over the years they had become an arm of the river or quiet back waters. Along the banks or at the end there were small club houses, their boats moving up and down to the main stream. One reason I was anxious to learn swimming was that on the other side from us was a large grass area ideal for playing games. To be able to be part of and participate I had to swim across the narrow arm of the river to the opposite bank. You can see now why I learned to swim as soon as I had the opportunity. A mile or so up river was a lake surrounded by woodland and forest, its name appropriately enough, Lehnitzsee. Whenever younger cousins that could not yet swim were with us for the weekend and the weather was fine, warm and sunny, we all went up to the lake usually taking the path along the river carrying a picnic lunch with us .It was an ideal place for a family outing. With sandy beaches, shallow waters and trees nearby to provide shade. With a loving, caring family around you, who could have asked for anything more. The route home, as on the Isle of Ruegen, was through the woods, again picking berries on the way.

Growing up in such an environment was bliss. All the cousins got on well together. As we grew older, we became also more adventurous, swimming further out on the lake, away from the shore, with parents, especially our mothers, watching anxiously. We climbed trees as high as our courage would allow with no adults in sight and cycled on dangerous slopes. Add to this the skills we learned in the Hitler youth and in school, yes, I had a good, sound upbringing and for that I am eternally grateful.

Developing and maturing into a teenager was not just physical. Interests in the life around you widened, partly because, as academic and general knowledge increased, life began to make more sense and also you learned from your mistakes as you went along. Suddenly you realised your tastes became more expensive, you found yourself looking enviously at the latest fashions .Your pocket money was not enough to buy all you desired. To increase one's spending power one needed to earn some extra money. It was made easy for me; my father as well as my two brothers suggested I keep their shoes clean and polished an offer I readily accepted. How did I spend my money? Well at that time in my life there was nothing I wanted that needed saving up for. I was happy and content with simple things and still am. In the early thirties talking pictures had not been in the cinemas all that long and as I had all the toys I wanted, thanks to my father who made them for us, I found myself in the cinema most Saturday afternoons during the winter. During that time Hollywood pictures dominated the market in Germany as everywhere else in the world. Gauleiter Goebbles tried his utmost to counter Hollywood's influence, but to no avail. American films were very popular. Stars and the films were well known and so was the music that went with them. Names, such as Clark Gable, Jeanette McDonald, Nelson Eddie, Jean Harlow, Fred Astaire, Ginger Rodgers, Laurel and Hardy, to name but a few, were household names at that time.

Surprisingly American films were screened in German cinemas until the U.S.A. entered the war in November 1941. These films certainly made a great impression on me and when I saw them, years later, here in the U.K. I knew the story, what to expect and what was coming next. Why I ask myself? There can be only one answer! They had a good story line, were well acted and excellently directed. Indeed they don't make pictures like that anymore. It also shows what a hopeless romantic I was and still am, so my friends tell me. Seeing people dancing both on the screen and at family parties made me longing to join in.

At most birthday celebrations the younger generation sooner or later began to dance. Sitting around just talking seemed boring, so the girls asked us boys to roll back the carpet and started to dance. After a few dances they wanted to change partners and the boys were drawn in, not that we minded, we just were too shy as the girls were so much better at it. My sister Elli and my cousins taught us boys the basic steps of the Ballroom dances and we grew confident enough to enjoy dancing with family members, yes, with my mother and aunties as well when it came to the Viennese waltz at which they were very good. We danced to the latest hits of the day from home and abroad, many from across the Atlantic needless to say. Even the Charlton was still popular in the thirties and so was the Lambeth Walk.

None of us had a lot of pocket money to buy the latest hits and releases. We decided to buy one record a week and take turns to buy them. With seven of us in the group we could all manage it. After a while we had quite a good selection of songs and dances. With so many birthday and other parties going on they were much in use. It also kept the family together. The reason we had this many parties in the home was because after war broke out, dancing in public places was forbidden. The reason given, with soldiers dying for the Fatherland and their families in mourning it was only right we should refrain from dancing in public. Nonetheless the bands in these places carried on playing for entertainment. Although dancing in public was not allowed, dance schools could continue to teach. To become more skilful and improve my dancing I decided to take dancing lessons. Encouraged by some of my aunts, especially by one of my Godmothers, I enrolled at a dance school in September 1939. If ever I enjoyed anything in my youth it was my time at dancing school. In the first two weeks we were taught proper and correct dancing holds as well as good manners and courtesies. At the time when I started my lessons, the war had not caught up with the world of dancing in Germany. Girls 14 and over were looked upon as young ladies and we had them to treat them as such on the dance floor. We were required to wear white gloves when dancing with them. All these things were looked upon as basic skills to be learned before beginning dancing lessons. When we got round to dancing lessons proper as it were we started off with the polka followed by the Viennese waltz. After that the foxtrot, followed by the quick step. Then, the tango, which I loved, and I still adore to this very day. Unfortunately it was short lived. In the spring of 1940 both teachers, who were husband and wife, were called up for war work. We never had the end of season ball which I had so looked forward to. At Christmas in 1939, with all quiet on the Western Front, the ban on dancing in public was lifted and remained so until the spring in 1940 when dancing in public was banned again after the occupation of Denmark and Norway and remained in force, as far as I know, until the end of the war.

There is something else young people in Germany will always remember, their Confirmation into the Christian church. It is a great day with much rejoicing and a great family gathering, second only to a wedding. Most boys will wear for the first time a long trouser suit. Until now it was shorts and long woolly socks in winter. The girls, after confirmation, were looked upon as young ladies and wore smart black dresses for the occasion, in the Lutheran church that is. In the Roman Catholic Church the girls were confirmed much younger and wore white dresses and a veil. Our clergy took the preparation for confirmation very seriously. In my case it was a two hour weekly session. It took place after school hours in our class room. It was during my last year at school, beginning after the Easter holidays in 1939, no sign of war yet, at 2pm on a Wednesday afternoon, so a very long day at school, concluding the end of February 1940, well into the war by then. Most of my class mates were part of the group that was being prepared. The only break was during the school holidays. The Conformation Service itself took place during Lent the following year. In villages and country churches it was on Palm Sunday. In towns and large cities such as Berlin, depending on the numbers, Passion Sunday and even the 4th Sunday of Lent were needed to deal with the large numbers of candidates.

On Palm Sunday in 1940 I wore my new suit with long trousers for the first time and very proudly too. No denying, one felt grown up. With the new suit I had a new white shirt and a suitable tie to go with the occasion as well as a new pair of shoes. The last items were presents from my Godmothers. One was my mother's sister the other two were my mother's brother's wives. They saw to it I observed all the seasons on the church's calendar and understood the meaning of it. Now they were presenting me to the Minister of our church to be admitted as a full member. The sermon the Minister preached impressed my father very much I recall. With the war in its seven month now it was very timely. The text, John 15:13; "Greater love has no man than this, that a man lay down his life for a friend". He likened it to a stricken submarine where some members of the crew may well give their life that others may live. As these services took place during the morning we got back home in good time for the celebration lunch. These gathering were very much like a family birthday party only this time, as a church service was part of the celebration, everybody wore their Sunday best. During the meal a small band of musicians, usually three or four, would call and play appropriate tunes and suitable songs. Meal over, most of the adults and younger cousins would go home, leaving the teenagers to get ready for the party in the evening to which friends were invited and a good time was had by all. Indeed it was, and still is by many families, looked upon as the beginning of a new phase in a person's life.

It my time, confirmation coincided with leaving school. Most of my generation left school to learn a trade or find work to start earning a living. Some of course went for further education with a view to entering a profession. With Germany now at war, planning for the future was not as straight forward as it used to be. In the past you chose your career, had your training or continued your studies, obtained your qualification, gained experience, then worked for promotion. Not so in 1940's Germany, no one knew what kind of a Germany would emerge after the war. We all hoped it would be victoriously, Hitler said so time after time. So far all his predictions had come true why doubt him now. As for the immediate future, all who entered the labour market at that time knew, sooner or later we would end up in one branch or other of the armed forces. The Hitler Regime made a few changes in existing schemes they had introduced before the war and brought in new ones. The most significant change was that, what used to be known as the Voluntary Labour Force had become the National Labour Force, this meant, that every fit and able young male, having finished his basic training, had to serve six month in this renamed labour force, working as before on road improvement and land drainage, improving the productivity of the land, they now also received basic military training. The new scheme was, that every boy teenager, before he reached his eighteens birthday, had to attend a three week residential course in an army camp preparing him to carry arms. The young ladies, when leaving school at fourteen, were encouraged to spend a year working in the provinces learning rural crafts.

With these prospects ahead of us we planned our future. We knew before we reached our eighteenth birthday there would be interruptions in our training and study. As there was nothing one could do about it I went ahead with sending applications to become a fitter. One was to an aircraft factory just outside Berlin at the western end of the city, the other to one of the four railway works we had in Berlin. The one I applied to was the newest of the four. It serviced and repaired the carriages of the city's transport system. In the end I accepted the one from the railway for two reasons. Firstly it was much nearer home, and secondly I had the advantage of free rail travel in the city and three rail passes a year to anywhere in the country. This made me the third member in the family working for the railway. I left school on 31st March 1940 and started work as an apprentice the following day, 1st April at the railway works in Schoenewide, (Beautiful Meadow).

As with the school timetable we made an early start in the morning. We had to be at our workbench at 06.45. Work finished at 16.00 on Monday to Friday. On Saturday the working day was 06.45 to 12.00. The apprentice workshop was set apart from the main workshop, quite a distance in fact, about a three or four minute walks away and run independently. It was purpose built and still quite new when I started. Fully equipped with machines, drill, lathe, plane and a blacksmith shop with two furnaces, two anvils and every tool one may require when working there. We were all given a set of basic tools, if we needed special tools they could be obtained at the material supply counter. In our second year we would have six months training at the machines and three months in the blacksmith's shop. The first year however was given over to learn skills of a locksmith and electrical physics, building on the basics we learned at school. For that purpose we had one day a week at Tech. School which also was within the grounds of the works and again we made an early start. The day at school was from 07.00 –

14.00; on that day we had our breaks and meals in the canteen of the main works with the other workers.

We were in groups of 12 and each group had a foreman who stayed with us for the first year and taught us how to use tools properly, what type of tool to use on different materials. The first task set was to form a cube from a round piece of iron 4 inch in diameter and 2 inch long, using hammer and chisels only. It was done in three stages and for a good reason. We were young, inexperienced and had very soft hands when we started. By the end of the day however we all had sore hands with blisters and bruises. On the second day we laid hammer and chisel aside and picked up the files in our workbox and were taught how hold them correctly to achieve a level surface. That done the items were marked with your work number and safely stored away. At a later date they were brought out and we repeated the procedure. At the end of the second stage we had a very rough cube indeed. Again they were stored away to be brought out for the third and final time to make into a dice. That was in December of that year when we filed the sides down to the required size, rounded the corners, bevelled the edges and then carefully marked the sides with the correct number of dots for opposite sides to make up the number seven before using the drill gently making shallow sunken holes to indicate the number of dots on each side. That successfully done we polished the dice using silver steel rods and oil and finally put a tiny drop of black paint in the shallow holes to show up the numbers on each side. We were allowed to keep them as a Christmas present and I still have mined to this day. In fact I made the dice into a paperweight by mounting it on a piece of suitable scrap iron I found in the waste metal box.

From time to time other test pieces to measure our skills were required of us. Towards the end of our first year we were given two pieces of flat iron of suitable length and thickness to be made into   pliers. Again taking two or three stages, the final one being in the blacksmith's shop in our second year when we bent the handles and hardened the completed tool. They were later used in the main works. We made locks and keys all from scratch and on one occasion the main workshop requested a number of keys for the use on trains given to drivers as they left the works with their trains after their biannual service to resume regular service.

The third year of our training introduced us to the electrical side of our trade. It began with the simplest wiring job and progressed to electric motors, great and small. We started with the small motors. The copper wire required was not much thicker than a strong cotton thread. One needed to count the windings accurately and most of all be very careful not to break the wire. To complete the job the loose ends had to be soldered into the collector. If ever there was a fiddly job, this was it. Thankfully there was no time limit on this job number. Patience and endurance were called for. In the summer of 1942 we started on our final test. Again it was in several stages. As before, we were given all that was needed for the project, consisting of a lump of copper, suitable pieces of iron, a length of electric cable, a wooden handle, electric heating element, screws, nuts, bolts etc. and finally the drawing of an electric soldering iron with all the important measurements on which we were finally marked, judged and our passing grade given.

In the first stage we were asked to shape, reduce in size or whatever was needed to be done to the individual parts so that they could be recognised as to which part of the completed piece they are to represent. However, before we got to the second stage I had my call up paper to report to a Wehrertuechtigung's Lager for a three week training course. We all knew we had to attend; it was just north of Berlin. As expected, it was run on strict military lines by N.C.O's with just one officer as acting camp commandant. The days were given over to lots of military drill as well as field work with some weapon training. The only reason I could think of, was that were asked to do this course was to make an early start to knock us into shape and make us fit for military service which was not all that far away. Some of the chaps there needed it, no doubt about that. It was a very intense training course with very little spare time between sessions, at the same time it must be said, the instructors were well aware of our age and pushed us not quite as hard as they might have done had we been an older group of recruits. The day in camp started at 06.00 and finished at 18.00 with our evening meal. After that we had free time until lights out at 22.00. After supper we stayed in our rooms playing cards or just talking to each other, learning where we came from and what we were doing. Talking among ourselves we discovered we had someone training to be an opera singer in our midst and what a delightful discovery it turned out to be. Towards the end of the evening he entertained us singing well known arias, setting the scene and explaining the story of the opera to us before he began to sing, ending the day on a delightful note. There was one evening that really tested our stamina and endurance. It was the night they transported us back to Berlin to attend a big rally at which leading party members gave moral boosting speeches. This was after a long, hard day's training and a hurried meal before marching to the station and the journey to town. After arriving in Berlin, to get to the assembly hall meant more marching followed by two hours of cheering and singing. Rally over, we did it all over again in reverse order arriving back in camp about two o'clock in the morning. All this time we had nothing to eat or to drink. This night we needed no one to sing or rock us to sleep. The only reason I can think of why the authorities went to all that length and trouble to stage this costly exercise, was to fill the assembly hall to capacity to show the world the nation was supporting the war.

Back at work we continued with our training which included working on carriages in the main works to a time limit as they were part of the assembly line and had to be ready on time to be tested and certified as safe before entering service again. That quarter train, two carriages, were entirely serviced and repaired by apprentices, under supervision of course. We noted the numbers down carefully in case we should see the carriages sometime in future, or better still, travel in them. Then we could proudly say:" I worked on that train!" Now with our final test piece (Gesellenstueck) completed, we were waiting eagerly for the results to be posted on the notice board. When eventually they did come out, after being independently tested and assessed, I was surprised my marks were higher than expected. As I said before all soldering irons were used in the main works. On our final day as apprentices we assembled in our canteen, our foremen came to say 'Good Bye!' and gave us final hints and advice for the future one of which I have never forgotten. It was this: 'We have taught you all we could and all we know. Now as you go out into the world you begin to learn.' The day did not end there. As was the custom, that evening we had a graduation party in our social club with all the newly qualified fitters present, quite an elaborate affair. It was in the style of a cabaret with two presenters of which I was one. An evening to remember if, for nothing else, that I wore formal evening dress for the first time, hired of course! Little did I know it would be over 50 years before I wore one again. The joy of that evening was short lived. We graduated on a Friday. The following Monday I was leaving home to report at one of the main railway stations for my six months in the National Labour Service. The camp we were taken to was in the middle of the Polish country side. As expected it was run on strict military lines with an oath of allegiance to be taken by all. Any punishment dealt out was of military nature. Military training included using live ammunition on a shooting range. We had our own rifles to look after and to keep clean. The work we were assigned to was to drain agriculture land. That involved laying drains that emptied into a canal constructed earlier by chaps who did their six months service before us. We had no leave of course, the only day off was Sunday when, if we felt like it, we went into the little town nearby where we were not all that welcome. At the end of September our time was up and we happily turned our backs on that camp. All one hoped was, we had done some good. On my return to Berlin I took two weeks holiday before reporting to work. I was welcomed with open arms as qualified labour was beginning to be scarce. Being young and unattached I was put on night work which I happily accepted. It meant I had to leave any party I was at before anyone else to get to work on time. This lasted until I received my calling up papers 25th November 1943, my 18th birthday. Which stated "I had to report the following week, 2nd December at the barracks in Nuerenberg". Rail pass enclosed.

Chapter 5

University of Life

All the while as an apprentice I learned the skills of a lock smith and fitter in the railway works, out in the University of Life I learned social skills and graces. There may have been no dancing in public but dance halls and night clubs carried on much as before the war. Granted, the number of drinks you could obtain was limited and tobacco products rationed, nevertheless the troops that came home on leave wanted some night life and they got it in one form or other. In any case those based in western countries e.g. France, Belgium and Holland brought back plenty of drinks. These could not be consumed in public places of course but they made parties at home go with a swing and there were plenty of them. You needed no excuse to give or go to a party.

Going to work meant I met new people. My social life expanded. So far my life was family based and now the world was opening up. The family was there, birthday parties continued as before but there was more life beyond the family circle I discovered. Although, let it be said, I missed some of the regular outings and activities. One was an early trip to the fruit and vegetable market. One uncle of ours was a market trader and the family also ran a small greengrocer's shop. As my uncle went to market most days I had many opportunities to go along with him. Yes, I had to rise at an ungodly hour but it was worth it. The fresh smell of the fruit and flowers, the atmosphere itself mixing with the traders made me feel grown up. It made me feel big to talk about it to other children; certainly it was something none of my school friends experienced. When all the dealings were over we collected our purchases, took them to the van and after everything was stowed safely away made our way to one of the pubs to have that longed for breakfast. Boy did that taste good. For me it was a warm drink, a freshly baked roll with a Beefburger you can only get in Berlin. That lovely taste and flavour was revived on a recent trip to my home town. For the grownups drinking began early. They too had a roll and Beefburger but accompanied by a glass of beer. These outings understandably enough could only be during the school holidays. It also meant I had to sleep over with my uncle and aunt and cousin Dorchen. We were like brother and sister anyway and good playmates.

The first tender steps I took going out on my own was during the brief spell of calm between the autumn of 1939 and the spring offensive of 1940, when dancing in public was allowed again. All was quiet on the western front, the only front there was at that time. I had just started work, had my first weekly pay packet and burning to spend it. Not a great amount but it topped up my earnings from cleaning the family's shoes. As I had never been to the West End, here was my chance to find out. Confident I could dance, after all I had taken lessons, I made my way to a well known dance hall. Having got there it was much as I expected except the girls were much older than my cousins and girls I knew. When it came to dancing I was out of their league. Enviously I watched them and hoped one day I could dance as well as them, I just needed more practise I told myself, after all, I had plenty of partners to practise with. My courage to ask a girl for a dance vanished immediately and completely. Even so, I enjoyed watching the more experienced dancers both male and female and in the end was not too disappointed with my first evening out on my own.

Dancing was not the only activity I enjoyed in my leisure time. As I said before, swimming too was high on the list. As with all big organisations and institutions, the railways had a very active and well supported sports club making provision and providing facilities for any discipline you care to name. Yes we had a swimming club, not far from the works as it happened, about two miles away by the River Spree. It was situated in about four acres of wooded ground a short walk away from the station. There was a large club house with restaurant facilities and changing rooms on the ground floor and sleeping accommodation upstairs for anyone who wanted to stay the weekend. These facilities were much in demand when we hosted a tournament. As members of the club we needed to be up nice and early to set up everything for the various races and prepare as much as we could for the last event, water polo. There was also a large play area suitable for all kinds of ball games. Being sandy ground made it ideal playing bare foot if you liked. The 50 metre long pool was along the river front, with 8 lanes but no diving facilities. Well, 1 and 3 metre boards but no 5 or 10 metre platforms. I spent many a weekend there and a good many summer evenings as well during the three years I was with them. Usually I went straight after work with a dip in the river when I got there and then joined others playing ball games with another quick dip before going home, tired but happy. The grounds, pool and club house were open from April to September. During the autumn and winter months we had arrangements with the Post Office swimming club to use their indoor pool one evening a week for training purposes. Occasionally we had a competition between the clubs just for fun and a bit of banter.

During all this time I grew closer to my sister Elli. She spent a year in East Prussia as part of the government scheme to help the social services in the country before she started her training to become a secretary. Now at 18 she had met a great number of people and made many friends. She was invited to lots of parties and whenever she could she asked me to be her escort, not for the whole of the evening but only the early part as later on we had found our partners for the night. The tricky bit came when the party was over and time to go home. I wanted to take my girl of the evening home and Elli's beau of the evening was expecting to take her home hoping to make another date. Most of the time we found a way round it. The only problem with the two girls from Elli's office, they lived too far out of town. Pity really, one of them, Elvera was truly a beautiful girl and I would have loved to take her out more often. Then there was Gretchen, my brother Reinhold's youngest Sister in Law. She was lovely too and lively. I was sweet on her for a while and we had great fun together on family outings. They were usually on Sundays in summertime as most of us worked Saturday mornings. One such family outing was sometime in May at apple blossom time with a visit to Werder, a large fruit growing area such as places in Kent, Hereford or the West Midlands in England. It was about an hour's train journey away from Berlin. Then there was the annual outing to the Spree Wald, a delta formed by the river Spree upstream from Berlin. Again just over an hour's ride away from town. There, in that delta area you found peace and tranquillity as there were few roads and little traffic to be found. The stillness was breath taking. You could almost hear a pin drop. What as children we were looking for, was to mess about on the river in the flat bottom boats they used in the delta for most of the day, with little fear or danger of being drowned as the water was very shallow and quiet flowing apart from the main channel. As I said, there were few roads; almost everything that needed to be transported went by punt. There were other outings of course, but whenever we went out together we had lots of fun. Only once had I taken Gretchen out for the evening, to see a variety show. Then there was Lise, the only girl the same age as myself, all the others were older. We went to the same school and although segregated, we walked to and from school together whenever the timetable would allow. We went for walks in nearby parks, talked a lot and enjoyed each other's company but lost touch after leaving school. She was my first girlfriend one might say. Now that is going back in the past.

However, we must not forget there was a war on. As we got deeper into the conflict life became quite difficult at times. Not only was food rationing introduced but after the successful occupation of Denmark and Norway and the successful outcome on the on the Western front, overrunning France and the Low Countries, Hitler and his cronies became more daring. With the aborted invasion of England, air raids seemed to be the answer. By bombing British cities, Hitler's hope was to force the

British government to surrender. As we know, things did not turn out that way. Over the years air raids increased, especially during the winter months. If the weather was right you could expect nightly raids, thankfully they were never to the same city two nights running. That gave us time to clear up the worst damage and got things moving again. After a night's raid you made your way to work as soon and as best you could and carried on working as long as required, then made your way home hoping to get there before another raid perhaps. One just never knew how long a journey would take.

With communication severely interrupted, keeping in touch with the family proved difficult at times. There was only one answer, you went on foot. Boy, did I walk miles over town. Past burning and collapsed buildings. People trying to identify houses they were looking for anxiously hoping their loved ones managed to get out and away in time and were save somewhere. The joy when you get to your destination and find all are alive and well truly lifts your heart. Yes, your heart jumps for joy. You experience that all over again when you get back and tell the rest of the family at home that all is well. It takes hours of course when you have to do it on foot as a bicycle is not of much use as a lot , if not most, of the time you would either have push it or carry it even with so much rubble and other debris about. The air was full of smoke and soot and foul smelling. By the time I got back home my hands and face were black and clothes almost untouchable. Who cares, the family was still together. Strange as it may seem, in the end you take it all in your stride. War was everywhere and total, but was it as Hitler visualised? Bad and sad as things were there was always something to be thankful for, mostly just being alive and not being a Prisoner of War. Many were used to clear up the rubble the following morning. Most of them came from the Ukraine and were very poorly and roughly treated by their guards. How their eyes sparkled when my father gave them a packet of tobacco from their own country which soldiers, returning from the Russian front often gave him as a tip when he helped them on arrival back home, having been a prisoner of war in Russia himself during the 1st world war knew how they would appreciate the gesture. Horrible stuff to smoke I must say having tried it myself. How different the French prisoners of war were treated that were unfortunate enough to be captured in 1939 or 1940. Our coalman had one working for him for a time, replacing his workers called up to serve in the armed forces. He delivered coal to our flat every week, living on the fourth floor my mother thought he deserved a drink and gave him a cup of coffee each time he called, accompanied by a sandwich or a piece of cake or biscuit. These experiences were part of my growing up as well as the social side. As the future was uncertain and tomorrow may never come parties in the homes continued. No wild parties, just getting together, have a drink and a dance.

Night air raids, sleepless nights, shortages, even no public transport to get me home after a night outdid not stop me going out when I had the opportunity, especially after I got sweet on my boss's secretary at work, Ursula by name. Soon after she arrived I took the courage to ask her out one summer's evening and we went for a lovely walk along the river. As we talked we found we had much in common and shared the same interests. Later that evening, before we said good night, we had made another date. This time it was to a theatre. The government organisation 'Strength through Joy', administered through the Trade Unions, offered tickets for theatre, opera, ballet, cinemas in the West End as well as concerts and sporting events with a discount. My cousin Herta, who was a distribution agent, could get me tickets for most performances and if I struck it lucky even for the evening of my choice. It was an operetta by Franz Lehar, The Count of Luxenburgh. This was the first of many theatre visits we went to. It was not long before I invited her to family parties where she was well received. Meeting Ursula at the station to take her to a party, theatre, show or concert was not always convenient or practical. As I finished work an hour earlier it seemed more sensible to go to her home and go from there. That was when I met her mother of course, who always made me very welcome and wished us a happy and joyful evening as we left. If we were not too late I went in for a night cap. So over time I stayed longer and later, sometimes leaving it rather late to catch the last train home, resulting in me having to sprint to the station. You'll not be surprised to learn that once or twice I missed the train and had to take another line which meant a longer walk home. They were sweet romantic days and happy and carefree too. We partied together with all other friends who could make it on the last Sunday before the following day I left home to join up.

That Monday was a rather sombre day at home. My mother was sad, understandably, as I was her second son to go to war. She already had two brothers on the Russian front, one missing, and presumed dead. Bravely she got on with the daily routine as best as she could. Cooking my favourite meal and pudding and had a good cry, praying I might be spared. My father simply embraced me wishing me well and stressed not to do anything foolish. So I left home in good time not to miss the 22.50 overnight train to Nuerenberg.

Chapter 6

The Signal Corps

On arrival at Nuerenberg's main railway station, the first thing I noticed was the military police; they were very much in evidence here. They were of course out in large numbers at every main railway station in Berlin, so I should not have been surprised. But the situation was different now, before too long I would have to take my oath of allegiance and that would bring me within their jurisdiction. As I looked around I spotted two sergeants, standing by a stand serving as assembly point, waiting for the new recruits. They were arriving by every train. After the last expected train had left and the sergeants were satisfied there were no more newcomers to look out for, we were directed to a truck and taken to the barracks at the edge of town. As it turned out they were occupied by the Waffen S.S., recognised and looked upon as Hitler's elite', a show force. The Waffen S.S. was the military wing of the Nazi regime, in contrast to the S.A. and the S.S. who formed the political wing of the party. The Waffen S.S. was formed long before the war and used to guard Hitler and his official residences e.g. the Chancellery in Berlin and his mountain retreat in the Alps at Bergesgaden, the Eagle's Nest. They also formed the guard of honour when welcoming foreign heads of state or other dignitaries and there were many, I should know, because we had to turn out to a good many during my time in the Hitler Youth, enthusiastically greeting the visitors. That is how the general public saw the Waffen S.S., a kind of Brigade of Guards. Here was I, about to become a member of it. As I liked military music and military pomp, what better unit was there to serve in. I had forgotten there was a war on and times and circumstances had changed. I still had the image from before the war of soldiers Hitler was proud to show off. It was not until many, many years later that I read about the atrocities and ruthless tactics employed by the force in keeping down French resistance fighters and realised how war can and does change the character of a person, an army, a nation. The individual is driven to retaliate because of a lost comrade or friend. The commanding officer is driven to succeed and achieve fame and glory no matter what. A nation, not to have suffered and sacrificed in vain, will accept the unexceptionable. Be that as it may. Here was I, beginning a new phase in my life.

Once inside the barracks we were shown to our quarters where we left our belongings. Then off to be registered. Names and identities were checked. Next of kin names recorded. After that, we went across the square to the mess hall for a bite to eat: Soup, bread and mug of coffee, 'Ersatz Coffee' of course. A while later, the permanent staff having had their lunch and returned to their stations, we were kitted out: All done in a military fashion, including the unavoidable but orderly queues. It has been said that half the time in the military is spent queuing for one thing or the other, well, in the German Army anyway. During the afternoon we were issued with boots, socks, blanket underclothes, pullover, drill pack, military uniform and mess kit. The rifles came later. We took it all back to our rooms, stored everything in our lockers and then had a little time to get know each other before we assembled and were taken to our evening meal, which was as expected the usual stew. It's always tasty and well balanced but not very exciting to look at. But when you are young and still growing, hungry with a healthy appetite, it all tastes good. The pudding course was a milk pudding, rice or semolina, or some fruit, mostly an apple, occasionally a piece of cake. We were not short of sweet savouries as one or the other of us in the room had a parcel from home containing sweets, cakes and chocolate. Sunday lunch was more of a traditional meal, meat, gravy and vegetables, just as we were accustomed at home. But of course it was nothing like home cooking.

Before we returned to our quarters we were issued with a loaf of rye bread to be used for breakfast in the next two days. Bread was given out three times a week. Under military rules loaves had to be at least two days old before they were handed out but not older than five days and not to be eaten after six days. At the same time we were also given a lump of 'Kunsthonig', a substitute honey. Bread and honey to be our daily breakfast with coffee to be fetched from the kitchens and taken to the accommodation blocks where the team on duty would transfer the coffee into jugs. We were also introduced to our sergeant and corporal and the daily timetable. Here our military training began in earnest, although the training received at the Wehrertuechtigung's camp, the three week course in defence awareness and the six months with the National Labour Force stood us in good stead. Taking a rifle to pieces, cleaning it and then reassemble was a piece of cake and impressed the sergeant as did other basic things in the training course we had already been taught and practised. We could now concentrate on automatic weapons and the branch of the military we were to enter; the signal corps. Our intake of recruits was to be trained as signalmen in tanks. We also had a thorough medical check-up on our second day in the Wehrmacht, including a dental examination, which was not good. I was told to come back as soon as possible.

Here at the barracks, as everywhere in Germany, we made an early start. Rising bell was 05.45. By 06.00 we had to be in place for the daily roll call and a quick medical inspection. Every now and then, unannounced, a doctor would be present looking for sexual infections or diseases. Anyone who for any other reason needed to see the doctor or go to the medical centre that day had to say so now. The next 45 minutes were always a bit of a rush, if not hectic, as we had to fit in our ablution as well as our breakfast, which, as I already said, was a very simple one, rye bread and substitute honey issued three times a week. There were eight men to the room and we had our breakfast there. One of us fetched the coffee from the central point in the jug that was standard equipment in each room as were brooms, brushes, pans, buckets and mops. We also had to make our beds, clean the room and leave it neat and tidy before we made our way to the place of instruction or lecture room.

Being part of the Signal Corps, the first activity every morning, six days a week, 07.00 sharp was learning and practising the Morse code, yes Saturday included. The training was not unlike learning the time table. We had to make the Morse code our own, being able to tap out a letter or number without thinking. There were a number of little rhymes that were very helpful and made it easier to learn the alphabet in Morse. There was a rhythm to it that made it almost fun to learn the code. The reason for the early start and being the first lecture or activity of the day was, we were told, that the mind was at its most receptive at that hour in the morning. After a week or so we began to use the proper equipment for our training, hitherto we only tapped out the signal on discarded old Morse keys. From now on accomplished and fully trained signalmen were our tutors, which included N.C.Os. Our progress and achievements were constantly tested and assessed. It proved that chaps with a musical ear made quicker progress, certainly as far as taking down messages were concerned. It also helped when sending out messages.

Not surprisingly progress was slow in the first two or three weeks, but after Christmas and in the New Year we all made good progress. Not that we had much Christmas or New Year celebration that year. We had only just settled in and got to know each other in the room and in our group as well as the platoon. But now as the daily rhythm became part of you it became easier and almost enjoyable and fun even, including learning the Morse code. It could be compared to sequence dancing I suppose; you remember the individual moves but find it difficult to do them in the right order. If you practise them frequently they become part of you. So with using the Morse code, practise daily and the rhythm becomes part of you. By the end of January that year, being 1944, I was quite good at sending messages, 70/75 letters a minute was considered very good. A top signalman could send about 90 letters a minute. One is able to do this because before transmitting a message you have time to read the message and prepare yourself before sending it. Receiving and taking down messages can be more problematic. Not knowing what letter comes next, the moment it takes to think what is was and to write down the letter might, just might, make you miss the next letter or two even. Most of the time you could guess what they were. Missing a letter in a coded message could prove to be a disaster. As every dancer knows, having your feet in the wrong position, or as in a quick, quick move, miss a step altogether, and you are in trouble. The music goes on, the drummer beats out the rhythm; you are all behind and feel stranded. If you have a musical ear you might pick up the dance after a beat or two. If not, you have to wait a moment or two and start the sequence from the beginning. In the heat of battle that is impossible for the signalman to do. At the end of the course I was able to take down about 70 letters a minute correctly.

Learning the Morse code was only a tiny, although important part of our training. The early morning sessions lasted 50 minutes. We then collected our gear for the next training session of the morning which could be anything from light firearms or the workings of a field telephone exchange. On other days we may go out into the woods laying field telephone lines, looking for the best place to position the transmitter and receiver, in which direction to lay out the aerial. There were days when we had field training in basic skills of infantry warfare including tackling the obstacle course. There was even 'Square Bashing' once a week, intended may be for the victory parade, who knows? After lunch there was always a two hour break and then we went across to the tanks for training should we ever find ourselves posted to a tank unit. In most types of tank the signalman doubled up to load the gun. Sometimes we had instructions on basic maintenance of our equipment. By and large our intake of recruits did extremely well, in the field and on the range. As our captain once said to us he never had a better intake. Well drilled and well skilled. That could only have been because all of us had basic training and drill on previous occasions, in the Hitler Youth, Wehrertuechtigungs Camp (Armed Forces Awareness Camp) and in the National Labour Force. Saturdays and Sundays were slightly different. After our morning session in Morse code we joined the rest of the chaps scrubbing the floors and washing the walls along the corridors, toilets and washrooms. Then when the N.C.O. on duty was satisfied that all was to his liking we went to our own room to give it a thorough cleaning. The afternoon and evening were free and we could get a pass to go to town. Not that there was all that much to do or see. In any case we did not have all that much money. Sunday was very similar. Roll call was an hour later and breakfast you could have at your convenience. But of course if you had it late you only had cold coffee such as it was. Most of us took the opportunity to wash our shirts and smalls as well as writing letters to family and friends who were anxious to hear from you.

As we were there for only three months basic training we were not taking part in guard duties but were on twenty four hour standby as fire fighters. By 1944 Allied air raids had penetrated deep into Southern Germany. Munich was the main target but Nuerenberg did not escape entirely. Whenever there was an air raid warning, we made our way to the trucks which were pulling up by the main gate at the double. Within minutes we were on our way to some strategic point in the city which could be a government building or museum. Sometimes it was the main Post Office or main railway station. It was midwinter when I was there with long, dark evenings, our night's sleep was often interrupted but we were spared an actual air raid during my time in Nuerenberg. Occasionally we were also on all night fire watch in buildings that close down at the end of the working day e.g. Rathause, Record Office and other government buildings of this kind.

Then one morning in February we were told that our group was to be posted to Holland to a newly formed Tank Division. As signalman we were to relay messages from the commander of the group to the captain of our tank. In addition we were to be assistant gunners, which meant feeding shells into the gun. Whilst we were beginning to be kitted out for the move, disaster struck. On a regular basis each platoon had a set time to use the shower room. On the day disaster struck for me, we were undressing and when ready, jubilantly rushing towards the showers I slipped on the wet floor, fell heavily and hit my left thigh on the sharp edge of the draining channel and it became badly bruised. Worse was to come. I was unable to get up and realised I was paralysed on my left side from hip to toe. Help was summoned and I was carried to the sickbay where a doctor examined me and diagnosed a bruised nerve. He assured me and all those who stood round my bed that the paralysis would only be temporary and I would be up and about again in a few days after which light duties were recommended. That proved to be the case.

Whilst I was recovering from my fall, the rest of my intake was frantically getting ready to leave to join their unit in Holland. The complete course of injections had to be given as well as a general health check including another dental inspection. Some of the equipment issued to us on arrival had to be handed in at the Quarter Master. Here was I, doing light duties helping the gardener getting the flowerbeds ready to be planted later in the year. It was a strange feeling having to stay behind, as we had got to know each other quite well during the weeks we were together. We had become friends and comrades in that short but intense time of training. A sad day for me it must be said, as I watched them getting onto the lorries and driving out of the barrack gates on their way to the station. There was just one other chap left on our block, Joseph Birnbaum, he had been called up three months earlier than me and came from Bavaria. Joseph had suffered a rather more serious injury received in training, from which he had now fully recovered and deemed fit for active service. Like me, he was put on light duties for the time being and, ordered to join me helping the gardener. So we moved into one room, wondering how long it would be before our fate would be decided. We had not to wait long. Five days later, first thing in the morning, we were summoned to the company's office and told we were posted to a newly formed tank division in the south of France and we had less than two days to be ready. How we managed to tick all the boxes on the list of the things that had to be done I just don't know, but we did it. How the body coped with all the injections and vaccinations was quite remarkable. The amount of equipment issued when posted to an active unit is unbelievable. We were assured it is all needed and necessary. How to get it all stored and packed into one's rucksack is quite an art, but in it went somehow. The last box to be ticked off on my list was the dentist. This was in the afternoon of the day we were to catch the overnight train to Paris from Nuerenberg's main railway station. Not having done as I was told on an earlier visit only eight or nine weeks earlier, I wondered what kind of treatment I could expect. I need not have worried, not only was the dentist attending to me young, but also understanding, gentle, kind and efficient. It was late afternoon before he finished with me, having cleaned my teeth, put temporary fillings in a number of teeth and finally extracted a tooth that was beyond saving. Amazing how he achieved it all in one visit. His parting words were I had to see a dentist as soon as possible after reporting to my unit as the fillings were only temporary. It was more than two years before I saw another dentist.

Chapter 7

The French Connection

Needless to say it was not the most comfortable rail journey I had ever made. Joseph and I left the barracks in good time. As there was nothing to delay us, that did not prove very difficult. All our friends had already gone and there were just the two of us left. Joseph was senior to me, so he was put in charge of our mission. We left Nuerenberg on time and as expected, the train was crowded, as all trains were during the war. There was standing room only by the time we boarded it. No seats for two young soldiers, one in his early twenties the other in his late teens. Standing in the corridor besides other travellers with their luggage and now adding our two packs as well as our rifles, the passage was almost blocked. People wanting to use the toilet had great difficulty in getting by. After an hour or two on the train the painkilling injection I had after my tooth extraction, began to wear off. The gum was inflamed and sore, my head aching and I felt cold and shivery. As neither of us had any Aspirins there was nothing I could take to ease the pain. As the night went by, with nothing to eat since early evening the previous day when we left Nuerenberg, Joseph began to feel peckish. With the corridor packed one could hardly move and it was impossible to get near our rations. That did not bother me as I felt like nothing on earth most of the night. Anyway, I was used to going long periods without food.

Fortunately we had access to our flasks to have a drink albeit only 'Ersatz' coffee, which was of some help.

Early in the morning, with dawn just breaking, we arrived in Mannheim. The train was stopping for twenty minutes which gave us a good opportunity to stretch our legs and get a hot drink to go with our pre packed meal of pumpernickel and cheese. We had to do it in turn so as not to leave our packs and rifles unattended. But before that, with a number of people getting off the train, we secured couple of seats for ourselves. When we started rolling again it was daylight and for the first time we could see the scenery we were passing through. I had never been in this part of the country before so it was quite thrilling for me, not least, when soon after leaving Mannheim we crossed the Rheine of which until then I had only heard of. It was not long after crossing the Rheine we came to the German/French border, again all new territory to me. Then entering France we passed through Alsace and other disputed districts which were given to France in retribution after the First World War and now joined once more to the 'Father Land' after the Spring Offensive in 1940. It was all very new and exciting to me. Eventually nature took over and I fell sound asleep. When I open my eyes again it was time for another bite to eat. This time it was the standard issue of army bread and salami. Having secured a window seat in Mannheim, we could now enjoy the scenery as we travelled through the French countryside munching away on our salami. The next meal, we said, would be in Paris hopefully. The big question, where in Paris and what would it be like?

It was late in the afternoon when we arrived at one of the main stations in Paris; I cannot recall which, too overwhelmed with it all I guess. Before we left the carriage we made sure we had left nothing behind and then made our way to the Station Commander's Office, where one of the clerks on duty checked our credentials and travel documents before issuing us with a number of vouchers. There was a voucher each for an evening meal near the station and a travel warrant for each of us that would get us across the city to a hotel quite near the station from where we would depart the following morning. For the hotel itself, a credit note was issued that would cover the bill for bed and breakfast for the two of us. Finally a railway pass that would get us to Bordeaux the following day. As I said, Joseph was in charge and he got on well with it all.

Having been 36 hours on our feet by now with very little sleep, we both began to feel tired. We were longing to get to our hotel and the rucksack off our backs as well as a bath or shower and a good night's sleep. At the same time we were hungry and looking forward to a hot meal. The reality was we had no choice. With no French money in our pockets once we used our travel warrant there was no going back. Nor did we have any idea where else we could redeem our meal vouchers in the city, so the hot meal near the station it was. A lovely tasting beef casserole as it happened with potatoes and greens, and semolina pudding to follow. The coffee too tasted much better than of late. We enjoyed the meal as well as the atmosphere and took our time before we set out on our journey across the city.

The network of the Metro took a little sorting out but we got there in the end. We were looking for the station we were to depart from for Bordeaux the following morning, so that helped us for the next day. The hotel we were to stay in for the night was indeed just around the corner from the station. We checked in and were received rather indifferently, shown where the dining room was, taken up to our room and then left alone. Again this was quite a thrill for me as it was the first time I was to spend the night in a hotel room and in Paris of all places. During the last twenty four hours on our way to Paris I wondered what we might do in the evening. Going to a café maybe or to a night club even? We did neither. After we had a bath and shave and a general sort out we felt too tired to go anywhere or to do anything. The desire to see Paris by night faded fast, so we had an early night and went to bed instead and just as well, the next day could be demanding and strenuous as we had find our way to Bordeaux first and then to a little town called Mirebeau.

After a good night's sleep we both felt rested and refreshed ready to face whatever the day may bring in its wake. My gum, where two days earlier a tooth was extracted, was still inflamed and swollen, but thank God the pain had gone. When we were ready and had everything packed again we did as we were told, took all our gear and went to the restaurant for breakfast which was of course a simple continental one and it went down a treat. Chewing was less troublesome than it was the day before. Still a little tender but much improved. Meal over, we went along to the station where all documents were thoroughly checked again before we were directed to the platform where our train for

Bordeaux was waiting. As we were early we managed to secure two window seats, with no Officer or N.C.O. entering the compartment, we remained seated to our journeys end.

It was an interesting journey, totally different from what we had seen so far. There were a lot of French civilians on the train, unlike the train to Paris, which was crowded with people from the German Military. As we were nearing Bordeaux, Joseph and I were talking and wondering what the setup in Mirebeau would be. Just before we left the barracks in Nuerenberg we were told when we arrived at our new base we were to be in charge of the telephone exchange there. What kind of an exchange would we find? What size of a telephone exchange would we have to deal with? What was expected of us? Our training in this field had been very basic. Yes, we had laid telephone lines, we had repaired broken and faulty lines, connected terminals to exchanges in training, but this was real.

After arrival in Bordeaux, we went through what had by now become an established routine. First call was the Commandants office. After our papers had their stamp of approval we were told to wait in the canteen, where we could have a meal, whilst the office was arranging transport for us to our final destination. In due course we were called and introduced to the driver of a lorry that came from the unit we were to join. He took us to his vehicle. We tossed our belongings in to the back of the lorry, except our rifles of course, joined the driver in his cab and off we went. It was quite a lovely ride through rural France. The scenery was totally different from what I had known since my childhood in Berlin. On the way our driver filled us in as to what we would find when we joined the company. It was the maintenance unit of the newly formed tank regiment. After an hour or so we arrived at the little market town of Mirebeau, south of Bordeaux in southern France.

The driver dropped us outside the company's headquarters, in one of the hotels in the market square, which was quite picturesque. Before he drove off he welcomed us to the company and made sure we left nothing behind in his lorry. We went into the building and were shown to the office where we met the company clerk, who seemed more than pleased to see us. We handed him our papers, at which he had a quick look before he took us to the Sergeant Major who was equally overjoyed to see us. After a little chat to make us feel welcome and relaxed, he himself took us upstairs to the room where the newly installed exchange was situated. It was in one of the hotel's single rooms, enough space for a single bed, a small wardrobe, acting as a locker and the equipment that makes up the exchange. He then took us along the corridor to another single room simply furnished with single bed, wardrobe/locker, chair and small table. These were our two rooms to share. One of us had to be at the exchange, while the other rested. We had to work out a plan that suited us, as long as one of us was on duty. As we were part of the headquarters' staff we took our main meal with the others in the hotel restaurant. All other rations were issued to us from the kitchen. Officially our duties would start the following morning, 06.00. That gave us just the evening to sort ourselves out.

How did they manage to operate before our arrival? They didn't. The post had only been established two weeks earlier. Everybody was still settling in. Internal memos were sent by messengers and external mail, messages and orders from higher command posts delivered and taken away by road. While unpacking our few belongings, Joseph and I talked about our rather unusual situation. First we talked about the shift pattern and decided a twenty four on and twenty four hour off routine with a break over the mid-day period. It would work as follows; shift would start at 18.00 and continue through the night till 10.00 the following morning. The one who had the night off would take over until 14.00, when the one who had been on duty since the previous evening would finish off his shift and be relieved at 18.00 by the one who had most of the last twenty four hours free. That gave the one that came off duty the evening free to do as he liked, not that there was much if anything to do. We had no entertainment other than the home produced, as it were, so we could not expect much on that front as there was very little time and opportunity to meet socially and to get to know each other. We were a new unit and had to find a place to store the new equipment that arrived daily now, somewhere in town safely and securely. Half the men were on guard duty most of the time anyway, which made it almost impossible to get them together for any kind of rehearsal.

After all, there was a war on. We were the occupying power. The enemy was all around us in the form of French resistance fighters. One could never totally relax even if the locals seemed friendly and some were. Apart from drinking, smoking, talking or playing cards there really was not much one could look forward to. So the working pattern we worked out suited us very well. The two of us were very lucky really. We were excused daily roll call and were we expected on parade at any time. Neither did we any guard duties. What a cushy posting!

Operating the telephone exchange was not very demanding either. We started our duties at 06.00 the morning after our arrival. Joseph, being the senior, took the first turn. I stayed with him observing and taking notes hoping to offer a smooth running service when I took over at 10.00 and handed the ear phones back to Joseph at 14.00. He then saw his shift out and handed the phones back to me at 18.00. We were pleased that our first twelve hours went without a hitch, thanks to our training back in Nuerenberg. I was wondering now what the night shift would bring. I need not have worried. Most of the time the exchange fell silent after 6 p.m., as did the town. Any calls after that usually came from officers requesting a drink or light refreshments from the kitchen. After ten in the evening we were able to stretch out on the bed, ready to answer any call that came during the night, which was very rare. Towards the end of the night we went and spruced ourselves up, tidied the room ready for inspection by the officer of the watch soon after six in the morning. But at 06.00, come what may, we tested the outside lines. There were four of them. They were to neighbouring units stationed at nearby towns. These lines had to be tested every morning at 06.00, partly to make sure the lines were not down and partly for security. We were always relieved when we heard a cheerful voice at the other end. We need to remember we are talking here of Spring 1944. Things were beginning to stir beneath the surface and the atmosphere quite tense at times. All the other terminals at the exchange were internal connections to various offices in town and depots on the outskirt of town.

As for internal calls there were two lines that had priority over all others, the Captain's personal line and the Company Office; next came the officers, then any other line. Once the morning rush was over, usually about ten in the morning, the workload for the rest of the day was light. Joseph and I got on well together. When we were not manning the switch board then we stayed in the second room allocated to us in the hotel, mending socks or cleaning boots, washing smalls. We may have been excused many things but we still were subject to a surprise inspection by the Officer and N.C.O. on duty. In fact the second room we had was our restroom. That is where we slept the nights we were not on duty. There were no other private soldiers billeted in the hotel only the officers, if we wanted company when off duty we had to do go to one of the two dormitories in town where the rest of the company had their sleeping quarters, or should it be raining, look in at the guard room for a short while. Walking the town would have been ill advised and foolish, given the circumstances.

As I said, we were newly formed and things were changing all the time. We were supposed to be a repair unit, but as yet had no work shop as far as I knew, nor anyone to work in it. But these were early days for the company and in any case there wasn't anything that needed repairing. This easy life was not to last for long. To make the unit complete and serviceable, one morning in early April I was called into the office and told to get ready to go on a fortnight's course for electro and motor mechanics in Dresden, leaving at once. So back to Germany I went.

This time the train ride was not nearly as exciting as the one only a month ago. I was quite used to getting on and off trains now. The countryside I travelled through was still pleasant but nothing as exciting as the first time round. Nor did I touch Paris on the way east. The route back to Germany took us through Lyon, Dijon and Mannheim where I had to change trains. It was the middle of the night by now and quite chilly which was not surprising, after all it was still early April, as well as draughty as all railway stations are. The waiting room was not too crowded and I found an empty seat in the far corner of the room. It was very quiet for a place that is usually buzzing with noise I must say. Obviously it was past our bedtime. All we had to do was to wait till our designated train arrived and hopefully on time, something that could not be guaranteed, then continue with our journey. I did not have to wait too long before the train that would take me to my final destination rolled in. In fact I was looking forward to seeing Dresden again, as not so long ago I spent a wonderful holiday there with three of my fellow apprentices. It was then still a quiet, open, beautiful, clean town. What would it be like now? Had the war changed it I wondered?

It was in the forenoon when finally we got to Dresden. With my travel documents checked and cleared I made my way to the barracks. From my previous visit to the city I remembered in which direction to head and what tramline to take. So it was not long after I left the station that I reported my arrival at the guard room, from where I was shown the way to the accommodation block where the members of the course would be billeted. Once there, I was shown to a room where one fellow participant had already settled in. It was a room for four, so there were still two more to come and join us. Both of them arrived during the afternoon. As it turned out I was the youngest of the four in our room, which did not really surprise me. Not that it mattered; we were there for just two weeks, the duration of the course.

After the evening meal we gathered in one of the lecture rooms where we were introduced to the staff and what the course was all about. As it turned out, some of the course work on electrical motors I was already familiar with. That meant I could pay more attention to maintaining and servicing petrol engines, specially two stroke engines which were used in the field and diesel generators. It was an easy paced course. As usual the morning work was in the classroom, starting at 09.00. There was a compulsory rest period after lunch and two sessions in the workshop, one before the evening meal and one after, finishing about 21.30. No time in the evening to go and paint the town red.

At the weekend we did go and have a walk into town. There were no concerts in the park by the music students from the music academy this time: as it was too early in the season. All the same it felt good being away from barracks for a while admiring the sights as well as girls and have a drink or two.

There was one facility at the barracks which, as far as I know no other barracks sported, a Sauna! Wednesday afternoons, at 14.00 we were marched across the square, a vast one I remember, towels under our arms to the sauna, where we stripped and when ready walked, carefully this time, into the sauna room. It was an experience of a lifetime. The attendance poured water over the red hot stones which produced the hot steam that opens the pores and cleans the skin, makes you perspire, drains you of your energy and makes you feel very, very tired. I cannot remember how long we were in the sauna itself, what I shall never forget is the plunge into ice cold water as we came out. All part of the treatment we were told. At the end of it all we marched back to our quarters, somewhat weak at the knees now, and told to go to bed but be up in time for the next session in the workshop at 16.30. I had the good fortune to experience this treatment twice whilst in Dresden.

At the beginning of the second week it was suggested that we might try and get permission from our commanders for a short leave whilst in Germany. My request was granted I am happy to say, as were the requests of all the other chaps. We all were sorry to leave Dresden as it was such a relaxed atmosphere. No square bashing, no guard duties, no field work, what a place to be. It was quite timely therefore to remind ourselves there was a war going on and we had to play our part that is why we came to Dresden in the first place. The course finished on Friday of the second week and checking out did not take too long as we brought all we needed for personal use and comfort with us. Just after lunch we left barracks, made our way to the station and hey presto, Berlin here we come.

Not having a telephone at home, I phoned our landlord and told him of my good fortune. He said he would be very happy to go upstairs and tell the family I would be home Friday evening. In fact I arrived home early evening and was greeted joyfully by my mother with tears in her eyes, happy to have one of her boys home, if only for a short while. We talked long into the night, catching up on family news. The two younger uncles, young enough still to be in the armed forces, were on the Russian Front, one of my brothers was in the air defence around Hamburg, the other somewhere in occupied Europe. My older sister worked as an auxiliary nurse in East Prussia. That left only my sister, the baby of the family now nine years old, at home under mother's wing. My cousins, being younger than me, most of them in their teens, were still at home. Mother had contacted them to tell them I would be home for the weekend and there would be a party Saturday night. She managed to get hold of some our young friends including Ursula and told them I would be home over the weekend and invited them to the party. Some could not make it, but those who did had a wonderful time. We danced long into the night and in fact had to run to the station to catch the last train. I took Ursula home and had to walk back the four miles or so to Lichtenberg where we lived. Before we had our last 'Good Night Kiss' we arranged I would come to her house on Sunday night as her mother would like to see me as well, that would leave all day Sunday to be with the family at home.

That was how I spent the last weekend in Berlin with family and friends for many years.

Monday was a lazy day. As my train for Paris did not leave till 19.50 that evening I stayed in the building and spoke to the neighbours, thanking them for being so tolerant the night before. I also called on the landlord and thanked him for taking the message to my mother on Thursday. In the afternoon, with my sister home from school, I played with her until supper time. The meal over, I got ready and, when it was time, made my way to the station.

Night travel seemed to have become a habit with me. With the evenings beginning to draw out we could see more of the countryside we were travelling through. This time it was a straight run from Berlin to Paris where we arrived about eight the following morning. Now familiar with the routine and what to expect at these terminals, I was quite relaxed making my way through various checks and inspections. Even making my way across Paris in the Metro to the other side of town to pick up my train for Bordeaux I felt quite relaxed. I made the connection alright and the journey too was smooth and uneventful. Not that one wanted it otherwise. It was late afternoon by the time the train pulled into the main station at Bordeaux. Having travelled now for over thirty six hours I hoped it would not be too long before I was on my last leg of the journey back to Mirebeau, to get a bed to lie on and stretch out. Luck was with me, as it has been all my life. I got back to the company about 19.00 that evening and was pleased to see some familiar faces. This time I was assigned a bed in one of the dormitory blocks and told to report back to the office at 09.00 in the morning.

Chapter 8

D – Day Plus

That was not the only change. Not having that cushy job in the telephone exchange any longer I now had to be on parade for roll call every morning as well as being regularly on guard duty. With French Resistance Fighters becoming more active and more daring by the day, one almost had to have eyes at the back in one's head. Orders were that guards at night had to be doubled, which in reality meant a lot of the time we were on guard duty somewhere in town with little spare time to do any work or have any free time. Even before I reported to the office the next morning I had noticed some changes that had taken place during the two and a half weeks I had been away from the unit. Firstly, Joseph had been seconded to Divisional Headquarters which did not surprise me, as he was really good at sending and receiving messages by Morse Code. He was wasted as a telephonist, certainly at a small exchange such as we had in Mirebeau. Our places were taken by two veterans who had seen action on the Russian front as well as in France. In the office the Sergeant Major told me that my colleague in the workshop had arrived and would be waiting for me in the garage across the town square which had been commandeered to be our workshop. His name was Werner Fleischer. As expected he was older and at twenty-four years old, had six years more work experience than me. As it turned out, he was a good and patient teacher in the weeks that followed and I learned a lot from him. Werner told me we had a truck we could call our own and a driver to go with it. Just as well, as neither of us could drive. In the garage we had all the tools necessary to repair the communication equipment that came into our workshop, which mainly involved replacing faulty components in radio transmitters, receivers and field telephone sets. The work involved testing the faulty set and after identifying the problem, replacing the faulty part. Portable radio sets had recently come onto the market and occasionally one of the officers would bring in a set which had stopped functioning to see if we could get it working again. Here I was in a nine to five job, what else could one ask for?

With guards doubled during the night half the company was on duty, whist the other half got drunk. Those on duty made up for it on alternate nights. It was only cheap 'Vin Ordinaire' from the local farms let me hasten to add. When you were on 24 hours guard duty you were on from 18.00 in the evening to 18.00 the following evening. The extra guards for the night mustered at 18.00 as well but came off at 06.00 the following morning, then had three hours off before it was back to work. That alternated, your 24 hours duty came every fourth night. Two days later you reported for duty as extra night guard. That too came round every fourth night. We were very glad that summer was on the way and the nights were getting shorter. That meant only one of our watches would be during the hours of darkness when naturally visibility is restricted.

With the bombing of railway lines, bridges and roads for weeks now, the invasion of France by the Allied Forces did not come as a surprise. All along it was just a question of when. As the world knows now, it took place on 6th June 1944. Our unit had been on standby for weeks and ready to move when ordered to do so. Now the day had arrived we expected to pack up and go. Not so. It took several days for the High Command to decide which fighting unit our Division was to join. We as the work and repair unit were stationed furthest south and west. The tanks with their supply unit were to the north and east of us, the waiting time was tense. After D–Day we had to be more vigilant than ever, especially at night, not knowing where French Resistance fighters would strike next. From the residents of Mirebeau we had not much to fear we thought except that they might hide or shelter members of the Resistance and so aiding and abetting their fight for freedom.

By the middle of June we had our marching orders to make our way north. With everything ready and packed, we destroyed what we could not take with us; we made our way north to rendezvous with other units of our Division. In convoy we made our way north to join the fighting units in Normandy. Progress was very slow; at times it seemed we were only crawling along. After two days we came to the fringe of the fighting zone and within reach of Allied fighter planes. From now on we could only travel by night. Fighter planes strafed the roads and fired on anything and everything that moved which caught out many of our chaps which were careless or foolish enough to move, as well as some French civilians in the early days of fighting. The outcome of this, before dawn we had to find a suitable place, a wooded area or an orchard, to hide in. Before daylight everything had to be camouflaged to avoid detection by the fighter planes. With the sky full of these planes, we were told to move only when absolutely necessary as a keen eyed pilot might spot us. This procedure was repeated day after day. The routine became, you slept during the day if you had the chance, guards still had to be mounted, equipment to be checked and maintained, vehicles serviced and made ready for the next night's journey travelling in the dark hours of the night. With a total blackout it was not always easy to see the vehicle in front of you, even with three pairs of eyes as it was in our case. With the nights getting shorter we did not travel very far in any twenty four hour period. There were times when we struck it lucky when looking for a suitable place to hide. Once or twice when we were near villages we found empty barns or large buildings we could drive in and be out of sight. We had to make sure doors were completely shut or else. Any military hardware showing and the buildings were attacked regardless of what it might cost the farmer. The French farming community suffered heavy losses anyway. Much of their livestock was killed by straying bombs or bullets when bolting during air attacks, running out into the open. As we neared the front line we found the farms forsaken, houses and outbuildings empty, frightened animals roaming the roads. Parts of the horrors of war you can only imagine unless you experience it yourself. All this was confronting me totally unprepared as no one talks about this side of war. All that is ever published is the human cost of the war and quite rightly so. In some respects we should be grateful to our politicians for having the courage to do so.

There were other reasons for our delay and slow progress towards Normandy and the front line. Shortage of fuel was one of them. Sustained bombing of roads and railways by Allied Air Forces in the run up to the invasion seemed to have paid off. Many of the fuel and ammunition dumps were badly damaged or destroyed altogether. The outcome, shortages of everything needed to go into battle, including food. Once or twice we had to lay up for two days waiting for fuel to be delivered which could only be delivered by night. Every now and then we ran short of food supplies. It was here that our Company Sergeant Major showed his worth as the mother of the company. He would go into the nearby town, village or farm in search of food, requisition supplies, issue the store or farmer with a credit note to be honoured by the German government. What a hope, but he made sure the men in his care had something to eat. On one such occasion we were sheltering in a barn with a brook running through a nearby wood. We saw this as a good opportunity to have a thorough bodily clean up. When the air space above and around us was free of planes we dashed across to the wood and sat down by the fresh, life giving water and savoured the moment.

We also experienced the complete opposite. There were days when the thundery rain never seemed to end. Our misfortune was to be out in the open. Then, the only way to get out of the rain and to keep dry was to crawl under the lorry. Even then it was no feather bed, the ground under you became wet and then the three of us climbed into the cab of the truck for shelter hoping to get some rest. Not easy under such cramped conditions. You dreamed of your comfortable bed back home or even the last time you stretched out on straw in someone's loft somewhere.

Eventually we made it. By the middle of July we were near St. Lo. Rumour had it the advance by Allied forces had come to a halt or even stalled on some sections. Be that as it may, our orders were to halt the line until reinforcement arrived. Reports from the front reported that German forces had suffered heavy losses that to some extent explained our predicament. It was hoped that reinforcement was on its way. Looking back on this time I cannot recall ever having been employed as a Division. All I can recall is we were sent in small groups, platoon strength, to fill the gaps. Anyone, that could carry a rifle and was not needed anywhere else, was sent to the front line. To slow down the enemy's advancement, on our section of the front anyway, the order was to halt any advance during the day and then make an orderly retreat in the night to a point where a new line of defence had been established, always hoping we could check the advance of opposing forces for at least a day or two. Once we reached the new line of defence we were directed further back to a point where the next line of defence would be established should we fail to hold our line. This went on for the most part of July 1944.

There was just one occasion when we were withdrawn for a forty eight hours rest which was spent in a good clean up and a good sleep. We were very tired, so much so that I found myself sleeping as we marched along the road. In fact I could drop off to sleep almost anywhere. This forty eight hours break nearly proved fatal to our detachment. By then we were almost an unrecognisable force, made up of men from each and every unit that was in the area, led by a young officer. During our rest American forces surrounded us and blocked our route to the new line of defence which we were to have established by daybreak. Goodness knows what happened to the chaps that were to hold on to the line during the night. We clashed just before dawn that morning and a battle developed between us. We had nothing but small firearms, mostly rifles, as well as a few automatic weapons including one or two machine guns mounted on selected trucks. The skirmish started soon after it was fully daylight and continued for two or three hours. Why we were not captured, or killed, or even wounded I shall never know. All I know, with our rapid firing we managed to keep their heads down. The Americans themselves may have had only small and limited arms, who knows. Possibly the American Command may not have been aware of the situation which we know developed over night. Being so very early in the morning would have been another factor. That too might explain the absence of fighter planes, being soon after day break. We managed to hold on and survived until the German force that came to our rescue opened a corridor for us to make our escape. The Colonel in command was pleased we made it back behind German lines as we were urgently needed to strengthen the defence to prevent a rapid advance of Allied Forces in our sector. There was a lot of shelling from both sides that day. After attacks by American planes, scouts came out from behind their cover to test our defences but were hurrying back when we opened fire. We managed to hold our position that day as well as the following night.

As our replacement arrived we withdrew from our posts to have a day away from the frontline, hoping to find somewhere to stretch out and have some sleep. We lost all track of time by now and when we inquired what date it was we were told, 31st July! Towards evening, after having spent some time during the day cleaning and oiling our weapons, we were getting ready to go forward again and take up our position once more, when some of our comrades coming back from the front line were passing us looking tired, hoping for a hot meal and find a place to get some sleep. Then along came a Captain whom I had not seen before, the replacement I assumed for my old Captain who had been seriously injured a few days earlier, with a young Lieutenant beside him. He ordered us to follow him. We left the main road, marched along a narrow lane with banks on both sides. A few minutes later we left the lane, went across a field where on the other side the Captain placed us in a ditch that ran along a hedge. He left the young Lieutenant in charge with the order to hold the position for the next twenty four hours, then left. So far, in our section, we were able to hold on to our positions and restrict the advance of the Americans to the dark hours of the night or very early morning. We all hoped we could do so again. Two nights earlier we sustained heavy casualties, our Captain among them. We just had to wait and see what the dawn would bring.

At dawn the next morning, 1st August 1944, we were heavily bombarded. First with mortar fire that made us keep our heads down. That continued for a considerable time. When the bombardment ceased, we were experiencing continuous air attacks. The Lieutenant, about four yards to the right of me, was experiencing his first shelling. He looked somewhat frightened I must say and in a way I really felt for him, as only six weeks earlier I suffered the same experience. The flash of guns, the whizzing of bullets, exploding bombs, the acrid smell of gunpowder, the sounds of battle and war do make you scared and frightened when first encountered. As with everything else, if you live through it you get used to it. At first you duck every time you hear a bullet whizzing past you. Then you remember, the bullet that hits, injures or kills, you don't hear. You get battle hardened. That was the experience the young Lieutenant went through at that moment. But take it from me, you get used to it.

When eventually it stopped we took the risk to lift our heads and look across the adjoining field expecting to see American soldiers coming across the field attempting to take our position or at least firing at us as we looked over the hedge, instead we heard a noise behind us. Looking round we were staring into the rifles of half a dozen G.I.s. They must have found a gap further along our thin line and managed to get behind us. To resist would have been suicide, so the Lieutenant surrendered and we laid down our arms. There were just three of us besides the Lieutenant. Remarkably, none of us were injured. Then we heard for the first time the words we heard a hundred times or more; 'Come on! Let's go'! What happened in other sections along the line we had no idea. They may have suffered heavy casualties, we never found out. The four of us were taken behind the American line and marched to a holding compound. On the way I wondered what would happen to us. Images of Russian Prisoners of War in Berlin came to mind and how they were treated. Would we experience the butt end of a rifle on our backs cramming us into a railway goods wagon? Where would we be taken to? What would life be like in a prison camp? My father never talked about camp life when he was a P. O. W in Russia during the 1st World War, only about the three years that it took him to get home after the Russian revolution.

My feelings were rather mixed, my mind confused, but I was not frightened.

Chapter 9

The Prisoner of War Years: The Early Stages

As soon as we arrived at the holding compound the young Lieutenant was taken away whilst the three of us joined the two soldiers already in the compound. When talking to them we learned they too had been taken prisoner that morning, a little earlier then us under similar circumstances, expecting to hold a thinly defended line. It was not long after we got to the holding compound we were taken to our first interrogation. It was a strange feeling I must admit, never even having contemplated such a situation, but here I was facing an American officer. As instructed and as it was drummed into us I just stuck to name and number. I could not have told him anything that he did not already know of that I am certain. The mix of soldiers they captured and took prisoner over the last few days would have told the American Command that all is not well behind the German lines. I was taken back to the compound wondering what next. The other four who were with me in the compound and had also been taken for interrogation returned one by one having been asked identical questions; which Unit, which Division, name of commanding officers, how many men, how many tanks? As I said, they knew as or even more than we could tell them.

Round about mid-day we were handed a packet of army field ration of a strange mixture. The first problem was how to open it. Neither of us had an implement to use as a tool to break into the pack. Eventually we found a strong enough piece of wood to leaver the seal and break it open to gain access to the food which looked strange to us but smelled good enough to eat and that is exactly what we did. A little later we were given a mug of coffee which went down extremely well. It was the first drink we had that day. Soon afterwards we were taken one by one for another interrogation to be interviewed by a different officer who adopted a different approach but asked basically the same questions. When the five of us were all together again, no other prisoners arrived during the day, towards evening we were taken by truck to a more substantial enclosure. We joined those who were already there, which I estimated round about the thirty mark. All of us looked somewhat tired and forlorn by now having been on our feet for most of the day with little rest or food and drink. That was put right soon after we got to the camp. We were given a drink and an evening meal, U.S. army ration and a blanket each. So ended my first day as a Prisoner of War, going to sleep rolled up in an army blanket, under a starry sky in Normandy, France.

Being tired and exhausted sleep came quickly, not that it was the most comfortable night I ever had, but at least one could lie down and stretch out a little, but not for long, the cool night air made you curl up like a hedgehog, so helping to retain the body heat to stay under the blanket. Early in the morning the chilly air woke me as well as nature's call and I could not help wondering what would come next. Where would we be taken from here? How would we be treated? How long before our folks back home would learn of my fate? All these questions remained unanswered for a while. Understandably, pictures of how I saw Russian prisoners of war from the Ukraine were being treated by their German guards back in Berlin came to mind again. These thoughts were soon blown away as soon after our morning count and breakfast, which was identical to the ration pack we had the previous day in the holding camp, a G.I. standing by the gate beckoned me to come to him, which naturally I did. He selected three more and then took the four of us to an open army truck with a number of rolled up stretchers on it. After about half an hour's drive along a road on which we could see plenty of evidence that fighting had taken place recently, we drove into a field and stopped. We were ordered off the truck and through an interpreter were told what we had to do. It was to search the fields, ditches and hedgerows around us for corpses, American, German, civilians. We were told it was most unlikely we still would find anyone alive. In pairs, with guards to keep an eye on us and a medical orderly, we set out across the field not knowing what we would find.

What confronted us was almost unbelievable. I had no idea where in Normandy we might be. The area we were in must have been heavily bombarded by artillery and from the air, but did it matter? All I know is, what we saw is seldom if ever reported or written about by reporters or journalists. It really was an unrecognizable mess. First impression was that German forces suffered heavy casualties, these were only the corpses we saw, there must have been at least an equal number of wounded. We hardly knew where to start. Apart from the corpses, both German and American, there were cows bloated, lying stiff where they fell with their legs stuck up in the air, in the meadows around us. Horses still in their traces, broken loose from their wagons, then suffering the same fate as everything and everyone else as they ran wild, lay dead in the fields. In the sweltering, blistering heat of July and August corpses and carcases covered with maggots and flies, not a pretty sight. The smell, no, the stench was almost sickening and hard to get used to but after a little while we did. Our task then was very urgent clearing the fields, ditches and hedges in this area to avoid an epidemic. With only gloves as protective clothing we started work, handling the corpses very carefully as directed by the medical orderly and as the decaying bodies would allow. When we had them safely on stretchers, a team of G.I.s who had joined us would take them off somewhere else, we had no idea where. We did this for about six hours with a break in between and to my surprise a meal as well. We had access to a drink of water at any time.

At the end of the day we were taken back to the holding camp, where the number had almost doubled, just in time as the evening rations were given out. We washed our hands thoroughly and then joined the others who eagerly wanted to know what we had been up to whilst away. That evening someone suggested that it would be better if we slept in pairs using one blanket as a groundsheet so to speak and the other as a cover. We did this and it worked, so we used this method for the rest of the time we were in France using the starry sky as a canopy. Fortunately it kept dry all the time whilst I lived under those conditions. The next morning the same G.I. came into the camp and picked the four from the previous day to resume the job. Off we went, this time knowing what we could expect. We found far fewer corpses than the day before for which we were very thankful. As on the previous day, we had a mid-day break with a meal and a drink which those who remained in camp did not have. They just had two meals a day.

As the fourth day of captivity began for me I had got to know some of my fellow prisoners a bit better and learned that all of us were taken prisoner in groups of three or four holding the thin line. We assumed from this and as far as we could tell, it was still an orderly retreat. Whilst wondering what today would bring, a different G.I. came into camp, looked around and after he found what he was looking for beckoned me to come over to him. After he had found the other three that were with me the previous two days we went out to a waiting jeep this time and off we went, ending up at a military cemetery. A different smell welcomed us here, chloride. Chloride was the dominant smell for the rest of the day. What the four of us found so very touching and in some ways very surprising was the care and trouble that was taken by the American Authorities to identify the decaying bodies and that is not an easy task when at times it was difficult to keep the body together or when the skin is peeling. When no military identification disc was found on the body they were carefully checked for other identification, e. g. photographs or private addresses that might give a clue to the authorities who this might be. Valuables were removed, rings etc., carefully listed and put into a bag. The teams, there were a number of them working in the cemetery, were also looking for maybe a birthmark still visible that could help. Slowly and painstakingly they went over the body and when all was done that could be done and everybody on the team was satisfied, the bodies were handed over to us. Our task was to dust the corpse, or what was left of it, with chloride. We then carefully put it in a body bag and took it to an assigned grave where once more it was checked to make sure the earthly remains of the deceased went into the right numbered grave before we lowered it to be buried. The cemetery was divided into sections and whatever conclusion the examining team came to, it was up to them to decide to which section we would take them. I had no idea what the criteria was that decided the section of the cemetery in which the remains should be buried nor did I care. All I remember it could be quite a way off as it was a very large cemetery. As the day before, we had a break around mid-day with something to eat and drink. The four of us were called out the following day to do exactly the same task. So far the events and the experiences since being taken a prisoner turned out altogether differently than I expected.

That evening when we returned to camp numbers had greatly increased. Looking around I still could not see a face I recognised. But we were a mixed bunch alright. Some, as myself, in combat gear, others still had their uniform on and that is all we possessed except perhaps a picture of a loved one from back home, which our captors let us keep in our pocket. All my personal belongings were left on the truck with our tools, drawings and other equipment.

On the fifth morning after being captured, August the 6th, the guards came into the camp very early urging us to get up and have our food which was waiting to be issued and to get ready to move. As there was nothing to pack and get ready, all we had to do was have our food and we were ready. It was not long afterwards that a number of soldiers arrived to march us down to the beach where a landing craft was waiting for us to board. Those among us who knew about ships and the sea soon realized that our destination would not be America, so it had to be England, somewhere along the south coast. As soon as all who were to sail with us were aboard the ramps were raised and at that moment one of our lads attempted to escape. A patriotic act no doubt, but foolish under the circumstances, as there were at least half a dozen G.I.s with guns at the ready to stop anyone of us attempting to make a break for it. He was shot in the leg and immediately hauled back in and taken to the first aid post on board where a doctor attended to his wound. We were told he was not seriously wounded and would live. Now of course the speculation began, as to where we would land. I did not have a clue nor at that moment did I care. All I wondered was, would I be seasick or not.

Chapter 10

The First British Encounter

Never having been to sea before I had no idea what seasickness felt like, what its symptoms were, what it looked like. When I heard people talking about this condition either having suffered it themselves or observed others going through this experience said, the nausea really makes you feel very sick and you wished you could die. People around the sufferer will tell you they look green and grey and in severe cases, like a dead person. These were the thoughts that went through my mind as we pulled away from the beach on the Cherbourg Peninsular heading out into the English Channel. As when on other occasions, not knowing what would befall us, I settled down and left the future in the hand of God and fate.

After a very early start to the day, a hurried breakfast and the Channel calm, with no one on board showing any sign of seasickness, we all began to feel a little peckish. We had to wait a little longer though before we had any refreshment. It must have been two hours or more, at least it felt like it, before we had a drink of coffee and a cookie, gratefully received I might add. As an eighteen year old with a healthy appetite whatever the situation, I could eat anything at any time. After several hours at sea we noticed signs that we were docking, but where, that was the big question. As we were in the hold of the landing craft or cargo deck throughout the journey we had no idea what we would see when we emerged from below. The wounded we had on board, including the one of our own, who was shot when he tried to escape just before we cast off from the French beach, as well as any other Allied personal, disembarked first. That task accomplished, we were ask to stand and form a marching column. While all this was taking place a group of British soldiers came on board to take over from our American captors. When the handover was completed the order to march off was given by the British officer who was now in charge. It was very striking how much more relaxed the whole atmosphere had become from the moment the British army had taken on the responsibility of seeing us safely to our journey's end. We lined up into a column, walked up the ramp onto the slipway and waited until all the prisoners were ashore. When our new guards were satisfied everything was as they wanted it, we marched off. Just before we moved off we were told that we were in Southampton, England. What we noticed as we marched along the streets was that the traffic was mostly none military, which we had not seen for a long time. Along the route we saw a row of what seemed to us private houses as well as larger buildings of commercial type used for storage and the like. Something else that was new to us was our escort, the British Tommy, the first any of us had seen. In fact there were quite a number of them, none of them carrying firearms. That was an amazing sight. So very different from what we had experienced so far.

As we marched along we also noticed heavy bomb damage in downtown Southampton as well as in the dock area as we approached it. We learned later, the place we came ashore was the Town Quay. Marching through downtown Southampton gave me a strange feeling I recall. I cannot put my finger on it and tell you why. Maybe I expected hostility from passers-by, sneering at us as we went along, or showing animosity. But no, they ignored us, minding their own business. Perhaps they have seen it a number of times before in the last few weeks and had become used to it, who knows, but it certainly felt strange to me. As we went along, the houses were receding and we entered a more open space area. There were roads and railway lines as well as sheds and other industrial buildings; obviously we were in Southampton Docks now. We also spotted a large fenced off section to which we were making for. It was very obvious we had reached our destination, a substantial holding compound. There was a large shed to which we were taken. As we entered we were handed a mug of hot tea with milk and sugar, the first I had ever tasted. Oh boy did that taste good. Hitherto the only tea with milk I ever tasted was on an occasional Sunday at home when my father was not on duty. He requested tea in the afternoon, reminding him of the years in Russia. All I remember the tea was weak and tasteless and looked insipid, but this tasted totally different. We were also handed a large sausage roll which tasted gorgeous. No doubt this would keep us going for a while. When all had finished their drink and bite to eat we boarded a waiting train and continued our journey into the unknown.

It was not a long journey, only an hour or so, when the train came to a halt. It appeared to be in a country area. Apart from the station buildings there were only a few houses to be seen. As ordered we got off the train, formed into a column and off we went, marching through a country lane this time. It was not a long route, ten minutes or so when houses and other buildings appeared. It turned out to be a grandstand on a race course. I was familiar with such a sight as I had seen them in and around Berlin. The first thing we were given when we got there was a registration form. Having filled it in and handed it back to German speaking clerks, we were taken to a shower room and told to strip. Our clothes were taken away to be de-loused and our heads inspected for lice. After that we had a nice, long shower and felt all the better for it. We were handed a lovely large towel to dry ourselves with. Then every one of us received two pairs of socks, two vests and two pairs of underpants and a small kitbag to carry it all. Our clothes were returned to us but before we were allowed to wear them we had to see a doctor, of which there were quite a large number in attendance.

By now daylight was fading, the evening was coming in and we were beginning to feel hungry. We had no idea as to when or where we would have our next meal. We did not have to wait for very long. Once all the necessary procedures were completed the sergeant in charge gave orders to line up and then took us a short distance to a large tent where a cooked meal was waiting for us, as well as a nice hot milky sweet mug of tea. Unfortunately it was rather a hurried meal as we had to be back at the railway station at a given time and before complete darkness. As it was not too far away we made it in time. On arrival at the station we immediately boarded the train and soon afterwards started rolling into the night. A lot had happened to us in the last twelve hours from disembarking at the town quay in Southampton that morning till now with night falling, setting out from a race course somewhere in the south of England to our next destination. Only our military escort knew where we would finish up the next day. In truth no one really cared, we were far too tired to worry about it. The rhythm of the wheels running over the joints of the rail, the gentle swaying of the carriage and the long day, soon rocked most of us to sleep.

Not having a watch I had no idea what time it was when I woke up during the night. The carriage was dimly lit, the blinds pulled down, after all, I may be out of the fighting now, but the war was still going on. The black out in Britain was very strictly enforced, as it was in other countries where air raids were a possibility, that much we had already detected, even so we had been less than twenty four hours in the country. I requested to go to the toilet, which was granted by the Corporal in charge of the guards in our carriage. From what I could make out through the frosted glass window in the toilet, it was still pitch dark outside. So I had to wait a little longer before getting any idea where we might be. After a while the fellows around me began to stir one by one and soon afterwards it began to get light. The guards indicated that we could pull up the blinds and that gave us an indication in which direction we were heading. Looking through the windows on the right, the sky was very much brighter than looking out to the left where the horizon was much darker. That told us we were heading north, but where to? Rapidly it became full daylight and we could see we were travelling through rural England. By the evidence of stooks in the fields, the grain harvest was in full swing and a number of lads who came from farming districts in Germany wished they were home helping their folks, knowing how important it is having the corn safely gathered into barns. That just was not to be and worrying about it would not help either. The breakfast that was served was quite simple; hot, sweet, milky tea and a bowl of porridge.

As we journeyed on, the scene changed from time to time. There were little towns and villages we passed through. Hamlets, farmsteads, cottages and clusters of buildings could be seen in the distance and from time to time barns and other farm buildings out in the fields. It was not long after we had our breakfast that we pulled into a station, not very large, just two platforms. There were some soldiers on the platform waiting for us and once off the train we were lined up and counted again, which became part of daily routine from now on. Numbers proved correct, we were handed over and with our new kitbags on our shoulders marched out of the station onto the highway en route to our next destination. We were looking for place names but could not spot any anywhere. Someone suggested they may have been removed for security reasons, so we accepted that explanation and in step this time, went on our way. It was a lovely morning, a little chilly I recall, but that may have been due to lack of sleep. The station must have been on the edge of a town or village as only after a minute or two of marching we were in the middle of the countryside. We met a few locals walking, or on their bikes, making their way to the place we had just left one assumed. They all exchanged greetings with our guards but took very little notice of us. Much the same as we experienced in Southampton. We assumed seeing German Prisoners of War was nothing new to them. I dare say they seen it all before. The march through the countryside certainly warmed us up as well as the sun climbing ever higher in the sky. After half an hour or may be going on for an hour, we spotted a camp site ahead much to everyone's relief. As we marched through the gates we spotted three men in German military uniforms wearing sergeant's epaulettes and wondered what they were there for. We soon found out.

Once inside the gates of the camp they took charge. The senior of them, a sergeant-major, introduced himself and the other two sergeants, neither names can I remember, what I do remember though is, he told us that the three of them were in charge of the camp and responsible to the British Commandant for the orderly conduct and discipline of all ranks within the camp and that all orders by the British Military Authorities were observed. The P.O.W. section of the camp was comprised of Nissan Huts except the mess hall, toilets and washrooms, as well as the administrative building which were of a more permanent construction. The military part of the camp was mainly wooden structures. The first order given by our N.C.O.s was to fall into groups of twenty four, being the number allocated to each hut. By now I had formed some friendship with one or two chaps and we tried to keep together. To a large extent we succeeded and managed to get into the same hut. The accommodation as well as furnishings was very basic. Camp beds with a pillow and a blanket for each bed, two tables and four benches. At least we had somewhere to lie down and stretch out at night. On one of the table were twenty four small cakes of soap and also a hand towel for everyone in the hut. We had just over an hour to slip down to the washrooms to freshen up and then be ready to assemble, to be counted and then make an orderly entrance in the mess hall. Quite honestly by then I was ready for whatever was served up for our meal and I cannot for the life of me recall what the food was like in that camp. All I can say it must have been agreeable, had it not been, I would have remembered.

As we had free time in the afternoon we looked around and noticed that the camp was built on a slight slope overlooking quite a large valley. The main camp was along a busy road with the P.O.W. section at the back. Being slightly elevated we had a very good view across the valley. The weather having been kind to us so far since we landed in England made it quite a pleasant afternoon. The most obvious thing we saw was that we were in farming country. Being August the corn harvest was getting into full swing. We could see a binder, pulled by a tractor, cutting the corn and binding it into sheaves. There were six or eight people in the field picking up the sheaves then making stooks of them by putting eight or ten sheaves together in a row. After looking at the scene for a while we could make out that it was mostly women working in the field and as I said before, the men among us who lived and worked in rural areas, could not help wondering how folks at home were making out. After having a good look around and seen what we wanted to see, one by one we made our way back to our huts and started talking as to where we came from , what unit we were in, where we were taken prisoner. We talked about our families, education, hobbies and other interests in life. There was quite a difference in our ages as well, which was not surprising. Being only eighteen years of age I was among the youngest of course. Anyone in their thirties was an old man as far as I was concerned. Most men were in their twenties, but what did it matter, we were all in the same boat. Having said all that, I must say we got on well together.

At 18.00 that evening we were again lined up to be counted and then went for the evening meal, after which, as we left the hall were handed each a parcel donated by the International Red Cross. When we got to our huts and opened them we found they contained a safety razor, a comb and a toothbrush, how thoughtful we felt. As far as I knew no one possessed a razor, certainly not among the men in our hut, nor a toothbrush, only two or three combs that were passed around in the morning and then back to its owners. These three items were a most welcome gift indeed, not only useful but also most needed. As for evening entertainment, we did not look for any on this first night in our new surroundings. All we were looking for was a good night's sleep in a bed, albeit on a camp bed. As we bade one another a 'Good Night' once again I began to wonder what tomorrow would bring.

Morning came all too soon. In typical Military fashion Reveille was at 06.00 and the sergeants went through the huts to give us the morning call. Then the usual rush to toilets and washroom to be ready on time to be on parade to be counted. The Camp Commandant with his adjutant and three or four other ranks came into the compound to make the count. When they were satisfied that all were present and all was correct, we stood to attention, the officers saluted and left. We then returned to our quarters to make our beds and tidy the hut ready for inspection, which was to take place after breakfast.

After breakfast, which was not until eight, the sergeants made their hut and kit inspection after which we assembled once again, this time to be detailed into working parties. Half of us worked inside the P.O.W. compound, the other half, under escort, went outside to work in the British section. The jobs included cleaning kitchens, mess halls, washrooms, toilets, offices and places that were used by soldiers when off duty as well as attending the flower beds, picking up litter, sweeping paths. That was our morning task. By twelve thirty we were back in our huts getting ready for the mid-day meal. As far as I can remember that afternoon we assembled in the mess hall and were given an official Red Cross letter and envelope and a post card to write home but no address at which we might be contacted. That could mean only one thing, we were in transit. Still, just to write home and tell our families that we were alive was a great relief all round. It was amazing how that simple task of writing a few lines home lifted the morale in the camp. After supper that evening, back in our hut, someone produced a pack of playing cards, which lifted the mood even further. Naturally, with only the one pack of cards, the number of chaps which could play was limited. So we let the four keenest card players get on with it, whilst the rest of us looked on. Before we knew it, it was time to get ready for lights out. The following morning, 06.00 the sergeants came round to wake us up and the routine of the previous day was repeated except writing a letter home of course. That meant we had the afternoon completely free and most of us took the opportunity to catch up with washing under clothes and attending to personal needs, such as having a shave or cutting toe and finger nails etc. This went on for a week or so, except for the Sunday, when only the kitchens, mess halls, washrooms and toilets were cleaned. Neither did we have any inspection on Sunday morning, only the two roll calls. The morning one was an hour later than usual, at 07.00. Then one morning at breakfast (August 27th we were told by the chaps who were keeping diaries) we were told to go back to our huts, pack our few belongings in our kitbags, clean our quarters, leave them clean and tidy and be on the parade ground at 09.00 ready to march off. A final count before we were handed over to the officer in charge who with the guards under his command would take us to the next destination. We guessed it would be a train ride away. Soon after nine o'clock that morning we were on our way. The way back to the station seemed not quite as far as when we first arrived, but it must have been, as it took us an hour to get there. The train was waiting for us at the station and we noticed an additional number of guards that would accompany us. As before, those who had formed friendships tried to keep together as we boarded the train. Speculation began immediately as to where we might be taken. I had little knowledge of the British Isles. I knew about England of course and had heard of Scotland and that it was part of Great Britain. There was Ireland. Yes, I knew it was divided, but where did Wales fit in? In all honesty at that time in my life I had never heard of it. That conversation went on a bit as it was quite a while before the train pulled out of the station to begin its journey across the north of England.

As we travelled through rural England, we could see again people in the fields gathering the harvest. After a while the scene changed and it became more urban. The areas we were travelling through now seemed more populated as well. There were tall chimneys indicating some kind of factory or industry. But we had absolutely no idea where we were. No place names were to be seen anywhere as we travelled through towns and villages. In due course we had our lunch consisting as before of nice hot, sweet, milky tea and a sausage roll. With some food inside us and an ever changing scene outside, the rhythm of the train trundling over joints and points made us drowsy and before long one by one we rested our eyes. What woke us was the sound of clinking and clanging. The regular rhythm had gone. Looking through the window it was quite clear we were in a city. But which one? We saw quite a lot of bomb damage which reminded us of what we left behind in France. Then someone spotted a sign; Liverpool! Obviously, a sea journey was on the cards. But, where was the big question! One of the Scottish Isles someone suggested. I could not care less; all I could think of was seasickness. Slowly we pulled into the station and for the first time saw the name of the station, Lime Street. We were very surprised to see a large number of policemen all over the station. Did the military expect a large break out from our ranks? I heard of no such plans, not in our carriage anyway. After the train had come to a complete halt the order was given to get off the train and to form an orderly column. As we were getting into line we noticed a fleet of double decker buses at the end of the platforms. The first time I had ever seen one. On our short walk from the town quay to the new docks in Southampton we had not seen any buses. Here we were now in Liverpool about to board these buses. The police, in large numbers, closed ranks as the people of

Liverpool tried to break through the line, shouting abuse at us. So it was for our protection that the police were there in large numbers and not to prevent any planned escape. Quickly we board the buses and as soon as all were on board we left the station in convoy. As we emerged onto the street, stones, bricks, sticks and more abuse were hurled at us as we drove past the crowds. Windows were broken on both upper and lower decks. The bus drivers speeded up to get away from the station to avoid more damage to their buses and any injuries to us. As we went through the city we saw a great deal more bomb damage and began to understand why the people of Liverpool were so angry with us. The bomb damage became worse as we came into the dockland area and as we entered the dock gates, more protesters were waiting to hurl missiles and abuse at us but we got safely through, as I said, no injuries, but the buses appeared badly damaged. As we approached the waterside we saw a number of ships berthed. Among them tankers, cargo ships of different tonnage and a passenger liner alongside where we drew up. It seemed big to me compared to the landing craft we came across the Channel to England. Those who know about such things told us she was only about 25000 tonnes and nothing like the really big liners such as the Queen Mary or the Bremen or Europa. I took their word for it as I had not seen any of these ships and did not know anything about them. The only sea going ships I could recall were the ferries that crossed from the Isle of Ruegen to Sweden and they were nothing compared to what I was looking at now. This one was huge in comparison.

As soon as the buses stopped we were getting off one bus at a time, and in single file boarded the liner and with it returned my concern would I be seasick? By now I did not care very much where I would end up. When on board, we were taken to our quarters, which must have been one of the dining rooms when the ship was in commercial use. It was a large room with double bunks all around the room. The middle was laid out with tables and benches and at the centre were stations at which were stored the hammocks. The chaps that boarded the ship first made straight for the bunks understandingly enough, the rest of us were left with the hammocks. Here was something that I would never have dreamed of in a thousand years being on an ocean going liner with the prospect of having a hammock for my bed. It was not long after we came on board that the ship cast off and moved to the middle of the river. The first order given was that we were confined to our quarters at all times except when taken on deck during the daily time allotted for exercise. Hammocks had to be taken down during the day and stored in the designated places. Boat drill was in half an hour and we had to be ready with life jackets on to await further instructions.

Chapter 11

Life on the Ocean Wave

Exactly half an hour later an announcement in English came over the public address system for the whole ships company to assemble at their designated emergency station as indicated in their cabins or sleeping quarters. The notices in our quarters were all in English not surprisingly, but one or two chaps with knowledge of the English language had a look at them and summarised them for us. Not that it was of much help. Confined to our quarters we could not explore the ship on our own, we had to wait for an escort to take us wherever we needed to go. At that moment however, the guards arrived and led us to our assembly point, which was on the open deck. Daylight was fading by now and a warm summer evening breeze greeted us as we stepped out on the open deck. Whilst we were waiting for further orders and instructions, we had time to look around. Apart from our group there was another group of prisoners of similar number. We estimated there were about 300 P.O.W.s altogether on board. The two groups were kept well apart throughout the voyage. Most other passengers were Canadian soldiers, many of them wounded. There were also some civilians on board and a detachment from the Royal Navy in charge of the ship's safe passage. When all were assembled, an interpreter gave us instruction in German as what to do in an emergency. The assembly point, at which we were at the moment, would also be the area where we had to gather for our daily exercise. Thus we would not find it too difficult to make our way there, without help, should the need arise. Looking around while all this was going on, we noticed quite a number of ships at anchor all around us. Tankers of all sizes, cargo vessels large and small, some Navy ships too, our escort no doubt. With so many Canadians on board the speculation where we were heading for changed from somewhere on a Scottish Island to Canada.

By the time we were through with the emergency drill it was almost dark. With the deck only dimly lit we were glad to go back to our quarters ready for our first meal on board. All the meals were to be taken in our quarters. As I said, we had enough tables and benches, sufficient for all to be seated at meal times. On a rota system a group of men went to the kitchen to collect the food and then served it by going from table to table. They also had to take the dishes back to the scullery and do the washing up. The meal over, it was not long afterwards, that we were getting ready to stretch out and get some rest. By then we would have been about twelve hours or more on our feet. It was quite an eventful day after all, what with the journey across northern England, the rowdy reception in Liverpool and maybe crossing the Atlantic in an ocean liner. It was rather a lot to take in for one day. Being tired emotionally and physically, I had no idea where to begin and what to do to secure my hammock safely, but friends came along to give a hand and I could stretch out if I knew how to get into it! I was not the only one being naïve on how to cope with getting in and out of a hammock! Our dilemma caused a bit of fun and eased the tension. We cracked it in the end and, as with most things, it's easy if you know how.

Upon the bench we stood, hands on the beam, hauled ourselves up with bottoms above the edge of the hammock and the gently lowered ourselves in. Similar procedure in reverse when we got out. We hauled ourselves up on the beam, careful not to move the hammock too much, swung over the side and lowered ourselves onto the bench. All part of the University of Life, learning as you go along.

I had no idea when we set sail, all I knew, a stronger vibration could be felt throughout the ship and there was some movement. Come breakfast time I did not feel too good at all nor did most of the others on our deck. But breakfast was taken by those who could tackle it. They of course had to do their own fetching and carrying from the kitchen and clear up afterwards. We just about managed to fold our hammocks and made up the bunks before an officer arrived with two sergeants and a translator in attendance. They asked if anyone felt ill, apart from being seasick. None raised a hand, so it was assumed all was well in our section. Come 11.00, the order was given to put our jackets on or warm clothing as well as a lifejacket, as we were about to be taken onto the open deck. Never having been to sea before I thought it was rather rough. Those who had experienced such conditions before assured us it was only a heavy swell. Whatever it was, I felt sick and with many others rushed to the rail and fed the fish! It was cloudy but dry and there was quite a strong wind as well. However poorly we felt, we had to stay on deck for the whole hour. Once back in our quarters those who had bunks fell into them, the rest of us made do the best we could, either slumping over the tables or even lying on the floor. Few had a mid-day meal. Many who had a bite to eat brought it up again. This went on all afternoon. With great difficulty and help from some friends I managed to get my hammock in place, swung into it and before long began to feel better. The ship continued to rock and shake and roll throughout the night. Next morning it became even worse. Thankfully we were allowed to keep the hammocks up and the men with bunks could stay in them if they felt poorly. But come 11.00 the order was given to get ready to go on deck. Swaying from side to side and unsteady on our feet it took quite a time and great effort to make our way on deck. What we saw and experienced was horrendous. Severe Gale force winds or Storm force even. Our ship pitched and rolled and swung in all direction. We felt it rise and then drop into a trough, waves were goodness knows how high, I had no idea. All I know, in spite being seasick and I can see it even now, the other ships in our convoy at one moment were riding on the crest of a wave and the next moment had vanished. Then up they came again only to disappear once more. Some of the smaller cargo ships, they might have been of the Liberty class, I cannot say but when they were on the crest of the wave we could even see the propellers spinning out of the water. We observed this for about an hour before we were ordered to go below and boy were we glad to get to our quarters and lie down again. I have no idea how I got back into my hammock but I got there as I did the day before, with the help from my friends. Soon after I lay down I began to feel better and before long was asleep. When eventually I woke up I felt much better. My hammock hanging from the beam was gently swaying and looking, at the ceiling, I noticed still a lot of movement in the ship but nowhere near as much as earlier when we came down from the open deck. I lowered myself out of the hammock and slowly made my way to the washrooms without any ill effects but still felt dizzy and strange but thank goodness the sick feeling had gone. On the way back from the washrooms I smelt food cooking and all of a sudden I began to feel hungry. It was not long afterwards the call came to collect our rations from the kitchen. Several of us went along to collect the food and drink for our boys, who were beginning to sit up and take notice. Obviously, most of us were getting over our bout of seasickness. Meal over, we took pots and pans, jugs, cutlery etc. back to the scullery, cleaned and washed them up and then returned to our quarters. I must say I felt much better with some food inside me if still a little drowsy. With the ship still having a battle with the ocean waves, no one in authority checked up on us how things were. So most of us opted for an early night and went to bed.

The following morning the sea appeared to have calmed down. Just a slight movement in the ship could be detected from time to time. Fellow P.O.W.s, as well as the many other passengers, could be heard and seen around the ship including those in charge of us. We were informed there would be an inspection at 10.00 after which we would be set to work cleaning our quarters as well as toilets, washrooms and other areas of the ship, before we had our hour on the open deck, to be followed by lunch. What a difference as we stepped out on deck. There were broken clouds in the sky but the sun was also shining and the sea was moderate we were told. Whatever the state of the sea, it was much, much calmer and we enjoyed being out in the open looking at the other ships, at least on the starboard side where we were. That was the side reserved for us. The forward side to port was where the other group of P.O.W.s took the air every morning. Midship and aft was for the other passengers. The afternoon was free of any activities and so was the evening. With no entertainment provided by the military and not knowing one another all that well, nor what hidden talents there might be around, we just sat and talked speculating where we might finish up. As I already said there were a few packs of cards around and the keen players soon gathered around the tables enjoying a game or two with the rest of us looking on.

This routine became the daily programme:-

06.00 Call by the guards

06.30 Early inspection by the N.C.O. on duty

07.00 Breakfast

08.30 The officer on duty with his sergeant and a company clerk, who also acted as an interpreter, made his inspection.

Anyone who needed medical advice or a doctor could request one. After that was over we were then put into working gangs and set our task for the morning somewhere on board. At 11.00 we were to assemble to be taken out on the open deck for an hour's exercise. At 12.30 lunch and the rest of the day was ours. We were now allowed to hang up our hammocks after lunch, which we did and enjoyed a lovely snooze every afternoon. We left the talking for the evening.

As we could only move as fast as the slowest ship in the convoy, progress across the Atlantic was slow and we lost all sense of time. On the days we had the stormy weather we could not care less what day it was. Anyway, what did it matter, the future lay not in our hands nor was anyone waiting for us on the other side of the Ocean. So we took every day as it came. Fortunately the weather kept calm from then on. In fact the nearer we got to North America the calmer the sea and lighter the wind. If the truth were known, many of the younger and unattached among us in many ways began to enjoy our sea journey, especially as it was at someone else's expense. Then one day when we were out on deck we noticed that a number of ships had left the convoy including most of the naval ships. That told us two things. Firstly we were in safe waters and secondly we were nearing our destination, but we still had no inkling where it might be.

Then one morning everything appeared unusually quiet. Very little vibration could be felt throughout the ship, just a little humming noise. We also noticed some excitement among our guards and the wider crew. Obviously they were pleased at whatever the place we were. As expected and not surprisingly, in true military fashion we went through the morning routine. After breakfast we were told to tidy our quarters, gather our belongings and stand by for disembarkation. Having been surrounded by water for the last 14/15 days we looked forward to stepping ashore and seeing buildings again.

Chapter 12

New York, U.S.A.

As we were lining up to disembark the official interpreter told us we had arrived in New York and were to be handed over to the U.S. Military. Slowly we made our way to the gangway and onto the quayside from there we were directed to a very large shed with a wide open door a hundred yards away with what were to become very familiar words to us: "Come on! Let's go!" As we hurried along, dock workers watched us and looked at us rather curiously we thought. I had no idea what they were expecting to see, whilst we were wondering what would come next. As we entered the vast dockside shed we saw plenty of G.I.s as well as civil clerks waiting to begin processing us onto government files. The routine was similar to the one we experienced in England. Stripped of all clothing, a good long shower, delousing, followed by a medical inspection. After that we were issued with two sets of underclothes (vest and pants), two pairs of socks, two shirts with the letters P W on the back of the shirt and a pair of boots. We were also given a larger kit bag to store our new belongings. Once clean and tidy the registration began with yet another number given, the third in less than a year. There were no official interpreters about, as many of the G.I.s spoke enough German to make us understand what we had to do next. I noticed the number of prisoners had increased. Certainly there were more of us now then we had aboard our ship coming across to America.

What came next was our first meal on U.S. soil and an excellent one is was too. In one corner of this vast building there was a cafeteria style restaurant to which we were directed after our cleansing and registration process was completed. There were no holdups or long queues as only a handful of chaps at a time made their way across. We were handed a tin tray which had several compartments, a knife, fork and spoon and then went along the counter and were issued with meat, gravy and vegetables and an orange which neither of us had seen for a long, long time. By the time everyone had finished their meal it was getting on for three o'clock in the afternoon and we were free to mingle in the far corner of the shed. That gave us the opportunity to be with friends we made on the sea journey across the Atlantic. Keeping together might prove difficult as we knew from past experience, once we are on the move everything goes by numbers. We hoped there may be someone who was willing to step back or others come forward to make up the number in front of us, to enable us to keep together. We just had to wait and see.

It was not long after, that we were ordered to fall in and move off. We went out onto the street within the dock area to a landing place where one of the harbour ferries was waiting. The route was lined with armed guards and behind them some of the population of Brooklyn. That was the Borough of New York where we had landed and disembarked. The folk that stood behind the guards looked friendly enough and some, speaking in German, wished us well. On to the ferry and across the harbour we went. Then came, what must have been to all of us, the thrill of a lifetime. As we turned to make our way across the harbour to the other side of the

Hudson River, the Statute of Liberty came into view. More than that, we passed close by on our way to a railway marshalling yard in New Jersey. Never in my wildest dreams had I thought I would see the Statute of Liberty. The nearest I would ever get to the U.S.A. or New York would be watching Hollywood movies.

After we crossed the harbour we stepped ashore and marched two or three hundred yards along the railway tracks to three waiting trains where we were handed over to armed guards posted all around the trains. As we boarded the trains guards counted us into groups of thirty and pointed us to the carriage we were to occupy. So far the four of us that became friendly over the weeks on board ship were lucky enough to get on to the same carriage, but were separated because of the seating arrangements. Three men allocated to four seats. The seats were in groups of four with two seats facing each other, leaving one seat vacant in case someone needed to put his feet up. It also gave us some room to manoeuvre albeit in a small area. It was not long after all were aboard the trains and everything in place, that we started to roll. By then, daylight had begun to fade and we could see the lights twinkle as we looked out of the window. Slowly we made our way across the points to the track that would take us out of town and to our destination. Looking out of the window I saw a familiar sight that I grew up with, a scene you see on every railway marshalling yard, railway engines, trucks, goods wagons, carriages, side lined and waiting to be assembled into a train. Slowly we gathered speed and the scene changed from an industrial and commercial area to an urban one. Eventually we left the city lights behind and travelled through the darkness of the night with the occasional light in the distance.

By then it was time for our evening meal. What would it be we wondered? The food was brought and handed out by the G.I.s on board. First of all we received two slices of white bread, soft to the touch, smelling delicious. As we were hungry, we did not wait or care what else there was to come. This fresh, soft, white bread was irresistible, so we began to eat it straight away. It went down a treat and tasted like cake, something we had not seen or tasted for a long time. We were then handed a standard army mess tin and a fork and spoon and moments later served cold slices of meat or 'cold cuts' as it is known in the U.S. with some beetroot. After the meal we had a beaker of coffee and finished with either an apple or an orange. With food inside us now we were invited one by one to visit the toilets, one at each end of the carriage. We were then handed a blanket and settled down for the night.

As soldiers we were used travelling by night. We did so in Germany as well as in France and in England and now in the U.S.A, therefore it was not long before we were all asleep. Suddenly we all woke up, slightly dazed and somewhat confused. What was the cause of our rude awakening? The regular rhythm of the train had changed and we were moving quite slowly now and lights were all around us again. Where could we be? Chicago we were told. Minutes later we could see the stockades brightly lit being made ready for another delivery of beef cattle and other livestock for the Chicago slaughterhouses. What a contrast to Europe where it would be pitch dark at this time of night and one would be looked upon as a traitor if a glimmer of light showed from your house. But this was America, far removed from any of the Theatres of War, so no such precaution was necessary. The train came to a halt and before the train stopped completely some of our guards, on both sides of the train, were jumping off rifles at the ready just to show us, should we have an urge to escape, to forget it. It was quite a lengthy stay as I remember, as we had to take on board a fresh water supply. An engine change was also made and with it came a fresh driver, fireman and train guard to relieve the crew that travelled with us from New York. There were other activities going on as well and when all were satisfied we set off again rolling into the morning light as dawn was breaking. Soon after, breakfast was served consisting of this lovely smelling tasty white bread, butter, peanut butter and jelly spreads a choice of apple, blackberry or strawberry, all in little individual cartons and a mug of coffee. Looking through the window as we were speeding through the countryside we noticed a great change was taking place. We left behind the largely rural scene of 'Down State New York', the industrial district and suburban area of Chicago to the more open and hilly country of the 'Midwest', cowboy country if you like, which we had so far only seen in Hollywood movies. Can you imagine, here we were, seeing and indeed, travelling through the real thing excitingly talking of what we saw and pointing out to one another features we only seen in photos or read about in the past, such as log cabins, riders on horseback, cars outside every building whatever size or whatever state of repair. With all this excitement the scenery, as well as the time, flew by and, before we realized, it was lunch time. We, the P.O.W.s, weren't the only ones on board the train to feel excited, many of the G.I.s from New York, our guards on that section on our journey to goodness knows where, were caught up in this fever as well. In due course the mid-day meal was brought, served on a mess tin were chicken, vegetables and gravy with two slices of delicious white bread, followed by a fresh peach.

After lunch the scenery became more rocky and mountainous and at times quite stunning, similar, in one sense and yet altogether different from the Bavarian Alps, I remembered. It was quite tiring looking through the window all the time and the desire to have a nap was great, yet we were reluctant to close our eyes as we did not want to miss anything as the chances were we would never come this way again. Nevertheless, from time to time nature had her way and we dropped off to sleep every now and then and we shall never know what we missed, if anything. In due course the evening meal arrived being cold meats, bread, butter and a choice of fresh fruit; e.g. apple, orange or peach. The menu for our meals throughout the train journey varied little, not that it mattered to us as even the food and the way it was served, was a new experience to us all. Not long after supper, night fell and we prepared to spend our second night on the train.

As morning broke and we could see what it was like outside, we realised little had changed so far as the terrain was concerned. If anything, it might have become more mountainous and we may travel in a higher altitude as the vegetation was somewhat sparse. Sure enough, as the guards came to give us breakfast, they told us that most of the night we had travelled through Canada but that before long would be back on American soil. Soon after we re-entered the United States we came to a halt in a very large railway marshalling yard. As before, we changed engines, took on a fresh train crew as well as replenished our food and water. Our guards we noticed were outside stretching their legs. That was something we were longing to do. For us however, movement throughout the journey was restricted between our seats and the toilet. Because of this, the chaps that sat at either end of the carriage had very little exercise I am afraid, as we had to remain seated all the time. Because of this, some of us began to have swollen feet. When the doctor made his daily round this was pointed out to him, but all he could recommend was to keep our feet up, which was easier said than done as there was little room to manoeuvre. Even so it was quite interesting to watch the goings on. Eventually we heard the familiar; 'All aboard!' and we started rolling again. The scenery throughout the rest of the day remained stunning I must say.

This routine was repeated a number of times. We did not always spot place names, so we had no idea where we were, unless the guard on duty told us. Through these means we learned that we had crossed the Rocky Mountains and were making for the west coast of America. The scenery and terrain changed daily, from mountains and hills, to wooded slopes and forests, to agricultural areas. We saw farms and scattered houses, small settlements and little towns. We passed through open ranges and prairies, saw lots of cattle and even cowboys on horseback. As we left the Rockies behind, standing timber was very much in evidence, so the lumber trade was the main source of income here and the boys among us who grew up in such an environment in Germany became quite home sick. Through all this time we spotted just two place names, Missoula and Portland. There were others no doubt, but we just never spotted them.

Taking all this in, as we travelled through one State after another, was very tiring. But there was nothing else for us to do. We had no reading matter or board games and those who had playing cards and they were few, could only be played by the three that sat together. Not that we minded travelling through the U.S.A. on a free ticket. Who could have foretold we would end up in America? P.O.W. or not, it was a great adventure. Even so, after two or three days we began to wonder how much longer we would be on this train. We also realized now what a vast country it was. Eventually though, as all things do, the journey came to an end. Having travelled five days and five nights on this train almost non-stop, apart from the service stops, one morning, soon after we had had breakfast, additional guards entered the carriage. So we knew something was afoot. It could mean only one thing; we had arrived at our destination. It was not long afterwards the train slowed down and we saw houses, roads and cars at close proximity, all the time we travelled across the states, most things we saw were in the distance, far distance. Now we had come to wide, open land, on which there stood army barracks, hundreds of them.

As on previous occasions when the train came to a halt, the guards jumped off the train, rifles at the ready.

There were other G.I.s waiting for the train to stop, these guys were carrying no weapons, only truncheons. They were there to receive us once the handover formalities were completed. A few parcels and packages changed hands and then we were ordered to disembark. It did not take long to gather our few belongings, as none were added on this trip. Once off the train, we all had a great surprise, something none of us had thought of, that we might hear a command given in the German tongue. But there he was, large as life, a Sergeant Major of the German Army dressed in khaki. He was obviously a member of the Afrika Corps who had fought under Rommel. He introduced himself, though I cannot recall his name, and he reminded us that German military discipline would be maintained within and without the camp and gave the command to fall in. "Right Turn, In step, Forward March!" Off we went. To keep in step, the Sergeant Major suggested we sing as we marched along and to start us off began to sing a well-known song, which we quickly picked up. We continued singing the half a mile or so to the P.O.W. compound, which was a section, fenced off within this vast U.S. military camp. On our approach the guard on duty opened wide the large gates allowing us to march straight through and onto the parade ground. Then the command: "Company Halt, Left Turn, Stand at Ease. Stand Easy!" At this point we were joined by comrades who were already in the camp wearing either German khaki uniform or American army shirt and trousers with the compulsory white P.W. painted on it. They greeted us very warmly and were anxious to help. Their first task was showing us to our quarters. Here we were having travelled from New York now standing in the middle of the Prisoner of War compound, part of Camp White, Oregon, U.S.A., in warm September sunshine, waiting to be shown to our quarters. We were counted into groups of 50 and those of us who made friends on the journey could stay together and go to the same barrack. That was quickly done and off we went to the barrack that was to be ours for a while, accompanied by those who were already in the camp and happy to help to make us feel at home. With that, life as a P.O.W. in the U.S.A. began.

Chapter 13

Life on the other side of the Atlantic

What was the first impression of it all? There just is no comparison! The openness struck me most of all. Plenty of space, and nothing was cramped here. This was a far cry from military establishments in Europe! The accommodation almost luxurious from what we had experienced since we joined the armed forces in Germany. Let the reader understand, we are going back to 1944 and there was a war going on. There were few, if any brick buildings to be seen in this camp. Here in Camp White, Oregon, U.S.A., we had the standard army camp buildings as seen in Hollywood pictures or American television programmes. They were two story buildings and in our case 25 men on each floor with washroom and toilet facilities on each floor. On the lower level, the rooms reserved for N.C.O.s, remained unoccupied as there were no N.C.O.s among us apart from the three put in charge by the American's to keep discipline in the camp. We used the time before lunch to claim our corner so to speak, e.g. the bed and locker we intended to occupy, which apart from two large tables and a number of benches were all the furnishings. We introduced ourselves to each other as from now on we had to live together for better or worse. Towards one o'clock we began to make our way towards the dining hall and looked forward to our first meal in Camp White.

Surprisingly it was a very good meal consisting of meat, potatoes, carrots and gravy with a choice of fruit for dessert. Over the meal we had the first opportunity to speak to the boys who were in camp before us. They were few, as most of them were out working. They were anxious to know how things were in Europe. Did the Allied Forces really have the success they claim? What was the morale like back home as well as among the troops? We told them the situation as we saw it and what we experienced. There were conflicting views of course, some more hopeful than others. Meal over the senior of the N.C.O.s, a Sergeant Major of the old school and a regular soldier, a veteran of the North African campaign, a mother figure as one expects a Sergeant Major to be, told us he was the link between us and the American Camp Commandant. He was authorised by the Americans to keep discipline within the camp and had the Commandant's backing. It was also his duty to see to it that we had everything that was due to us under the Geneva Convention. We learned from the boys already in camp, that it was thanks to him we had most of the sporting equipment e.g. football, volleyball, darts and some outdoor apparatus for the enthusiastic gymnasts. There was a piano in the camp theatre as well as other musical instruments and, thanks to the sergeant; there was also a well-stocked canteen where we could purchase tobacco products, magazines, toiletries, sweets etc. He was a real champion of his men. There was also a weekly film show in the theatre with two performances. The first one was at 14.00, for those in camp during the day, and the second one at 19.30 for those out at work. The first film I saw there was 'Going my way' with Bing Crosby of course. Shall I ever forget it? No! One of the other sergeants then gave us a rundown of the daily timetable: Reveille 06.00; that gave us time to wash, shave, make our beds and tidy the barrack.

Breakfast was from 06.30 and we had to be on parade for the morning count and ready to leave for work at 07.30. Lunch was at 13.00 for those in camp, and the evening count at 17.30 with supper from 18.00 and Lights out 22.00. He or any of the sergeants could be contacted at any time between 06.30 and 22.00 apart from meal times. Sunday's reveille was one hour later.

At the end of the introduction to camp life we went across to the Quartermaster's shed to collect blankets, bedcovers and pillows. Back in our quarters we made our beds and made the place more user friendly, displaying family photographs by those who had them or some personal item of sentimental value that had not been confiscated at some stage on the journey. I had nothing as it had all been left behind when I was captured in France. As there was still some time before the evening count some of us had a walk around the camp to familiarise ourselves with the layout. Just as well we did as soon after five o'clock that evening what had appeared until now a sleepy place came alive. The first gangs returned to camp after a day's work somewhere outside the compound in this vast army establishment. Minute by minute other gangs returned whose working places were further away. There were several gangs that worked in orchards and they came back with their food containers laden with apples, pears or peaches. They were all windfalls and the farmers just did not want to know about them as none were of top quality. They were either bruised, maggoty or had some other blemish. Those who did not work on fruit farms were only too pleased with the additional food supply. Not that there was any shortage of food in the camp, but there is always room for a little extra. By half past five all had returned to camp and were on parade except a few that were employed in two or three kitchens. Their shift would not end before seven or eight o'clock in the evening. Count over, which proved correct, some went straight for the dining hall, others returned to their barracks first before having their evening meal. At supper we met those who were out working during the day and it was now their turn to seek news from us about the situation in Europe. We, the fresh men in camp, took the opportunity and put our questions to them such as, what was life like in the camp? How were we treated? What kind of work were we expected to do? How many of us in the camp now? Overall it emerged life was pretty good behind barbed wire, it just depended on the individual how he could cope with living in confinement. As for numbers, with our arrival the number went up to 518 of which 368 were in the main camp and 150 in a branch camp some 60 miles away, where life by all accounts was quite free and easy. At the end of the meal we thanked our new found friends and looked forward to playing our part in camp life.

Before we could do so we had to settle in and get used to this new life behind barbed wire, new to us fresh men that is. On our way back we looked in at the canteen to see what was on offer. Surprisingly quite a lot, it was a mixture of Sweet Shop come News Agent which was open from 18.30 to 21.30 and was run by a group of volunteers. Before, we, the newcomers, could buy anything we had to earn some money and then wait for the pay day, which as it turned out, only a few days away. We were told that we would start working the day after tomorrow, just two days after our arrival and we would find details on the notice board at lunch time tomorrow. That added a new topic of conversation as we set around the table mulling over the day's happenings, which had been very eventful. All of us were thankful that after seven weeks in transit we were at long last able to put our feet up for a while. With that comforting thought, most of us went early to bed hoping for a good night's rest.

Next morning the public address system told us it was time to get up. Asking around, most of us had a good night and wondered what the day would bring. Weather wise it was another fine day. As on the previous day the sun was shining, the winds were light and it had the promise of a warm day. What all of us wanted to know was what our jobs would be and where. But first we had to work out some morning routine. It needed a plan for all of us to have a wash and shave and tidy the room as well as have breakfast before morning parade and count. We needed to talk about it and devise a smooth and orderly routine in the morning as from the next day we had to be ready to leave camp after morning assembly. To get to know what was going on after dismissal we watched the proceedings at the main gates and were surprised how quickly groups were counted and send on their way. Lorries, trucks and other motorised transport was waiting to take the boys to their place of work. That over and in no hurry to go back to the barrack, I took this chance and had a look at our surroundings more closely. Yesterday I had to watch where I was going not to get lost. Today though I could take my time, widen my horizon and have a good look round.

What I saw impressed me very much as did most things at that time in my life. The army camp was at one end of a large valley with the hills behind us. In the far distance, all around the valley, more hills or may be even mountains. To the right of us was a mountain, Mount Ashland, high enough to have its peak covered with snow. As it was the end of September I wondered whether it was fresh snow that fell a few days ago or had it been there all the summer. I later discovered that snow covered the peak all year round. Close by and all around I saw nothing but army barracks and a little further off, sheds large and small of all description. Later that morning I noticed a group of eight chaps returning to camp, when inquiring why the early return, they told me that they worked in the camp's bakery and started at 4 a.m. to mix the dough ready to prove, knead and put into tins and left it to rise again. Then they started a second batch of dough to be dealt with by the next gang that joined them at 7 a.m. Their work completed they cleaned their tools and worktables and when finished returned to camp which was usually about 10 o'clock. Talking to these boys I learned that the camp was totally independent from the outside world. All repairs were done on site. The various shops or departments usually had the oversight of an army sergeant, manned by our boys who did most of the work supervised by a civilian employee. Here was some news I could tell to the lads with whom I shared the lower story of our barrack. They certainly found it quite revealing and we began to wonder, with everything so well organised and running like clockwork, what jobs were left for us to do. We had not long to wait. On our way to the dining hall to have lunch we had a look at the notice board where the details of the new working parties had just been posted. Some of us went to farms in the valley, others, were found jobs within the camp. I found my name among a list of four, one of whom I knew suffered from epilepsy. So what might our work be? No good guessing, we just had to wait until the morning.

The next morning we made our way to the main gate and waited until our gang number was called. Although we knew each other by sight we were not too sure about our names. We put this right whilst waiting to be called. On our way across the Atlantic, because of my very blond hair, someone started to call me Blondy. The boys soon picked it up and I was stuck with that name for the rest of my time as a P.O.W, so Blondy I was to one and all as I waited with Johannes, Klaus and Franz to be called and to be taken to our place of work. Klaus was the one with epilepsy. We were the last but one gang to be called as one of the smaller army trucks, driven by a civilian, drew up and invited us to go on board. One of the G.I.s standing by the gates was detailed to look after us and off we went. As we went along we had a look at what was in the truck and found a large number of fencing posts as well as other items and tools needed either to erect or to repair fences. It was but a few minutes before we reached the boundary of the camp where we turned left onto a bumpy track that ran along the fence until we came to a halt where the fence was damaged. The guard indicated we were to get off the truck and our foreman told us what equipment and which tools were needed at this point to repair the fence. Job done we moved on along the fence to the next point that needed repairing. When the stops became more frequent we decided to walk as often we could see where the next fault in the fence occurred. It was a sunny day, lovely fresh air, a bit nippy at first but it soon warmed up and before long we could take our coats off. Working outdoors and at the edge of the camp we were able to see what lay beyond. We spotted large wooded areas as well as farmland with people busily engaged with the harvest of some kind. In this corner of the camp the stillness and tranquillity all round us felt almost heavenly. We had a short break during the morning as well as in the afternoon, an hour for lunch and back in camp by 17.00. As we were among the first working gangs back in camp this gave us time to have a wash and get ready for supper before the evening count. During the next twenty minutes or so most of my roommates returned with their stories of the day's events. Most of them worked within the army camp doing odd jobs such as cleaning office blocks or empty buildings, getting them ready to be used again. One gang carried out some light road repairs, others, went to nearby farms helping mostly with packing and stacking as well as transportation and deliveries. That was our first test of what life as a P.O.W. in the States would be like. We also earned our first 80 cents, the pay for a full day's work.

This routine continued till the end of September. Klaus had three or four fits during the time we worked on this maintenance gang, which can be quite disturbing or even frightening when witnessed for the first time.

GEORGE GEBAUER

Fortunately Klaus could tell when an attack was imminent and able to warn and prepare us. After the violent shaking of the whole body, what always seemed an eternity, at the end of the attack sufferers are utterly exhausted and need a little time to recover. Johannes and Franz could not bear watching, I had seen worse, so it did not bother me too much. In the first week in Camp White we were also given writing paper to write to folks back home telling them of our whereabouts, a great relief to all of us new arrivals. On the first of October we also received our first pay packed a total of $7.40; $6.40 for services rendered and $1.00 for the full week we were in Camp White, due to us under the Geneva Convention Rules. One of the sergeant's and one of our office clerks were in the dining hall for the duration of mealtime and we could collect our pay either before or after we had our meal. After receiving my pay I went straight to the canteen and bought a carton of 200 cigarettes for just $1.20 as well as some chocolate, what a joy. More joy was yet to come. The next day we learned that 50 of the new arrivals were to go to the branch camp in Tule Lake in two days' time. Names to be posted on the notice board in the morning and guess what, my name was on it. I was thrilled and was looking forward to it. I looked upon it as yet another adventure; after all I had nothing to lose. The lads in camp who had been there the previous year were sure we would like and enjoy the time there. I, along with others who were going to Tule Lake, packed our kitbags the night before to be ready for the ride the next morning. I did not need a wakeup call the following morning. After the morning count I went to collect my bag and joined the others waiting for the transport to arrive which came just after

8 o'clock. The lorries, standard army trucks, came into the camp as soon as all the working parties had left. We had another quick count to make sure no unauthorised person would join us on this trip and off we went. It turned out to be the scenic ride we were told it would be. Not long after leaving camp we were on the mountain road leading to the Klamath Falls. First surrounded by woodland and forest, as we climbed the view became more and more scenic. Rocks and mountains and waterfalls were all quite breath taking. There where long sections en route where the lorries had to change into lower gears. Then through the pass on top of the mountain and down into the valley of Tule Lake. It was a vast area, not unlike the valley we had just come from. In the far distance and all around we could see yet another mountain range. Before long we spotted the camp built in a woodland clearing and very isolated. The accommodation was in single story huts of timber construction. For us, who came just for a short time there were tents in one corner of the P.O.W. compound. They were intended just to be dormitories. As for anything else we were to use the existing facilities of the camp which had just a simple fence around it and was divided in two halves, one for the G.I.s the other for the P.O.W.s. It was well lit by night I must say and had only ordinary pill boxes at each corner. As the boys back at Camp White said, life was very laid back. We arrived at the camp just after one o'clock in the afternoon and found the place deserted apart from the office staff and the cooks in the kitchen who had a wonderful meal waiting for us. After lunch we picked our tent that we were to sleep in for the next few weeks and then had a look round and made ourselves familiar with the layout

of the camp. The tents were very simply furnished, each having four camp beds placed on a raised wooden floor, a mattress, pillow, bedcover and two blankets. There was one naked electric bulb to illuminate the tent, which was welcomed by all. As for my first impression, one could not wish for a more beautiful and quiet place, but tomorrow we were to start work, helping with the potato harvest. We were told the valley had only been settled since the First World War by veterans of that war taking part in a reclamation project sponsored by the U.S.A. government. It was agricultural and arable.

We assembled for morning count, just to make sure nobody hopped it in the night and simply were counted out to go to the nearest farm truck ready to take us to the fields where we were told the recently spun out potatoes would be waiting to be collected. When we arrived at the field, which was enormous, we were greeted by the farmer, who explained through an interpreter what was expected of us and the target we had to aim at to be paid our 80 cents. The target, 80 sacks a day per person. The amount in each sack had to weigh not less than 23 kg., but no more than 25 kg. Spot checks were made on sacks which appeared to have either too few or too many potatoes. We were given a broad belt with two hooks at the back on which to hang five sacks. On the front of that belt were a further two hooks on which to hang a board on which we fastened the sack into which we gathered the potatoes. Sounds complicated? It really was not. As we stood around the weighing machine, we were handed 10 sacks each recorded alongside our names and then pointed to the row of potatoes that was ours to gather. Each man had his own row. The yield that year was heavy and farmers expected a good crop as long as the potatoes were in the barns before frost and snow arrived. That was the reason for our being there. What looked like an easy target at the outset was not quite so rosy after an hour or so. Our legs and thighs unaccustomed to such work began to ache and tire, but we did not give up hope, there were plenty of potatoes in each line that made it possible to achieve this target. The machines the farmers used were enormous. They were digging up two lines at a time and merging them into one row. So, plenty in one line and it did not take long and one did not have to move far, to get the required amount of 24 kg. or thereabouts. By the end of day I must say I had enough. The target is achievable but one needs to keep at it. The boys who picked up the sacks of potatoes felt they did a good days work as well. They worked in gangs of six to each lorry. As they went up and down the rows of sacks of potatoes, they lifted the half hundred weight sacks all day long and their day did not finish until all the sacks were safely in the barn in case of overnight frost. For that reason they made a later start than the rest of us, as they might not finish until well after 8 p.m. By then darkness would have fallen and the chilly night air could be felt. After a day or two we became somewhat daring. When at the checkpoint to collect a further set of ten sacks and nobody was looking, or the farmer's attention was somewhere else, we dropped a sack occasionally. That made it easier to reach our target at the end of the day. The weather throughout our time in the potato fields was dry and mostly sunny. Temperatures in the day time were quite warm, mostly up in the lower 20s °C. The nights however became very chilly and we could have done with some heat in the tents.

The potato harvest came to an end at the end of October and we then switched over to help getting the onions under cover. Here we worked in pairs with a target of five hundredweight of onions a day between us, which was just about achievable. Before long our time in Tule Lake sadly would come to an end. Life was so peaceful and relaxed in these mountains. Food was good and plentiful and also well prepared. With the hunting season just beginning our army rations and diet were supplemented by farmers bringing us braces of wild geese they shot during the week as these birds migrated to the south. It made a welcome change to our diet and it must be said our cooks made a jolly good lob of it. We usually had them for Sunday lunch. Four days into the onion harvest, during the night of October 31st to November 1st, we had a very heavy snowstorm. The snow, of the wet and heavy kind, brought the tents down round our ears during the night and we had to seek refuge in the dining hall. That needless to say, brought camp life into a state of confusion. The morning was a little chaotic to say the least, but we managed. It just shows what good will can achieve. During the morning we were told by the camp's Commandant that transport, to take those billeted in tents, back to Camp White, would arrive about lunch time, the rest would remain to clear up and moth ball the camp for the winter season and arrive back at Camp White for "Thanksgiving!" As for the moment, we just cleared away the snow from the tents so as to have access to our few possessions. That, I do not mind telling you, was a cold, wet and miserable job, but it had to be done if we did not want to lose all our possessions a second time in less than six months. Lunch was early for those returning to Camp White so as to be ready when the transport arrived. As nobody went to work that day, those staying behind at Tule Lake cleared the parade ground of snow so making it easier for the trucks to turn and not pack down the snow, thereby turning the parade ground into an ice rink.

A little earlier than expected, just after noon, the lorries arrived, the drivers had a short break whilst we were saying our 'Good Byes' to new found friends and off we went. If the journey coming up the mountain was beautiful and breath taking, the return trip was spectacular, almost indescribable. The mountain peaks and valleys as well as the trees, with the sun shining on freshly fallen snow from the night before, simply looked stunning. Slowly we made our way up to the mountain pass and after safely negotiating the pass, down into the valley on the other side we went. As we came down the mountain the snow rapidly disappeared. That explained why we had the rapid response to take us back to the main camp as driving conditions were perfect north of Mount Ashland. It did not take long from here to get back to familiar surroundings where we had a tale to tell to the boys that stayed behind in Camp White. The friends in my barrack found it all very interesting as well as amusing. They told me that nothing of interest had occurred in our absence and were happy to see us back again. The next question, what work would there be for us? The following day we would found out. In the meantime I made the most of a free day, especially catching up with my laundry and writing my monthly letter home. Before going to lunch I had a look at the notice board and there I learned I was going to be in one of the parties that worked a late shift in the Quartermaster's warehouse. That meant a late start for a week, leaving camp at 14.00 returning at 22.00 before we changed to the morning shift working normal hours 08.00 to 17.00. The work involved by the day shift was getting supplies ready to be taken to various companies around the camp. The task for the evening shift was to sort out the day's deliveries and take them to be stored in their assigned place. We worked these shifts alternate weeks. Were there any perks that came with the job? Officially none; nonetheless there were some. Those who worked in the Quartermaster's warehouse were the smartest dressed in camp. Providing numbers tallied there was no problem exchanging old items for new. After all, exchange is no robbery. So we exchanged our tacky boots for some smart new ones, or if we could rescue a condemned pair of old shoes we would exchange them for a pair of new ones, the only problem, how to smuggle them pass the guard into the camp. Whenever we engaged in such exchanges we waited for the time when we returned to camp at the end of a day shift, when the frisking by guards was rather more casual because of numbers, as we were expected to be lined up on the parade ground for the evening count. What was the reason for doing it? Vanity I suppose. We had a similar system for shirts. There were two in my locker, a standard khaki one and a dark brown one. It also added some excitement and gave us a thrill of sorts that we got one over on our captors. It felt good to wear something different at the weekend starting with Saturday evening and all day Sunday. Within our compound we were not obliged to wear cloths with the compulsory P.W. on it.

The warehouse was the place I worked for the rest of the year. It was a good place to be as we were always in the dry and out of the winds. There was also a social life in camp. Some of the men had been there since 1942 and formed quite a good band as well as a concert party. In early November the concert party alongside the social committee were making plans for the Christmas show and party. With the influx of a 150 new men they had hopes of producing something special for Christmas that year. The band on the other hand was rehearsing for a concert that was planned for "Thanksgiving". That was entirely new to me. At that time I had never heard of such a holiday. It just shows you how insulated life was in Germany under the Hitler regime. I now know what a big holiday it is in the U.S.A. having been a beneficiary as well as having taken part in it. As the world knows, each year on the fourth Thursday in November America grinds to a standstill. Everybody longs to be home for "Thanksgiving". I enjoyed the day as the U.S. army wanted it to be special for us as well. There was the day off work of course and as I said before we had standard U.S. army rations and as it turned out "Thanksgiving" was no exception. We had the full treatment. For lunch that day we had turkey with all the trimmings, pumpkin pie and as every serving G.I., a cigar. All that was missing was the glass of wine. Those of us who experienced the day for the first time surely appreciated it. As for entertainment on the day, we had a film show in the afternoon and the band's concert in the evening. It was good to hear again all the familiar tunes I grew up with. About that time, at the end of November was also my birthday and the boys in the room made quite a fuss over it which touched me very much, after all we had not known one another very long. I thought at the time, what a lucky guy I am that my comrades should spend their hard earned Dollars and Cents on me.

With Christmas only one calendar month away, the social committee began in earnest their rehearsals for the annual Christmas concert. By all accounts the theatre group in camp was excellent. It was blessed with a number of good actors and comedians as well as a good producer and director who over the years in captivity had put on some wonderful shows. This year, because of our arrival in camp, they were able to recruit new and additional talent. With new blood and new and different experience from the newcomers, the Christmas show was really good. It was produced and presented on the old style Music Hall production. As always, on the night of the performances, American officers and N.C.O.s were present to make sure no plots of massive breakouts or riots were planned. Looking across at them, they laughed heartily at the comedy sketches and enjoyed instrumental and vocal solo performances. The band was present, accompanying performers, as well as having a spot of their own in the programme of the evening. The verdict, by one and all, was an excellent evening of entertainment of home grown talent. On New Year's Eve we had another enjoyable evening when the orchestra royally entertained us once again to blow our blues away. New Year's Eve or not, lights out as usual at 22.00 and the next day, as always, was a working day. With wishing one another a 'Happy New Year' and a good night, we went to bed and to sleep, wondering what 1945 would hold for us.

At Camp White, Oregon, in a borrowed Luftwaffe uniform jacket. This is the earliest Wartime photograph that has survived of me.

Camp White, Oregon

(I do not appear in the cast)

This photograph was sent to me by Gerhard Schmidt after the war had ended with following inscription on the back:-

'Ich' in Maske 'Krumme Lanke'.

English translation: Me, in the costume of Krumme Lanke

In the Ballard of "A little creek of the river Havel"

Chapter 14

California Here We Come

With Christmas and welcoming in the New Year behind us we were set to pick up the familiar daily routine. Imagine, when like a bolt out of the blue, just a day or two into the New Year, an announcement was made that 300 of us would be transferred to a camp in California. Details, as to who would be on the transfer list, would be posted on the notice board the following lunch time. That announcement caused a great stir in camp and set the tongues talking. It was certain that at least 150 of those who were in Camp White before our arrival would be on the transfer list. Personally it did not bother me whether or not I would be on the list as there had been hardly any time to strike roots anywhere since I had been in America. In fact the whole of 1944 had been a year of constant travel, another journey would be just one more adventure in my young life. On our return from work the following day everybody made a beeline for the notice board. Yes, I was on the list. The camp was to be a temporary one in the Central Valley of California. What was the reason for our being moved? It was to help with the cotton harvest! In other words we were to become 'Cotton Pickers.' If there was anything pleasing about it, it was surely this, we were going south to warmer climes. As for the job itself, none of us had any idea what it would be like and what was involved, so we just had to wait and see. Going by past experience, we never had much notice as to date and time. So it came as no surprise that it was the day after tomorrow we were to leave Camp White for good this time. As it was going to be a long journey, an early start was ordered so as to get to our destination before nightfall. Unlike the African veterans, who had gathered quite a few possessions during their two years in captivity and needed a little while to pack their worldly goods, the Normandy veterans soon had their kitbags packed and were ready to go.

Well before six in the morning on the appointed day, we were up to have an early breakfast and collected our packed lunch and filled our flasks with water for the journey. Whilst we were having breakfast a fleet of Greyhound coaches drove into the camp ready for us to board. Those who were to be transferred had their own assembly that morning. We were counted and numbers proved correct. We then boarded the coaches as our names were called out in alphabetical order. As you can imagine extra G.I.s were present for this operation as time was of utmost importance for the convoy to get away on time. The logistics of moving three hundred plus P.O.W.s as well as the military escort by road, travelling in convoy, was quite something. This time we travelled in some luxury, which did not happen too often with the military in those days.

So, soon after eight, on a cold, dull January morning in 1945, the convoy of cars, jeeps, coaches and trucks left Camp White in Oregon for California. Before long we were on the highway leading south. The first few miles were familiar to many of us as we had driven along it on our way to Tule Lake. Only this time, travelling in the luxurious Greyhound coaches, the scenery looked even more stunning. Up here in the mountains there was plenty of snow, which gave the whole area a picture postcard effect. But it did not last, all too soon we came to the point where we took the route that lead down the mountain: we were on our way to Sacramento. From mountains, valleys and forest the scene began to change to an agricultural one. As the day wore on the clouds lifted and the sun shone, making the journey through northern California a very pleasant experience. As before, the scene and landscape we went through was forever changing, hills, mountains, valleys, farmland, forests, woods and open spaces. Our journey south took us through towns and small settlements as well as wide open spaces. We saw ranch buildings and farmsteads also some isolated dwellings of typical American design and construction. Soon after midday, we made a convenience stop at a military base somewhere near Sacramento. It was but a brief stop, just long enough to make everybody feel comfortable again. Within thirty minutes we were on the road once more to continue our way south. Round about that time someone on the coach opened his lunch packet and guess what, one by one we did the same, a simple snack consisting of two sandwiches of typical army ration: one was a meat sandwich, the other of peanut butter and apple jelly. We also had an orange to finish with.

As we came further south, the hills and mountains receded, the landscape was flat and the area also became more populated, and of urban in appearance. Most houses seemed to be along or near the highway. Behind the houses we could spot vast areas of farmland as far as the eye could see, on which were growing all sorts of crops. Being quite a distance from the road it was not always easy to identify as to what was grown here. Three hours or so after we left the military base near Sacramento, we slowed down to almost a walking pace and looking through the widow straining our necks to find out what the reason might be, we saw the coaches in front of us turning off the highway onto a farm track and not too far beyond, a camp site. The site was at one corner of a very large cotton field. There was not a permanent building in sight, except a cotton mill, the reason for that we found out a couple of days later. The camp then, tents and nothing but tents, were erected on a roughly levelled cotton field. There was no electricity in the tents except in the cook house (tent), dining tent and washroom tent. The tents that were used as sleeping accommodations were lit by a hurricane lamp hung on the centre pole. There were six of us in a tent. Latrines were in one corner of the field with no lights, as the security lights illuminating the camp were deemed sufficient. In fact the security lights were all that was needed to find our way around the camp in the dark. Outside the P.O.W. compound things were much the same, the only difference, G.I.s had electricity in their tents.

Nowhere was there any heating to be found. This camp was even more basic than the one we were in at Tule Lake. It was a sight that did not exactly cheer us up after a long day's travel. Still, it might have been worse. We had a bed to lie on, albeit a camp bed, two blankets each, a roof of sorts over our heads and three meals a day guaranteed.

As there was only an hour or so of daylight left when we arrived at the camp the first thing we did was to secure a bed for the night. We looked out for friends we had made in Camp White, formed groups of six and looked for an empty tent to move into. Having staked our claim, secured our bed, we made for the dining tent where a cooked meal was served, cooked by G.I.s who knew how to get the most and the best out of army rations. It certainly tasted good and so did the hot mug of coffee, the first hot drink since breakfast. Back in our tents we lit the oil lamp, made the beds up, took towel, soap, toothpaste and brush and made our way to the washroom tent, where we were informed by those who got there before us, not to expect any hot water, only cold water was to be had in the camp. Well, so be it. All this reminded me of the Hitler Youth camps before the war, where we found similar situations, or the six weeks in Normandy before being taken prisoner, when we used the nearest stream or brook to wash ourselves and do some washing. The difference being, these things happened in summer time, but here we were in the middle of January! There was little we could do to change things, so we accepted the situation and got on with it. With nothing else to do we sat and chatted for a while guessing and speculating what would come next. Before long we wrapped ourselves in our blankets and one by one fell to sleep.

Next morning we were woken up by a Corporal whom the Sergeant, the only N.C.O. among us, had chosen to be his deputy walking up and down between the rows of tents telling us to rise and shine. It was rather a chilly morning not far off from a frost I would say. The daily routine here was no different from that of Camp White, so there was nothing new to get used or to readjust to. From now on food was to be prepared again by our own chaps who were learning fast how to make the best of and to get the most out of U.S army rations. The day after our arrival here in Central California was free and it was decided to level the parade ground so that it can be used as a playing field at weekends. It was nowhere near as big as a football pitch but at least we could knock a ball about. It must be said here, that the camp Commandant was very understanding and helpful securing the hand tools needed for this task in a very short time. After all, the Sergeant only made the request after morning parade and by the time we finished breakfast and morning inspection of the tents, the tools requested were in our hands. By the time the evening count took place the job was completed. The next step, to have a think what games we could play on this ground and accordingly what sports equipment to ask for. We left that decision to the Sergeant and a small committee of sport enthusiasts. In the end it was decided to ask for a football, a volleyball and net, as well as table tennis equipment. All these requests were granted and in the camp by the following weekend. To make these sporting activities competitive, each row of tents had to provide a team for each sport we were able to play, in order to stage a tournament and as it turned out, it was a wise decision. We knew our time here was temporary, depending how quickly we harvested the cotton crop and that in turn depended largely on the weather. We counted ourselves very lucky, as we had just one wet day in the seven weeks we were at this working camp in the middle of nowhere. All three tournaments were very entertaining to watch and to take part in and in the end became very exciting too.

Sport was not the only activity we were interested in. Improving our life in camp above the basics provided, the first task we needed to set our minds on was to improve the lighting in our tents. Fortunately, with an unlimited supply of paraffin, we overcame the poor lighting by converting jam or other suitable jars into oil lamps. We achieved this by very carefully making a slit in the top of the jars, then cutting a strip of the camp bed, intended to hold the bed together when folded. Next we fed the strip we cut of the bed through the slit made in the top of the jar. Then we filled the jar with paraffin oil and put the lit back on the jar, left it soaking for an hour or two, and there you have it. Health and safety rules, nor army regulation, may have approved of what we did, but they never knew of it as we were very careful to conceal any evidence of their existence. Before we left that camp we had four extra lamps in our tent and so did most of the others. Some even had six extra lamps.   Those who took down the camp and removed the equipment after we left would have found that most of the beds had at least one strip missing.

Just as well we made the most of our free day making our surroundings more user friendly. After that it was six days a week cotton picking, apart from one rainy day. Looking back on that time in my life, it was just one experience after another. Some were more exciting than others but they all were part of a steep learning curve and cotton picking was no exception. As a townie born and bred I had no idea how cotton was produced. Here I was now to be introduced to the art of picking this valuable natural product and it is an art believe you me. I am talking here of a time before machinery was invented to do the job instead of people. What was so unusual about all this was that the whole camp, three hundred of us, went to the same farm and the same field doing the same task. The only difference being, half of us started at one end of the field, the other half a long way off, at the opposite end. We just could make out the chaps at the other end of the field, they were just small figures in the distance. Honestly, they were ever so small. They certainly were a long way off. When all was set we were each issued with a 12 feet long bag made of cotton. Next we were assigned to a row of cottonwood trees, more like bushes really, then told our quota for the day, 12 pounds of clean cotton wool. Clean meaning no leaves or twigs nor parts of the bud in which the wool grew and matured. To be able to get the wool out neatly and cleanly the crop needs to be ripe. One can tell this when the buds in which the wool is housed breaks open and the wool emerges revealing five chambers. As the bud opens, the top of each section is very pointed and sharp as a needle. To extract the wool you put you four fingers and your thumb carefully into the five chambers, being mindful the ends are pointed and sharp. Inexperience and anxious to get our quota for the day we paid the price, ending the day with sore fingertips and well under target. The farmer was not surprised and more or less expected it as we were all greenhorns.

Before the week was out I, as well as the rest of the boys cracked it. Why not, we were after all in California and the sun was shining. By midday the temperature rose up to 20 degrees centigrade and often we took our shirts off before we went back to work after lunch. Whilst in contrast, there were nights when we had frost hard enough to freeze our water pipes meaning we had to wait until after breakfast before we could use the washing facilities. Consequently it became rather a bit of a rush to be ready in time for work and morning parade. Any time we lost to reach our quota for the day was made up by putting into the bag an odd pebble or two. The day after we had the rain, we looked for a puddle and rested the bag in it for a while. Somehow we made our quota and got our 80 cents for the day. Surprising how quickly we all got used to it. In many ways it was an easy life if somewhat restricted. The only setback was the cotton mill nearby. Before we had our lunch we had our bags weighed, recorded and emptied into a trailer with very high sides. The morning harvest was then taken to the mill, the trailer emptied, contents dry cleaned and processed. All the while the cleaning and processing work was carried out, taking out the seed for oil, removing unwanted material mixed up with the cotton which was then blown out by an extractor, followed by compressing the cleaned cotton into bales. It was the extractor that made an unholy row each evening. The afternoon crop did not reach the mill till well after 5 p.m. so, understandably, work did not stop until all the day's harvest was processed, which was usually about 11 p.m.

Throughout our time in Central California the only entertainment provided was the weekly film show. Our spiritual wellbeing was taken care of by a Roman Catholic Priest who visited the camp on Sundays just after breakfast using the dining tent. He was followed by a Lutheran Pastor at 11 o'clock to which all other denominations were invited.

Early in March that year, all the cotton was picked and baled, ready for its next stage in its manufacture. We also were ready to pack our bags and to move on to our next destination. Some thought San Diego was a possibility as it was known to have a large Naval Base. I had no idea in which direction we would have to go from here as I had never heard of the place. In fact my knowledge of the United States was very limited. All I had ever heard of were a few big cities such as New York, Chicago, Washington D.C. of course, and only thanks to Hollywood, Los Angeles.

Chapter 15

On the Shore of the Pacific

Transport to take us to our next destination pulled up outside the camp gate the next day. It was half way through the morning before they arrived and it was standard U.S. army trucks we saw. It told us, that we were not going very far. Firstly, by the time we would be leaving the temporary camp site it would be almost lunch time, and secondly, the type of transport indicated a maximum of four hours on the road. Had it been a long journey, a much earlier start would have been necessary and also, coaches would have been provided instead of army trucks. With security very light, as it had been all the time whilst cotton picking, with not a gun or rifle to be seen, it did not take long for us to get aboard those trucks. The speed with which we vacated the camp was amazing. The reasons, for the first time we were not counted as we left the camp to board the trucks and secondly, we were only too glad to get away from this site and no tears were shed as we turned our backs on this place. We all knew things could only get better. Another reason, the guards were unarmed, because the authorities did not expect anyone would attempt to escape. There was no point attempting such an action. It would be foolish as in this wide, open, large valley there was nowhere to run to, and nowhere to hide. With everything clear and all aboard, the order to roll was given and of we went.

When we got to the highway and the convoy turned in the direction that would take us to our next place of residence, it became clear, being midday and the sun behind us, that we were heading north again, but where to? Two and a half hours later we knew, as we drove through a large gate of an army camp, noticing as we entered, a board with bold letters, welcoming us to FORT ORD! It was big. Huts, barracks, office blocks, buildings and sheds of all shapes and sizes as far as the eye could see. It took almost 10 minutes before we drew up outside the gates of the P.O.W. compound situated at the very far end, on the edge of the camp on a slight slope with older style army huts build on stilts and manufactured of wood. The camp was unoccupied apart from the G.I.s that would be responsible from now on that everything runs smoothly in the camp. To make the formal handover we assembled in the square in an orderly fashion to be counted and when, we were all accounted for, the officer in charge of getting us to Fort Ord, handed us over to the camp Commandant. We were then asked to form groups of thirty, so friends could stay together. That sorted, we were then shown to our quarters. As I said, they were the old type of army accommodation, telling us there had been an army camp on this site for a very long, long time.

Entering the hut felt quite cosy, well anything would, after the previous seven weeks under canvas. The huts, as expected, had all the basic furniture. Beds, tables, benches and we even had small bedside cupboards would you believe it! The next task, to collect our bed linen and fuel for the two stoves, before having a look round to see where we could find facilities such as toilets, washrooms , kitchen and dining hall, canteen and the common room. There were two large open spaces, each about the size of a football pitch. One was designated to be the parade ground, the other as a playing field. As our cooks had little or no time to prepare a cooked meal, we had a platter of cold meats with grated carrots and beetroot as well as 2 slices of bread and fruit. We also discovered at the back of the washrooms there was, believe it or not, a washing machine. Quite a novelty it must be said, as none of us had ever seen one before! What all of us appreciated most was, to have hot water on tap again.

The day we moved into Fort Ord was a Wednesday and that evening, during our evening meal, it was announced that we had the rest of the week to settle into our quarters and to get to know the layout of the camp. Looking around my new home, all the faces I saw were familiar to me. Most of them I knew by name and I was sure we would all get on well together. None of us were strangers to each other anyway, as we had come across one another already either in the cotton fields or when competing against one another playing in tournaments at weekends in the previous camp. There was quite mix of characters in our hut as well as of trades and professions. The talent that emerged once we had settled in, and the interests my comrades pursued in the life before the army, were amazing. For the record, there was no professional soldier among us. We had students, whose studies had been interrupted by war, teachers, journalists, carpenters as well as mechanics, engineers and musicians. There were also farmers and foresters, shop assistances, secretaries. In fact we had among us representatives from almost all trades and professions and all walks of life. Living in close quarters such as we did at that time and having only limited resources we could share in our leisure time, we learned a lot from each other as well as about each other. It must also be said, the older men amongst us were only too willing to help and teach us younger chaps whenever we went to them with our problems and queries.

So we made ourselves at home as best we could in the four days before we started work again on the Monday after our arrival in Fort Ord. Not having been able to spend very much of our hard earned Dollars during the last few weeks we made up for it now in the well-stocked canteen we had in Fort Ord. Most money went on toiletries, such as fancy soap, shampoo and hair cream. Some of us could not resist the sweets and chocolate in the shop. Most of us in camp were smokers, so we were very interested in the tobacco products on sale. Most varieties of cigars were in stock as well as the most popular brands of pipe tobacco and cigarettes. All tobacco products were cheap to buy, 200 cigarettes were only $1.20. With a day's pay one could buy a week's supply of cigarettes. Those who wanted to could also buy their beer ration of half a pint a day again, all these things we had missed since we left Camp White. As we brought our sports equipment with us the football enthusiasts started to kick the ball around first thing the next morning. The table tennis was set up in the Common room that Thursday as well, in fact we had two now. So was the dart board.

Most of us were anxious though to get our washing up together. Some were brave enough to try the washing machine; others were looking on with interest to see how it worked. It was very basic, consisting of a trough in which the drum was placed with an open top. There was a simple flap for loading and two water taps. Then you placed your washing powder or your soap in the water, pressed the button to start the machine and off it went. When you thought your washing had long enough in the machine to be clean you stopped it, drained the water and started the rinsing process. All very time consuming and yet surprisingly the chaps were queuing to do their laundry this way. Many of us found it much quicker though to do our laundering by hand. Some of the time we also spent on making our quarters homely looking and feel lived in. To a man though, we all waited and wondered what kind work there was lined up for us next week. Details were to be posted on the notice board Saturday lunch time. The two clerks that had already been doing secretarial work would not let on what type of work we were to be put to. Eventually it was revealed. Saturday lunch time, accompanied by the two sergeants, they pinned the sheets, bearing our names with gang number and time we had to report for work at the gate, on the board. It took a little while before I got to the front of the notice board to see my fate. I was to be part of a gang of seven. It was shift work and seven days a week. We had one day a week off, with mine being a Tuesday, and we had to be at the gate at 10.00 Monday morning. There were not many jobs we as, P.O.W.s, could be set to that required seven days attendance. Work in a kitchen or cleaning in the hospital, sewerage work may be? As the day went on and the weekend went by, we gathered more information as to what kind of work it that we would expect to do. It emerged that all of us would be working for the military either within the camp boundaries of Fort Ord, or, a few miles south along the coast from here at a convalescence camp in Monterey Bay.

The seven of us that were to work together in the near future met after supper that Saturday evening to get to know each other a bit better and to talk about what we had heard over the grape vine since the notices were posted. It was not a great deal we had learnt but what we knew now it was to be work in one of the kitchens. What kind of work no one had any idea. Before we broke up to go to our own quarters, we decided to arrange to meet the other gang as from the time table it was clear that over the lunch period both gangs would be on duty. The time pattern was quite simple. The morning shift had to be at the gate 05.55 and finished their shift at 14.00 to return to camp. The afternoon shift was to be at the gate at 09.55 and end their shift at 18.00. Every Monday morning we changed over, so when we were back in camp just after 18.00 on the Sunday evening, less than twelve later at 05.00 we had to be at the gate again, to be picked up. Meeting with our colleagues proved quite helpful as good comradely spirit would present a picture of solidarity to our captors. We needed it at the time with the situation in Europe not looking too healthy. The Battle of the Bulge had been lost the previous winter. Fighting was taking place all along the German borders, on both the eastern and western fronts, something unheard of since the beginning of the war in 1939. So the least we could do was not to look downhearted when we met our new bosses the next day.

On Monday, in very good time the six of us, remember one had his day off, gathered near the main gate waiting for our gang number to be called. There was only one other group, somewhat larger than ours, waiting to be collected. They too, we understood, were involved with kitchen work somewhere in the camp. Just before ten o'clock a jeep type truck pulled up outside the gate with a sergeant emerging showing his papers to the guard and immediately our number was called. We moved towards the gate as they opened; the sergeant said hallo to us in a very friendly manner and indicated to us to hop onto the truck and off we went. The relaxed way he dealt with us could only mean one thing, that the early shift must have made a very good impression. It was a brief ride, in just three minutes we pulled up outside the back of a standard mess hall barrack, build on stilts as most of the buildings in camp seemed to be, with six beaming faces greeting us. They quickly told us what we had to do. Three from each group were to work in the dining hall being responsible for overall cleanliness. The others had to clear the tables after each meal and to prepare them for the next. After breakfast each day, or earlier if necessary, the table cloths had to be changed. The dining hall team was also responsible that the coffee, or other drinks according to the menu of the day, were ready and served in time. The team had to check the cruets were full and clean. Vegetables, bread and gravy had to be served as the tables were filled. This was something we had not come across before; Food being served on plates instead of mess tins and Drinks in cups, instead of tin mugs. The Flowers on the tables were the mess sergeant's responsibility thank goodness.

Only breakfast was served in the cafeteria style. We just took a jug of coffee to the table.

The other three in the group worked in the kitchen mostly doing the cleaning and the washing up as well as keeping the kitchen spick and span. As time went by and the cooks and the baker got to know us better they requested our help, especially in the days before festivals or public holidays, when the workload was quite heavy for them with more courses and special dishes that were on the menu had to be prepared. It did not take us long to work out a daily routine once we knew what was expected of us. Before the month of March was out we had things down to a fine art, so much so that the sergeant as well as the kitchen personal left most things to us to get on with. We worked out a rota so that wherever we were stationed, dining hall or kitchen, with whomsoever we worked, and in whatever department, we knew what to do and so we got on extremely well together. There was never a disagreement in the group or between the groups in the twelve months we worked together in that kitchen. We worked so well together that by 10 o'clock, when the late shift arrived, the dining hall was clean and laid up for lunch and the kitchen neat and tidy. Equally so, before the morning shift returned to camp at 2 p.m. the dining hall was ready for the evening meal. That gave us time for some leisure activity. The barrack next to us was converted into a lounge, except the kitchen section which we used as a bakery twice a week. As it was never used during the day, or at weekends, we made use of it whenever we had the opportunity. Most of the time we were around the pool table with the radio on, entertaining us with the latest hits from the world of pop, or sentimental ballads to help the boys to dream of home, their sweethearts or their latest pin up. Names and voices such as Bing Crosby, Rosemarie Cloony, Ella Fitzgerald, Frank Sinatra, The Andrew Sisters, Gene Kelly, Dina Shore and many others one got to know and love. We heard songs from the latest Musicals on Broadway including Oklahoma. One way or another it helped the morale of the troops as well as us, as we never had it so good. As long as one of us was in the kitchen to help the cook on duty, if called upon, and to keep on top of the washing up of utensils used by the cook, all was well. In any case, once we got to know the cook's requirements for the menu he had to prepare, we got things ready for him as much as we could in advance, which pleased them enormously. Working closely with the G.I.s and listening to the stars of radio in their daily programmes, introduced us very nicely to American culture and the American way of life. All this helped us with our English as well. Certainly it helped to understand English if not so much to voice it.

With the two gangs working so well together, the sergeant soon left us to get on with things. The cook who came on duty at 2 o'clock in the afternoon took the late shift back to camp when work was done and also fetched the morning shift. So the sergeant did not put in an appearance until sometime after nine in the morning and then he still looked, very often, bleary eyed. He made himself a cup of coffee and had a bite to eat before he set out to collect the late shift from the camp. After his return he dropped four of the gang and, with the other two, he went off to collect the provisions for the next day. The round took us to all the food and cold stores, including the bakery, where everything was ready for our collection. Whilst he had a chat with his counterpart at these places we talked to our own chaps and had a look round their workplaces. When we were out and about we sometimes saw troops in combat dress being marched towards waiting trains to be taken to San Francisco to board the ships on their way to the Far East. Back at the kitchen we unloaded the truck and stored the food in the appropriate places. The sergeant made himself another cup of coffee and then checked the dining hall that everything was to his liking, saw to the flowers whether they needed changing or not, and then waited until twelve noon for the first G.I.s to arrive. Once lunch was under way, he vanished until just before 14.00, only to take the morning shift back to camp. Then we never saw him again until after nine o'clock the next day. The reason he kept out of sight as much as his position would allow was, coming from the state of Tennessee, the Hill Billy area, the cooks gave him a hard time, considering him a little simple, and he dare not criticize or make any comment about their cooking.

All this evolved during the first four weeks or so after we came to Fort Ord and after we started work in the kitchen that looked after the N.C.O.s, who were head of departments throughout the camp, e.g. Quartermaster's Store, Ware Houses, Food Stores, Motor Pool, Sanitation Department just to name a few. This explained the posh dining facilities that existed in our mess hall.

After returning to camp on the first evening there was much to talk about. The boys in the hut wanted to know what my placement was and how I got on. I wanted to know how they got on and what their day was like. Overall, everybody seemed quite happy and pleased with their jobs and posting. All of us were welcomed by those in charge of us and were very pleased to have the extra help. It was not very long before we were trusted in all departments to get on with our jobs without much oversight. As in previous camps, within the P.O.W. compound, we could wear whatever we fancied, outside we had to display the letters P.W. front and back on our clothing. All clothing issued by the army was marked accordingly. As only a few among us still had their German uniform, most of us had to wear what we were originally given when we were fitted out on our arrival in the U.S.A., both inside and outside the compound. To enable us to have a change, get out of our working cloths so to speak, we needed to get unmarked clothes from the outside. As the boys working for the sanitation department went to every part and corner in the camp collecting refuse, or garbage as it is known across the Atlantic, at least once a week, we developed a system by which they became our parcel delivery service. They collected small, unobtrusive parcels from one department and delivered it at another. After a while most of us wore unmarked shirts and trousers at weekends or any other time we liked, as long as it was within the P.O.W. compound. Most of us also possessed at least one pair of smart shoes which we wore inside instead of army boots. The boys also delivered freshly made sandwiches and fancy cakes from the kitchens around the camp to other departments to give the boys there something different and more exciting for lunch than the usual dull, monotonous hand out by our kitchen staff. They still had no idea how to get the best and most out of U.S Army ration. Yet they had the same food delivered to the camp as we collected from the warehouses for our own kitchen. They could have benefited from a visit to our place and just observing our cooks. In their defence it must be said there were many things we were not used to in our diet at home. Corn for instance was one such item in the American ration we received regularly. Most of the boys considered it to be chicken food. Grapefruit was another item most of us did not know what to do with in the early stages. Cranberries or cranberry sauce we had never heard of. Working in the kitchen, I was fortunate to have tasted all these foods after they had been prepared properly and for the right dishes. That made all the difference. The cooks too encouraged us to taste their creations, which they were rightly proud of. Before long we enjoyed all the best and finest cuisine the U.S. army had to offer. At the end of our time we always had the first pick of everything in the fridges, the larder and store rooms.

Life within the P.O.W. enclosure too, quickly settled into a routine. Those of us placed in kitchens were the only ones working at weekends, the rest finished work Saturday lunch time and had the rest of the weekend off. It was not long before the sport enthusiasts got going again organising various tournaments. Those not interested in sport could find plenty of other things to do this time, as the well-stocked shop provided plenty of reading material on a variety of subjects which might stimulate thoughts and lead to some interests one could pursue. One could buy popular magazines as well as a daily newspaper. The latter was only purchased by a handful of chaps with enough knowledge of English. For me the attraction were the magazines promoting light entertainment and containing the lyrics of the most popular songs of the day, such as Broadcasting Songs or Song Hits Magazine and Hit Parade. When you have the lyrics printed in front of you it made the whole experience so much more enjoyable. The song became so much more meaningful and made so much more sense now. It was amazing what one could find to buy in the shop.

There were evening classes for those who would like to learn or improve their English. A small number of the boys enrolled in a correspondence course with a University in California. One such was in my hut, a young lad in his early twenties, enrolled to continue his studies to become a veterinary surgeon, much encouraged and helped by one of the older men among us, who by profession was a journalist. In the evenings when there was nothing going on, we passed the time by writing home, or caught up with the washing and mending, or joined others in a game of cards or a board game. For whatever reason, we were never offered any musical instruments to form a band. The reason may well be that we never asked nor did there seem to be any enthusiasm in the camp to form a Concert Party. The sporting facilities we had seemed, to satisfy the majority, that there was enough on offer with which to occupy our free time. The highlight of the week was on Wednesday, when every week we had a film show. There were two performances each time. The first showing at 14.30 for those who worked in the camp, kitchen and office staff or those who had their day off from work; the second showing was 20.00 for all the rest. Those on late shift and working at the convalescence camp out at Monterey Bay just about made it. These films were the latest out of Hollywood, most of them were musicals or comedies, easy to follow and easy to understand. Some of the stars were familiar names to me as I remembered them from pre-war days in Berlin. Yes, apart from the confinement, life was easy and carefree. To have a change from what became a regular daily routine, we sometimes swopped jobs. We all longed to make a visit to Monterey Bay. Those who made the daily trip told us what a beautiful place it was and a scenic ride as well. The day I went out there was a day to remember. It was and, still is, a scenic coastal ride. I did the journey again in 1988.The campsite too was in a beautiful spot on the slopes of the Pacific. It was nicely laid out with lovely gardens, wide open spaces and oh so peaceful and tranquil. The view out over the ocean was breath taking. The other time I made a swop was nowhere near so exiting. There was a film with Bing Crosby showing in the camp hospital which was full of fun and music, pretty girls and dancing. After having finished the work on the ward clearing up after lunch we wheeled the patience into the lounge, settled back to see the picture, which was entitled 'Here come the wrens' was great fun and colourful and I enjoyed it.

Whilst we got used to our new surroundings and our new jobs in Fort Ord, things were happening outside too, both in America and in Europe. Allied troops were entering Germany on all fronts and with the war in Europe all but over. President Roosevelt, not being in the best of health, returning home exhausted after the Yalta conference never recovered. He died on the 12th of April after serving only 83 days of his fourth term as President of the United States of America. The people were stunned and shocked and in mourning. His coffin, I remember, was carried through many of the states before his funeral. Many people said they felt as so they lost a father.

The same cannot be said about Hitler when he was found dead after having committed suicide in his bunker in Berlin. Most people in Germany were only too pleased this unhappy war was over and regretted ever having listened to Hitler and his vision to transform Germany. The shocking discovery of the atrocities in the concentration camps added salt to the wound and many found it almost unbelievable that some six million Jews and five million Communists, Democrats, Clergymen, Jehovah's Witnesses, Gypsies, intellectuals and homosexuals had been exterminated. We in camp here found it hard to take in but had to accept the evidence as presented in the press and cinema News Reels. We wondered if there might be a backlash in our treatment by the military or the civilians we came into contact: our concern was unfounded. There was absolutely no change in the relationship with our captors either inside or outside the compound. The chaps who bought the newspapers kept us in touch now with what was going on in the outside world including the opening sessions of the Nuremberg trials. The dropping of the first atom bomb on 6th August, ultimately lead to victory over Japan. In the Far East the end of the war on V/J Day brought great rejoicing all over the States and much was made of the first Thanksgiving Day after the war.

Looking back over my time in Fort Ord, I found it was quite an enriching period. The fact of being in America, at all, was almost unbelievable. Also, being on the west coast made it even more exciting. Working with the G.I.s on a daily basis taught me a great deal about the

American way and culture specially the way they celebrate their public holidays. I was familiar with the Christian Festivals, of course, but had never heard of Thanksgiving or Independence Day, among others, before I came to America. We celebrated Thanksgiving in Camp White in 1944, of course, where we were told, by our comrades taken prisoners in the deserts of North Africa, what a great national and family holiday it is. Even in the war that public holiday was observed. Here now in Fort Ord, working in the kitchen, it was a working day as usual. In 1945, we experienced them all, starting with Easter Day. Preparation for these holidays began with an extra trip to the food and cold stores collecting the provisions issued for these occasions. With additional dishes to prepare an early start had to be made. Not knowing what help was expected of us, we just stood by watching and absorbing what was going on until we were asked to give a helping hand with all this extra food to handle and prepare. The preparations began the day after we collected the special issues from the stores by plucking and dressing the turkeys. Next we helped the baker with his cooking the traditional pies. This was on top of our daily routine work of course. On the day itself there was extra work in the kitchen in all departments as well as in the dining room where the tables were decorated with flowers and greenery. Additional cutlery had to be laid out and a cigar in every place. It was quite a challenge to get it all done in time, for the first time anyway. When preparing for the 4th July we had some idea where we were going and knew where our help was most needed and appreciated. Come Thanksgiving we were well ahead with our work as by then we knew exactly what help and where our help was most needed. By Christmas all the cook and the baker had to do was to turn up and to start baking or cooking. In the end, apart from the actual baking and cooking, it was all left to us to get on with it. Inspections by an officer were very rare anyway. Looking back on that time in my life, it was quite carefree and relaxing and in some ways a happy time too. I was happy to be alive and well and happy that the war was over even if Germany came second. I was lucky to share my prisoner of war years with such a friendly and happy bunch of fellows. I spent my 20th birthday in Fort Ord and received the customary birthday card, homemade of course, by one of our talented chaps in the barrack. By November we all had become good friends as well as being comrades still. This could not have happened before as we were never long enough together and in in the same place to form any meaningful friendships.

So 1945 drew to a close and with the war over. There was speculation what would happen next. In the middle of the January in1946, we were told. All those taken prisoners in Africa would be repatriated first. The date was to be announced before long. And so it was, that in the second week of February that year, we said good bye to our comrades and friends from the Afrika Corps who helped us so much in our early days to settle in and come to terms with our fate and a life behind barbed wire in America. Looking back, I must say, it was a blessing and very helpful to join an established order and disciplined way of life at the beginning of that period of my life. Not surprisingly then, life was not the same after the boys had gone. There were the empty beds in the room for a start, then their chatter and their anecdotes from a different theatre of war all together than ours had ceased. It was a sad day for us who stayed behind when we saw them march through the gates on their way to the train. At the same time we were overjoyed for them, that they were on their way home at last after such a long time away from home and their families. Some had spent over five years in captivity. Good luck to them all, we said. Our time will come. It was only a question when!

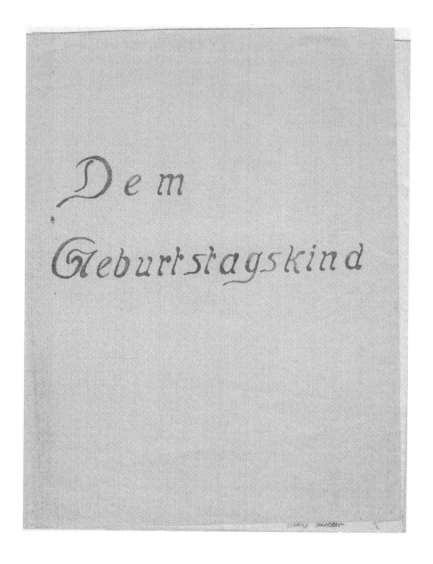

The Cover of my 20th Birthday Card given to me at Fort Ord POW Camp on 25 November 1945.

The two inserts are shown on the following two pages.

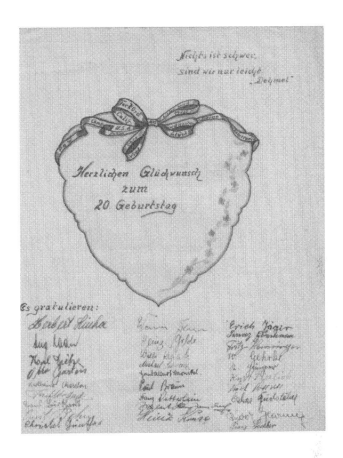

The first insert of my 20th Birthday Card. The reverse contained
another 15 signatures.
NOTE: The ribbon contains the following inscriptions:
Left side: P o W, Camp Fort Ord, Calif., U.S.A., Autumn, 1945
Right side: (translated: With love and good wishes truly your
comarades
other German inscriptions translate:
Top right: Nothing is too heavy
we are just not up to it.
Centre: Good Wishes
For
20th Birthday

GEORGE GEBAUER

The second insert of my 20th Birthday Card.
The English translation of the poem reads:

Dedication
Live Your Dream of Beauty and Luck
Dream about Love and Faithfulness
Always go forwards never go back
Change with Whatever comes your Way
Should fate not turn out as you had hoped it would be
Don't give up not all is lost
Bear in mind you will win through life
If you know how to deal with the situation!

My other 20th Birthday Card.

Signed by the gang I worked with for over 12 months at Fort Ord

Chapter 16

Homeward Bound

Four weeks later we were told that we would leave Fort Ord on 30th March for New York on our way home. We had one more week at work before we said our good byes to the sergeant and the cooks as well as the baker. They all were genuinely sorry to see us go but wished us well for the future. It must be said we got on well with our captors, be it the military personal or the civilians we came into contact on farms and warehouses or where ever we worked. There was never any ill treatment or even rough treatment at any the time we were in American hands. Certainly not as I had seen being meted out to the Russian prisoners of war from the Ukraine in Berlin. For that I am thankful to this day. Even the two chaps who escaped from Fort Ord were treated very leniently after their recapture. Everybody knew they did it only for kicks to liven up the routine life of the camp. They knew they would be caught before too long. Their hope was to get to St. Francisco and spend at least a day and a night there as they knew, from the outset, that there was no chance to get to Mexico, the nearest neutral country, which was hundreds of miles away. They just enjoyed their two or three days of freedom and the experience of what America by night looked like.

On the 30th March we all were up early checking through our belongings, which had increased enormously in the last twelve month, to make sure that everything was securely packed. It was amazing what we had accumulated in the time we were in the States. We also made sure that we took with us enough soap, toothpaste and above all tobacco and cigarettes. In fact most of us took as much as we could carry. Even none smokers took a quantity of cigarettes with them, knowing from past experience that such items could prove valuable commodity for trading. 10.00, the appointed time, we assembled on the parade ground for the final count. With everything in order, the sergeant who had been responsible for internal discipline was given permission to give the order to march off. With the kitbags on our shoulders and a tuneful song on our lips, we set out in step to march through the camp gates for the very last time. Once through the gates our escort fell in beside us as we went through the familiar avenues of the camp to the railroad tracks half a mile or so away, where a train was waiting to take us on the first leg of our journey home. Our destination was New York.

Knowing the routine, those who wanted to stay together kept close to one another as the final check and count was made before boarding the train, with luck, we might be in the same carriage. Those of us, who worked in the kitchen for the last twelve month, certainly had become very good friends: Horst Brinkman for one so was Heinz Gilde, Christel Guenter, and Werner Frenn. Teddy Brinktrine and Guenter Buchholz were also good friends of mine and we were really lucky to stay together on our way east. The arrangements on board the train were similar to those on our outward journey. Three men shared four seats. The great difference this time, we were allowed to get up and stretch our legs if we felt the need, which could prove very helpful to me. Or if we wanted to pop across to the other side to speak to someone, there were no objections either. Food distribution too, was left to us this time. There was only one guard in each carriage on this trip, armed with only a pistol kept in its holster and a baton dangling from his hip. Soon after midday we started rolling and after we had past the camps boundary, we gathered speed; our first meal was being served and was much the same as we had two years earlier on our way to Camp White in Oregon. So we headed east through what was now familiar terrain to us. By the time we had our evening meal we were approaching the Sierra Nevada mountain range which was quite a pleasant change from the Pacific coast shoreline we had grown accustomed to. With darkness approaching, I pulled down the blinds, unpacked the blanket, made myself comfortable and soon dropped off to sleep.

Next morning I was woken up by a rather hollow sounding rumbling noise. The train was moving, what seemed to me, at only a walking pace. Looking out of the window, after having pulled up the blind, I noticed a vast plain, almost as far as the eye could see, and this wooden structure of a bridge we were travelling on. The guard on duty told us that we were crossing Salt Lake at one end and soon we would be at Salt Lake City, where we would stop for a crew change and some water before continuing on our journey east. It certainly was a lovely sunny morning, if it continued to be sunny and dry we should enjoy our ride through the State of Utah. The route we were on was certainly different to the one we had travelled on before. After an hour's stop over we were off again with the lake to one side and open range on the other. The area we were passing through was cattle country with hardly any built up areas, or even the odd building, to be seen. As there was not much of great interest to be seen, out came the playing cards to pass the time away. Playing cards was about the only thing we could do, apart from looking at some magazines we had brought along with us, or sleep our time away. Reading matter in German was hard to come by, so we were content with looking at picture magazines. The following day the scenery became more interesting as we were travelling through the Mid-West now. More vegetation, more people, more activities along the track, more houses and more life altogether could be seen. The day after that brought stunning scenery and green country side as we journeyed on through Tennessee and Virginia. The last full day on board the train brought us to the outskirts of Washington D.C. and on to Baltimore were we stopped somewhere in the dockland area. With the windows open one could feel and smell the sea air distinctly. It was quite a lengthy stop here, as apart from taking on fresh food and water, a number of things on the train needed a routine check as well. All complete, we set off on what would be our last night on the train. As we made our way north now, along the Eastern Seaboard, towards New York, we could see this was a much more populated part of the country compared to some we had travelled through in the last few days. As night fell we could see lights twinkle near and far. The long stop in Baltimore made it quite an interesting day with so much to see, all be it only from the train. Not long after the evening meal, nature took over and one by one we fell to sleep.

As daylight broke we could tell we were not far from our final destination. We travelled through one large developed area after another. New York? We asked the guard. No! He replied, New Jersey. We were moving now at a much slower speed then we had for most of the time during the last four days. In the afternoon we slowed right down as we entered the Naval Dock Yard on the River Hudson in New York. As we were coming off the train we were told to line up outside our carriages to be counted and to make sure we had all arrived and that we were safe and sound after the long train journey. We remained in the same groups we were on the train as we were taken to our accommodation, where we joined fellow prisoners who had arrived the day before. The barrack blocks here were identical to the ones we had in Camp White. So we knew our way around them. On the way there the dining hall was pointed out to us, as well as the office block and the camp shop too in case we had any Dollars left to spend. Meal times were at the usual hours. Morning parade 06.30 and the evening count 17.30, and was all we needed to know. Any notices were posted at noon on the notice board. As this was a transit camp, we were not given any jobs to do except to keep the barracks and camp site clean and tidy at all times. With the induction over we were left alone. Not knowing how long we would be here in this camp, no one bothered to unpack. In fact most of us lived out of our kitbags all the time we were in New York. There was not all that much time before we had to be on parade again anyway, this time it was not to be counted, but in company with all Naval personnel on the base, for the daily ceremony of lowering the Stars and Stripes (Old Glory). That was to be a daily routine: morning assembly, the head count, during which the flag was raised, evening parade, the count and lowering of Old Glory. Morning and evening ceremonies over, we made straight for the dining hall which was a very large one here. Food identical to that of the U.S. armed forces. Good and enough, but nothing I was accustomed to in Fort Ord. Every day at lunchtime we could help ourselves to as much sliced beetroot as we liked. To this day I have not worked out why this generosity. Still, ours is not to reason why? The beetroot was available and supplemented the daily rations for those who needed it.

Two days after our arrival at the Naval Base things began to move. One by one, in alphabetical order, our names were posted on the notice board with orders and directions where and when to visit the clinic for a physical examination and the dentist for a dental check-up. Finally, over a number of days, we were to receive a full course of injections and vaccinations protecting us against all the known and common illnesses and diseases. That kept us on our toes for a while running to and fro to the notice board, checking and re-checking our appointments. The result of my own checks? Physically, excellent! Dental check revealed my teeth needed a lot doing to, which did not come as a surprise to me. I neglected the advice given to me by the dentist in Nuerenberg to see someone after my arrival at my unit in France. Those two teeth were beyond saving now, so out they had to come. As for the rest that needed attention, there was no time now to start any treatment. See someone as soon as you can when you are back in Europe said the dentist to me. 'Yes Sir!' Was my reply. Ten years later I did. With five hundred, or there about, of us in camp, it took several days for everyone to be seen and checked. But eventually it did happen. The day of our departure was announced, it was to be 20th April 1946.

With nothing to pack, everybody was ready and eager to go home. The day of departure was only three days away, yes, we could wait that long. On the day of our leaving America, after breakfast we had to be on the parade ground at 10.00 for a kit inspection. It was more of a security check than anything else. The marines that went through the lines looking through our belongings were searching for any kind of explosives, lighter fuel, gas canisters, sharp or pointed instruments, including knives other than pen or pocket knives. With the inspection completed, we were then called by name in alphabetical order, ticked off, boarded a truck and taken to the quayside where we boarded the ship. Sadly, doing it this way, we were parted from some our friends. Once aboard we were conducted to our quarters which were totally different to the ones on our way to America. This time we all had bunk beds, with not a hammock in sight. This, the chaps with maritime experience said, is a troop ship, or troop transporter, as there was provision made for kitbags to be stowed away. By one o'clock we were all aboard. Soon afterwards we were told to go to the mess deck for lunch. It was a cafeteria type layout. We entered the mess, picked up a tray, made our way along the serving counter, receiving our food and found ourselves a place to sit and eat. Here, on the mess deck, we had the opportunity to keep in touch with our friends. More good news was to come as in the early afternoon we assembled again on the mess deck for a briefing, followed by a boat drill. The boat drill took place in the designated area for us. Here we were to assemble should the need arise. In that same area we were free to go at any time during daylight hours. That was good news indeed as it meant we could meet with friends not only at meal times but also during daylight hours as well.

At 17.00 we slipped the lines and cast off to make our way down the Hudson River towards the sea. Everybody was on deck as we moved away from the quay to the middle of the river with Manhattan coming into sight. With daylight fading and the buildings being lit up, it was a marvellous sight indeed as we sailed passed the island. Looking north, up the river, with the darkening sky in the background, we did not notice the Statue of Liberty coming alongside. We had seen and passed by the Statue on our arrival in the States, of course, as we had crossed the harbour, but never seen it lit up. Now with darkness falling fast it really was a sight to behold. The Statue standing out clearly now, with the unmistakable skyline of Manhattan behind it, a sight I have never forgotten. It was to be forty five years before I would see that sight again.

So we sailed into the night, with some trepidation I must say, wondering how seasickness would affect me this time. But first of all we had to go below as doors were to be closed for the night and there was supper to be had as well. Then as we neared the sea, and one could detect movement in the ship, I made my way to my bunk to lie down as I remembered that being horizontal might help to overcome or lesson the effect of seasickness. Well it did the trick. The ship we were on now was less than half the size of the Empress liner we came to America on. I felt a little queasy, yes, but I kept the sickness at bay. As we were allowed on deck during the day, my friends encouraged me to join them as they felt the fresh air might help, especially when I lay down as well, which it did. It was after all only a small transporter we were sailing on, of some ten thousand tonnes, making a speed of some twelve or fifteen knots. So we would be on her quite a few days. Taking a more southerly route now would also add to the journey time. It was not only seasickness we had to fight, but boredom as well. Entertainment provided by the military authorities had to be limited, partly because of the size of the ship, and partly as far as we were concerned, any entertainment provided on board was geared to entertain the G.I.s and not German prisoners of war going home. Even so, what was provided for us were three film shows a week. They were all light hearted, either comedies or musicals, easy to understand and to follow. The weather too was kind. The sea was nothing like as rough as on the way over. We even had some calm days and one very calm day. Being on deck, helped to pass the time as we looked out for any wild life out there. On evenings, when we had no film show, we played cards or had an early night, depending on the weather. One thing that can be said, I was not seasick this time. And so, life fell into the new routine very quickly, as it always has done. Up in time not to miss breakfast, 10.00 deck and kit inspection followed by the daily count on the open deck. Lunch could be had from twelve noon. In the afternoons most of us had forty winks and then another breath of fresh air before the sun set and we were confined below deck. To close the day either the film show, or playing cards, had become the daily routine.

After a week or so we all longed to see land again as it become more difficult each day to keep boredom at bay. As we were nearing the English Channel we saw other ships and looking out to sea became very exciting all of a sudden as we were scanning the horizon for more ships. On the morning of the 5th May we entered the river Schelde on our way to Antwerpen. What a wonderful sight to behold. After all these days when seeing nothing but sea, the river banks almost close enough to touch, with the green meadows beyond. We had our lunch on board before we disembarked and there on the quayside to welcome us, the familiar uniform of the British Tommy. As we came off the ship, most groups of friends managed to stay together as we were taken by trucks to a very large tented P.O.W. camp, which we found was even more basic then we had experienced in Central California. After the good and easy life we enjoyed in America this would take some time to get used to again. The question everyone was asking 'How long are we here for?' No one had clue. All I can say in retrospect, it was an aimless existence. Fortunately the weather was kind to us with warm, dry sunny spring days, but the nights were cold and we had little sleep. So we made up for it during the day when the sun shone. The only good thing at that camp was that once a week we indulged in a nice warm shower when we were taken to the shower tent and had one minute to get wet all over, soap ourselves from head to foot with the water turned off, then three minutes to rinse ourselves down. After four weeks under these basic conditions, one morning after the daily count, names were read out, mine among them, to be ready at 13.00 the next day to be transferred.

At the appointed time we gathered by the gate as directed, after having said good bye to the friends, who were not included in this move, to be taken back to the port whence we came. So we were not going home just yet. We boarded one of the ferries that lay alongside the quay and in due time cast off and we were on our way. As it had been a long and tiring day I made myself comfortable in my seat and as the sun set in the west, went to sleep.

Chapter 17

Back on British Soil

It was the call of nature, brought about by the fresh morning air that woke me up. It was much cooler now than when we boarded the vessel in Antwerp and it was daylight, which meant we must have travelled all through the night. Somewhere in England, but where were we? Before long it became clear, we were on the river Thames making for the Port of London and not long after we saw the dockland and made for one of the basins to berth. It was in Tilbury docks where we made landfall and we noticed a number of ships tied up and a lot of activity in the area. Once securely tied up we began to disembark and went into one of the custom sheds close by where once again a nice hot mug of sweet tea and a bite to eat was waiting for us. It was the first food and drink we had since we left Belgium. Our stay was brief. Before long we were marched off to a waiting train and set out once more not knowing where we were going. After a four hour train ride, which was mostly through rural and farming areas, we came to a halt at a small station somewhere in England. It looked like a sleepy, peaceful little village. On the platform we were ordered to form a marching column, to shoulder our kit bags and off we marched out of the station on to a quiet country road. These were pleasant surroundings, it was early June, and the sun was shining. The trees were in full leaf now, the meadows a lush green and the corn fields were just beginning to show signs of ripening.

I had no idea how long we had been on the road, it was a hilly area and the road we were on went all along the bottom of the valley. Eventually the camp came into sight. It was of wooden structured huts extending up the gently rising hill. Once inside the camp, the count, and then we were taken to our sleeping quarters. Having been on the move for a number of hours by rail and on foot, some of the boys felt they needed freshening up before the evening meal, others, I among them, preferred some rest. Whilst having our evening meal we were told that morning parade would be at 06.00 and from 09.00 the registration would take place in the dining hall. It would be in alphabetical order. We had to listen to the public address system and go to the dining hall when our letter was called. My number was A 837 222; It probably still is and kept somewhere safely in the vaults of the War Office. This procedure took all day and with nothing else to do we had a good look at our surroundings which were very picturesque. After breakfast the following morning we assembled in the dining hall and were each handed two sheets of writing paper and two envelopes and a pencil. These were for us to write home to our families, and the sender's address would be name, number and the address; P.O.W. Camp, Morton-in-Marsh, Gloucestershire, Great Britain. That is where we were, but not for long. Over the next two days we were issued with two sets of under clothing, a pair of boots and the P.O.W. uniform which had a coloured, diamond shaped patch, sown in front of one of the trouser legs as well as in the back of the jacket. These were to be worn whenever and wherever we happened to be except in the confines of the camp. After a week at the camp in Morton-in-Marsh, on a fine sunny morning, we were on our way back to the station to board a train for our next destination. Two and a half hours later we stopped at a place called Romsey, in Hampshire. We were told to gather our belongings, get off the train, line up on the platform and after a quick check on numbers marched off into town. That was because the station is on the outskirts of the town and there is only one route from the station to the camp site one can take, and that route goes through the town of Romsey.

Again as it was on our first time in Britain during the war, there were just a handful of guards to keep an eye on us and not a weapon in sight. The people of Romsey, as the people of Southampton two years earlier, did not show any sign of animosity as we marched through their town. One had the feeling they pitied us. As we came to the outskirts of the town the road widened, the houses became bigger and were built further apart; a nice, quiet, peaceful area of town to live in but totally different to Morton-in-Marsh from where we had just came from.

Half an hour's march brought us to Ganger Camp at the very edge of the Borough's boundary. It was in a very pleasant setting, built in woodland with the nearest house a 100 yards or more away, a very quiet, peaceful, tranquil setting that greeted us as we marched through the gates. The Camp Commandant, with a number of his junior officers, stood on the steps of the office building seeing us arrive. One of the officers addressed us in German to say that the Ganger Camp would be our home for the foreseeable future and our treatment would very much depend on our behaviour. He then handed us over to the German sergeant who welcomed us and told us something of the daily routine in camp. There would be only one count a day, 06.30, followed by breakfast. We had to be at the gate at 08.00 ready to go to work. Details about this were on the notice board throughout the following day. Those who wanted to stay together were asked to form groups. As it turned out there were only two or three small groups because most of us had only known one another two or three days. So we made up groups to the requested number for each hut we were to occupy. All the huts in the camp were of standard British Army design. We were pleased to see single beds rather than bunks. There were two stoves and two long tables with a number of benches in each hut. That was all the furnishing there was. Food was the standard army ration, where again our cooks did not know how to get the most and the best out of it. As in the past, we soon settled into the new daily routine of camp life and quickly made new friends. As we got to know each other we discovered that we were all single, not a married man among us. As there was time before the evening meal we had a look around and explored the camp a bit further. It was not a very large one as camps go, but it was nicely laid out and landscaped. Neither was there a parade ground as such, just an open space near the gates where we gathered in the morning and from whence we were taken to go out to work. Neither was there a playing field for any sporting activities to take place. It was thanks to a neighbouring farmer, who owned the field at the back of the camp, who allowed us to use it after he had cut the grass to make hay. So, on Saturday and Sunday afternoons, weather permitting, we went out there and played a game of football, with just two or three Tommies coming along to keep an eye on us and to see fair play. That's how relaxed life was in Ganger Camp, No. 41 P.O.W. Camp, Romsey, Hants.

The next day, being a Saturday, notices were posted with details of names and work numbers. Work would commence on Monday morning and groups would leave camp at 08.00 and return at 17.00 or there about. As we had a lot of free time over the weekend, we nosed around the camp and discovered that the previous occupants had been Italian prisoners of war. Most of the evidence of their occupation could be found in the Common Room where they left behind a picture of Madonna and Child as well as a Crucifix. As the Common Room was used for Divine Worship on Sunday mornings these Icons were welcomed by those who attended these services. Here in Romsey, as in all permanent camps in the United States, ministers of religion were invited to come into the camp and minister to the faithful on Sundays and Holy Days. The Roman Catholic priest came early in the morning. The Protestant minister, usually a Lutheran pastor, came later in the day, sometimes even in the afternoon.

With the weekend over, on Monday morning we formed up by the gates for the daily count and then waited for our work number to be called. Outside the camp, lorries of all sizes and makes were lined up in an orderly fashion to take us to our places of work. These were provided by individuals under contract to the Ministry of War. It was not long before my number was called and with five other lads climbed into the waiting van as indicated. We had not far to go, half a mile or so. We drew on to the forecourt of a garage, Rolf's of Romsey, located just inside the town as one came in from the Winchester direction. But what would be our work here we wondered? We did not have to wait long before we found out. It emerged the garage was under contract to the Ministry of Agriculture to service all their vehicles, and Romsey being a market town in the middle of farming country, there were lots of them about. There were all types of vehicles that were waiting to be serviced. Our task was mainly to clean them inside and out before the mechanics got to work on them and then afterwards go round them with the grease gun. We understood that the Italians were here before us doing the same jobs. With no service bays or pits available to us, the vehicles had to be serviced where they were parked, which meant that half the time we were crawling under the cars on our tummy or lying on our back on the cold concrete. This was not the job for me I decided, by the end of the week I asked for a transfer, and as there were two or three chaps dying to get a placing like that, my request was readily granted.

As we had learned from our roommates during the week, most of them were working on farms, and a few in military or government distribution centres. I joined a group that was working on a farm not far away. It was an unusually large group. When working on the land, groups of six or more had an extra person added, someone with sufficient command of the English language to act as an interpreter and to make the tea at lunch time and in the afternoon. Each group detailed someone to collect the lunch pack from the kitchen which consisted of bread, sausages or sausage meat, margarine as a spread and a quantity of loose tea. Groups of less than six could detail off someone half an hour before lunch to collect fire wood to boil the water and select a sheltered spot where to light the fire and to have our lunch. For the rest of the month of June and part of July we were set to work to hoe between the rows of root crops and single out the seedlings, mostly sugar beet or mangel-wurzels. When the grain harvest started we joined the local farmworkers in the cornfields picking up the sheaves and putting them into stooks for drying and ripening. The grain needed a lot of drying in 1946 due to an unusual and exceptionally high amount of rainfall in the months of July and August that year. There were not many, if any, grain dryers on farms in the years immediately after the war. One or two Co-operatives may have had one. The average farm in England and Wales was under a hundred acres then and it would have been uneconomical to install costly grain dryers as they were very expensive. So there was no other way than to dry the corn in the traditional way, in the field. In September that year, due to the excessive amount of rain, many fields of corn were still standing, waiting to be cut. So the British government set aside a Sunday for prayers early in September of that year, asking the nation to pray for favourable weather in September to gather the harvest. The nation did respond I remember, led by the Royal Family, God answered the nation's prayer. The rain ceased, the sun shone, the sheaves were gathered in. Because of the urgency of getting the corn off the fields and into barns or ricks, we were ask by the military, as well as the civil authorities, to consider going to work the following two

Sundays, weather permitting of course. There was not much hesitation among the boys, we all agreed. The hauliers that took us to work every day were not at all pleased with our decision, as they had to turn out on Sunday to take us to work and bring us back to camp again late in the afternoon.

At that time our gang had begun to work for a farmer by the name of Stretton who owned a vast amount of land all around Winchester. We had started to work on his farm at the end of August and worked for him until all the crops were harvested including potatoes, turnips, carrots and mangel-wurzels. Our time with him came to an end late November of that year. During the three months or so we worked for him, he came to see us every day and brought us a packet of cigarettes, Woodbine was the brand, as well as a drop of milk for our tea. He never failed once and always inquired about our wellbeing and made sure all was well. At one time we were working in a field just off the Romsey road, close to the city of Winchester, with no copse or woodland anywhere near to gather wood to make a fire to boil a kettle to make tea. So we plucked up courage and knocked on the front door of one of the houses nearby to see if the occupier would be kind enough to boil a kettle of water for us. The young lady of the house was only too willing, so we handed over our kettle, tea pot and daily ration of tea and waited until the tea was made. When all was done she handed back to us tea pot, kettle and surplus tea. We thanked her very much and handed back the tea for which we had no further use, as we never made tea in the afternoon as it was too troublesome. With tea being rationed, our young lady was over the moon, so we went to her every lunch time as long as we worked in that field. It was of mutual benefit all round. These were the first kindnesses shown to us by the people of Hampshire. Mr Stretton, his workers, and the unknown young lady of Winchester. There were many more kindnesses shown to us as time went by.

With the work on the land having come to an end, different work had to be found for us. Not only for us but also for those who were billeted on the farms and were now returning to camp. In addition to that we were also taking in a small group of men that came from the P.O.W. camp in Southampton. That camp on the northern outskirts in Basset was closed down. So now our camp was full. Among the newcomers was a chap by the name of Alfred Bieniasch who became a very good friend of mine. In fact he became my Brother in Law! But here we were, wondering what our next assignment would be. It was in a small distribution centre situated in the New Docks in Millbrook, Southampton, supplying and delivering all sorts of things from office equipment to solid fuel to small government offices and establishments all along the south of Hampshire. The furthest east we went was Gosport and to the west was Bournemouth. One place we visited quite regularly with special manufactured orthopaedic mattresses was the military hospital in Netley. It was usually late morning when we got there, which might have been deliberate by our foreman. Having finished our delivery and loaded the old mattresses onto our lorry, we stopped for our lunch break by visiting the kitchens where a number of our chaps worked. They always provided us with a good meal, sometimes we even had a choice depending what was left by the patients. At other times we went into the dock area and shovelled coal delivered by lorries onto barges or railway waggons. We tackled a variety of jobs there and it was quite interesting work, besides having the good fortune to travel through the lovely Hampshire country side.

In November 1946 some restrictions of movement were relaxed. We were now allowed to leave camp unaccompanied and visit places within a radius of 5 mile of Romsey. We were also allowed to fraternise with the local population. It came as quite a surprise to us, as it was only just over a year since hostility had ceased. What would the locals make of it we wondered? On the first Saturday in November that year, we were able to go to town without an escort. Before the gates were opened, the sergeant reminded us we were guests in this country, and that it was a privilege for us to go out and we had to think of our reputation and behave accordingly. He need not have worried, we behaved ourselves and the folks of Romsey made us welcome in their town. Having been informed in the local press of government's relaxation of rules regarding fraternisation, some of our boys were invited into homes for afternoon tea, others, myself among them, were entertained by Christian congregations of all persuasions to Sunday afternoon tea in their respective church hall.

The walk into town became a regular weekend feature for most of us. It was not long before we discovered a shortcut taking the back roads through housing estates leading to different parts of town including the Abbey. This went on all throughout November and December that year.   Romsey folk relaxed and made us very welcome in their town. Some pub landlords, who found themselves with stale or warm beer at closing time on Saturday or Sunday afternoon, invited the lads in by the back door and offered it to the boys rather than pouring it down the drain.   As far as I know, it was never refused. Warm or stale beer is better than no beer at all; especially if it is the only beer that is to be had and you don't have to pay for it.

My first Christmas in England was a very quiet one. Before lunch I, with my friends, attended the Lutheran morning worship in camp. It was mainly a service of lessons and carols. In the afternoon we went into town, which for the day had become a ghost town. There were no bus services, cars were few and far between and in any case as petrol was rationed, people would not think of going for an afternoon drive in the days so soon after the war. The few cars that were about collected elderly relatives for the family Christmas lunch or came to the camp to take home with them the few lucky ones who had made friends with them and their families to experience an English Christmas. Some farmers came to take back the lads that were billeted with them throughout the summer for a traditional Christmas. They had to give a written assurance their charge would be back in camp by 20.00. For some that was quite an experience, most of us just thought of and talked about our childhood and remembered Christmas with our families and the good old days.

1947 started as 1946 ended. Five and a half days we went to work at our assigned places.   Saturday afternoon or Sunday morning we usually did our laundry and any mending that needed to be done or, if we felt like it, we went to town and said hello to the residents and passed the time of day with them. If Romsey football team played at home, those who were interested went along and watched them play; those who were not made their way back to camp again to be in good time for the evening meal. Not everyone went into town every time, some preferred a walk in the country or stayed in camp even. Then there were those who liked to play a ball game themselves, weather permitting they went to the field at the back of the camp and had great fun kicking the ball about. In the evenings we either played cards or board games or did some reading. Those who were interested in politics had the opportunity to go to Winchester and see how democracy works by observing Hampshire County Council in session. Much was being done by the British Authorities to get the grey matter in our brains to think freely and independently again, as it had been brain washed before by the Hitler Regime. Apart from the weekly film show, the pictures we saw were all British and we had no other entertainment. The reason we had no band or concert party may well have been that we had no need of one. Unlike in the United States, here in Britain we could get out and about and freely mix with the local population, which we did quite successfully. Every Sunday afternoon I, with some of my friends, took up the invitation from one church or another to have tea with the congregation and then go to their evening service. That made a pleasant afternoon and early evening and was much better than walking the streets of Romsey aimlessly in the cold and frosty weather the nation suffered in the severe winter of 1947. Some lads were brazen enough to go into the copse that were nearby and fell trees to supplement our fuel ration. Needless to say that activity did not last very long, but the severe weather did, 12 weeks in fact.

Aerial View

Ganger POW Camp 41, Woodley, Romsey

Row 2, Ganger POW Camp No 41

Taken at Romsey on 19.1.1947

When I was still 21½.

↕

Ewald Körner, Wolfgang Stein(Stone), **Gerhart(George) Gebauer**, Paul Villbrandt, Heinz Reiss(der Kurze)(translates Shortie),Hermann Mydeck

Taken on 19th January 1947

'Unter der Eiche'

PoW-Camp Nº 41

Ganger-Camp Romsey, Hants

England

English translation: 'Under the Oak Tree'

Postcard sent to me for my 21st Birthday

This card was sent to me on 16.11.46 by
my half-brother, my Mother's son from her
first marriage. Her first husband was killed
in the First World War. Translation reads:
**Hearty and Good Wishes for your
Birthday**

Obverse

Note: The card is sent from the Russian Zone of Berlin.
Translation reads:
And loving greetings sending you
Reinhold   [Brother]
Herter   [Sister-in-Law]
Gerd   [Their son]

Reverse

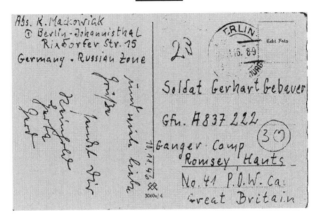

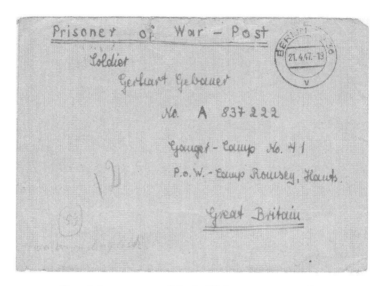

Sent to me on 21.4.47 by my cousin

Egbert Rósler, ① Berlin 0.34, Kopernikus Stra☐e 11, Germany

Sent to me on 2.5.47 by my cousin

Gisela Rösler,① Berlin N65, Tegelet Str. 37, Germany.

Chapter 18

Fraternization

The winter weather continued relentlessly. February came and went, well almost, before a change occurred in my daily work pattern which had remained the same since the beginning of the year. Every week, Monday to Friday, we were taken to the New Docks in Millbrook, now the Western Docks, to transfer a number of lorry loads of coal that came from a barge moored in a wharf somewhere up the river Itchen, onto railway trucks left on one of the sidings. The full trucks were moved during the night and three empty ones awaited us the next morning. On days when no coal was transferred, we were assisting with taking or replenishing supplies for small government posts occupied by various branches of the military. That took us all along the south coast in Hampshire, stretching from Emsworth in the east to Bournemouth in the west. This we had been doing continuously for seven weeks. Then on Monday the 24th February, as we returned to camp after the day's work, one of our office clerks was waiting for me and took me in the office where Erich Verhassel, a fellow prisoner, was waiting for me to arrive. We were told that the two of us would have a new assignment, starting in the morning. It would be agricultural work again. After three months or so working in town, it would make a pleasant change working on a farm again. We were not told where it was, neither what kind of work it would be. It certainly would not be harvesting of any kind at this time of year.

Anyway, the next morning Erich and I, having collected our lunch from the kitchen and a quantity of tea, assembled with the rest of the boys going out to work, at the main gate. When our job number was called we checked out and joined the others going in the same direction using the same transport. After a twenty minutes' drive, eight chaps got off in a place called Chandler's Ford. They were working in a nursery, engaged at that time preparing greenhouses for spring planting, or in potting sheds pricking out seedlings. That left five on board the lorry. It was not long after that we travelled through a town called Eastleigh. The outskirts, and suburbs looked neat and tidy and quite attractive. That appearance changed as we neared the centre of town and the railway station. The picture became more industrial with factory buildings along the road. We passed the town hall, the central park complete with band stand, and then through the shopping district.

As we crossed a large bridge by the station, we noticed large sheds and many tracks. On the other side of the tracks we entered an area which appeared very tranquil and peaceful. It had a village like look and feel about it. As we drove along we crossed a fast flowing river and after a while came to a place called Fair Oak where, in the centre of the village, we dropped off the other three men that were still on the lorry with Erich and me' we began to wonder how much further we still had to go before we reached our destination. We were on the road now for well over half an hour. Five minutes later or so we turned off the main road into a twisty, winding country lane, Shamblehurst Lane we noticed, as we turned into it. So it could not be much further. Then just after crossing a railway line by a hump backed bridge we pulled up and were told by the driver we had arrived. As we jumped off the lorry a young lady came out of a shed to greet us and to speak to the driver who handed her some papers and told her he would be back at four o'clock to pick us up. She then spoke to us greeting us with a warm smile. It was then just after nine o'clock. So it had taken about one hour to get here, to this our new place of work.

Erich and I were on our own now. As my English was almost none existent, I had to rely on Erich who spoke some broken and pigeon English. His home was in West Germany near the Dutch border where they speak what we call "Platt Deutsch" which contains some English words and phrases, so he picked up English more easily. The young lady then led us to the big shed and asked us our names. We told her Erich and Gerhart in the German pronunciation so goodness knows what it sounded like to her. "Oh my!" she exclaimed, "I had better call you Joe and George, that would be better and easier for all concerned." She introduced herself then as Gladys but said, she was known to everybody as Glad, which is what her parents had called her for as long as she could remember. As we entered the shed we were introduced to an elderly gentleman. Bill Gannaway, Glad's father, who had been sharpening saws that morning. Glad suggested that we take our belongings up to the house, along a path, just a few yards away.

As it happened it was a bungalow built on a traditional base, of concrete, and bricks and called Le Nid. The upper structure was corrugated iron on the outside, with asbestos sheets for the inner walls. Floors were of standard floor boards and doors the traditional type. There was a brick fire place in each of the five rooms. There was a kitchen-diner, which also contained a kitchen range, a sitting room and three bedrooms. Opposite the back door was the laundry, a shed which had a bricked in boiler in one corner with a fireplace underneath and next to it a small open fire, which was very useful we discovered later. There was also a table and two chairs as well as a mangle in one corner and three tin baths of various sizes. We put our bags, containing the standard mid-day ration of bread, sausage meat and loose tea on the table at which moment the lady of the house appeared and Glad introduced us to her mother. She asked us into the house and served us with a lovely hot, sweet cup of tea which was gratefully accepted by both of us as it was some time ago now since we had breakfast and secondly, the temperature outside was still below zero. Whilst enjoying the warm hospitality in every sense, Mrs Gannaway began talking to us, in English of course, of which I understood very little. Erich thankfully got the gist of it and explained what it was all about. When a young child, with her father away at sea for long periods, her mother working in Taunton most of the time, and her older siblings scattered all over Somerset, she was brought up by a children's nurse who was German born and very kind and caring. She felt whenever she could repay her kindness to another German she would do so. She had waited a long time for this, as she was now 75 years old and Erich and I were the lucky ones. By the time we went out to start work the morning was nearly over. By now the temperature rose just above zero, the sun was shining but the keen easterly wind kept the thermometer round about the freezing mark.

The main task, we were set, was to get some pruning done in the four acre orchard. A task much neglected in the last two or three years. Mr Gannaway was 79 when we started work on the holding in 1947. Nonetheless 79, or not, a gardener by profession, he directed operations. He told us what to do, how to do it and where. It did not take us long to get the hang of it and we were trusted to get on with it. We also noticed that Bill had a struggle to move the ladders, so we took over this job from him as well. He looked for the safest position and told us where to place the ladder and in such a way, should a branch break, the ladder would always fall into the tree. With the two of us getting to work on this task we got through quite a number of trees each day weather permitting. And just as well, once the temperature rose above freezing the sap would begin to rise and we would have to stop pruning.

There were days when we had to stop pruning because of strong winds. When that was the case we helped Bill cutting up branches to be put onto the bonfire. When it was snowing we brought the thicker branches into the shed and cut them into logs to go onto the fire next winter. On days like that, Bill stayed indoors but Glad kept us company whatever the weather. She could handle all the tools, hooks and crooks, saws and axes extremely well, quite amazing for a lady of such a slim build.

After a week or so the family had taken to us and, before starting work, we were invited into the house for some breakfast which comprised of a boiled egg and a lovely cup of hot, sweet tea. One day, when we were working in the orchard, Polly Gannaway, Glad's mother, had a peep at our rations and was appalled to find raw sausage meat among the bread and cheese for our lunch. So she took it indoors and cooked it for us. Remember we had our meals in the washhouse. It was not long before she kept the sausage meat and brought us some of the family lunch for our mid-day meal including freshly baked fruit pie and custard. All we could do, and did it gladly, was to hand over our tea ration for the day, and it was gratefully accepted.

In a very short time we settled into a daily routine which pleased all concerned. We finished pruning just in time before we lost the severe winter weather that had gripped the country for months. Having pruned the tree hard, there was an awful lot of clearing up to do. Whilst Erich and I cut out the branches and let some light into the trees, Bill kept the bonfires going day and night. It was quite interesting to watch him, selecting and cutting the branches and twigs to the right length so that the fires did not to burn hollow and leave a lot of unburned wood around edge of the fire. Next morning, he carefully opened up the ashes, placed some short thin twigs and sticks on the red hot embers, and hey presto the fire came alive again. There was just one day during that long severe winter when we stayed indoors all the time. We were in the warm, comfortable sitting room listening to the wireless. It was in mid-March, the snow had almost gone. With temperatures above freezing from late morning to early afternoon, it was warm enough for the snow to melt during daylight hours. On this particular day it was cloudy and there was a biting easterly wind. The frost was reluctant to go. Our journey from Romsey to Botley seemed colder and more miserable than usual. Soon after arriving at Le Nid, it began to drizzle and before long it turned into rain and the temperature dropped sharply. As a result, the rain froze as it fell. The water running of the roof formed long icicles in the freezing wind. Any outside work was out of the question, so we were invited into the house to spend the day with the family including sharing their meal. Our driver, anxious to get home before dark, came at three o'clock in the afternoon to take us back to camp. It was a slow, treacherous journey back to Romsey that day, as the roads had turned into ice rinks. Fortunately the other gangs were ready and waiting for us at the pickup points and the driver had his wish to be home before dark.

When eventually the weather became warmer, we were well into March and spring was arriving at long last. It was amazing how the gardens and the countryside were transformed in a short space of time. For months the fields had been white and barren and now, in a matter of days, were transformed with spring flowers to be seen everywhere. There were snowdrops, crocus, daffodils wherever one looked. In the orchard at Le Nid, between the lines of trees, thousands of daffodil bulbs had been planted many years ago, and were now all coming out in bud and bloom. It was quite a sight it must be said, especially so after this long, hard winter we had just experienced. Glad and her mother were experts in flower picking. The way the skipped through the rows was amazing. Picking of course is only part of the job. The ladies placed the blooms in boxes and Jo and I took them to the packing shed where Glad and her mother counted them into bunches and then tied them up ready to be taken to the wholesalers the next morning, all done very quickly and expertly. In those days bunches of flowers still were tied with raffia, instead of rubber bands as in modern times. By the time we went back to camp that evening, the shed was chock-a-block full of flowers with quite an overpowering scent. That routine happened twice a week for the next three weeks.

By early April that year Bill, Jo and I finished clearing the orchard of the pruned branches and began to prepare some ground for sowing seeds of various kinds. We dug a large patch, about half an acre, in readiness for early potatoes and peas to catch the early market. The rest was kept for cabbage type plants, mainly sprouts, primo and purple sprouting which always sold well in those days. With no machinery on the holding, a neighbour used to pop in when it was time and did the ground work, ready for the plants to go out when they were ready. Glad joined us whenever she could or when she was needed. Once a week we helped her cleaning out the hen houses, she had a small flock and was anxious to increase the numbers as soon as feeding stuff was more freely available. In 1947 animal feeding stuff was still strictly rationed. Polly Gannaway mostly did the housework and cooking, and what a good cook she was too. There was also a large front garden she attended which looked beautiful throughout the spring and summer and was admired by many.

With the days getting longer and warmer, visitors arrived to see how the family had survived the long hard winter. Not many people had telephones in those days and any communication was by post. Most were unaware that they had two German prisoners of war working for them. With food still rationed, everybody brought some home baked cake along for the afternoon tea. As it was about the time we packed up for the day, before returning to camp, and we having our last cup of tea, we met all these good people and were introduced to them. They offered some of the cake, and boy, that tested our finger licking, as it was so good.

By the end of May the work on the holding was well advanced, and there was need for only one hired hand to keep the work going. Glad explained this to us one day and asked me if I would like to be billeted with them. If so, she would then make an application to the camp. I was touched to be asked and felt very honoured. I was to have a room in the house, which was unheard of, as all others prisoners, who were billeted, were accommodated in farm cottages or caravans. The officer from the camp, a Major Ross, who inspected the accommodation and facilities said as he left: "You will never leave this place."

And so it proved to be!

Well, not for the next 24 years anyway.

Chapter 19

Steep learning Curve

On the morning of May 24th I packed my few belongings into the kitbag, said good bye to all my friends in camp, joined the crowd at the main gates to be taken to my place of work to be billeted there for an unspecified length of time. It was a lovely, late, sunny May day. When I arrived at Le Nid, only Bill was there to welcome me. It was Polly's 75th birthday, so the ladies had decided to have a day out in Salisbury. By the way, the name 'Le Nid' was given to the house by Scottish A.T.S. girls, stationed in a camp at the end of Shamblehurst Lane during the Second World War. These girls came to the house regularly to get away from camp life for a few hours whenever they could. They knew, whatever time of day, they would receive a warm welcome. They must have appreciated the homely atmosphere the Gannaway's provided, as many of them kept in touch with the family to the end of their lives. As soon as I arrived, Bill brewed a pot of tea for the two of us and boiled me an egg for my second breakfast. Breakfast over we set to work. I left the unpacking till later in the day, when work outside was done. The ladies came back in time to cook the evening meal and tell us all about their day in Salisbury. From the day I moved into the house I took all my meals with the family including the times when friends visited the family and stayed for lunch and tea.

Now with no other sound than English in my ears, I soon picked up the language. In fact Glad and her mother went to great lengths to make sure I understood what was being said. Being on my own now I had to make a greater effort not to be left out of things, as Joe was not there any longer to tell me what was going on. Bill too was pretty good, whenever we worked together with neither lady present, in his own way he made sure I understood what he said and what he wanted me to do.

Living in the house I was invited to join the family around the wireless after lunch to hear the news and listen to Workers Playtime, as well as in the evenings, when we settled round the radio set for the evening entertainment. Most popular were the comedy programmes such as ITMA, which was 'a must' in every household throughout the land. Not only was it funny, but it was also highly topical. Most other programmes were funny too, as well as entertaining: Up the Pole; Ray's a laugh; The Navy Lark; and later on Round the Horn. Monday Night at 8 o'clock, as well as Twenty Questions, were other programmes we all enjoyed very much. Thanks to Glad and her mother who patiently explained things and translated slang and phrases to me to me I soon understood perfectly what was being said.

All the time we were listening, the three of them explained in simple English what was being said, the meaning of it and what was going on. The greatest help to me to understand English were the B.B.C. News Readers at the time. They spoke such perfect English. They spoke slowly, their diction was good, they never used slang words in their reports and above all, their

English grammar was faultless. To me, a foreigner and immigrant, anxious to learn English, that was just what was needed. This is what, today's overseas students who come to this country to learn English, are looking for. Slang and bad grammar, picked up in the early stages, are difficult drop later on. To hear newsreaders and presenters using phrases such as 'Up for grab,' or even worse 'Up for Grabs,' makes me ask what are the people trying to prove? Or weather presenters saying 'Bits of cloud in the sky' or 'Bits and pieces of rain,' makes me sad as they should know better. We all know what it means, but it is not good English. People coming from abroad listening to them, not knowing any better, think it is good English. The English, I learned by listening to B.B.C. News and current Affairs programmes, helped a great deal to understand the vernacular tongue more quickly.

Listening to, and understanding English is one thing. Speaking it is quite another matter. The family never corrected my speaking. Partly they thought it might embarrass me, partly because it might make me nervous, and partly they loved me the way I was, they understood what I was saying. As my English vocabulary and my understanding of English increased, I enjoyed reading the newspapers and magazines which were delivered to the house. The daily newspapers were the Daily Sketch and Southampton Evening Echo. The magazines at the time were the almost obligatory Radio Times; every household seemed to have them, Woman and John Bull. Especially John Bull appealed to me as in the late 1940's it published in serialized form novels by well-known and acclaimed authors, unabridged. The first novel I completely understood and enjoyed thoroughly and eagerly looked forward to the next instalment, was Neville Shute's: 'A Town like Alice.' All subsequent novels of his which were published I read in John Bull or the books were given to me as either a birthday or Christmas present. I proudly possess all of his books. To obtain the earlier publications I went to every book shop in all the cities and towns we visited and I always went straight for the second hand book section to look if there were any books by Neville Shute I did not already have. Even in English speaking countries abroad I continued my search. I bought one, 'Lonely Road', in Victoria, Vancouver Island, Canada when we were on holiday staying there for a few days. I read other novels published in John Bull, among them; Forest of Eyes, Campbell's Kingdom and many others, including several of Alistair MacLean's books as well.

Something else I had to learn quickly was getting used to country life and country ways. Having been brought up in a big city and lived for a number of years having only men as friends and companions, residing in a family home in a strange land, was certainly new to me. Something I realized very quickly, farmers and growers and country folk in general, are a very caring community. They are always ready to offer help and advice to their neighbours. Be it on husbandry or live-stock management or breeding, there was always someone I could turn to. Something that needs to be recorded here is the kindness and warm heartedness the people of Britain shown to German Prisoners of War especially to me by friends and tradespeople in Botley, Durley, Curdridge and Hedge End. They showed me great kindness. One has to remember, scars of war were to be seen everywhere, families grieved for their loved ones who did not return home from this unnecessary war. I received endless help on many occasions in my twenty five years among them. We are talking here of 1947. Two years earlier we were still at war with each other, and here they were helping me to make good in life very often at some cost to their own. There was Ernie Crawford, our neighbour; all I needed to do was to pop across the fence to ask his advice. Jack Candy was a wizard with machinery. He could get any tractor going again, he did so for us on many an occasion. And there was Fred Taplin, a man who could never say no. Day or night, twenty-four hours a day, if you needed help he would give it. He was the 'Good Samaritan' of our time. There were times I knew when he did not have two halfpennies to rub together; even so, he would never refuse to help anyone.

Friends and traders made me equally welcome in those early days after the war. There were the Bailey's, the Maffey's, the Sciviers, Bertie West, the chemist in the village, and later Peter Fagg who followed him, as well as the West's, just to name a few. All these good people suffered losses in the war, if not in the family, then among close friends. None more so than the good friends of the Gannaway family; such as the Cozens and Hall families, who lived in Woolston in Southampton. Not only did they suffer bereavement because of war but most of them were bombed out of their houses more than once and yet they made me welcome, invited me into their homes and to family parties. No animosity, no hard feelings, just sadness and sorrow that this unhappy war ever took place. Being large families these parties seemed never ending. Most of the children of these families were of my generation, so we went to a number of 21st birthday parties and weddings.

Soon after my taking up residency at Le Nid we began harvesting the first crops. In early June there were the broad beans and first early potatoes, soon followed by garden peas. But before all that, just after we had finished with the daffodils, we pulled quite a large amount of rhubarb. As the season progressed, all the berries ripened. To start with there were the gooseberries being overlapped by strawberries, quickly followed by the raspberries. We were moving into July by then when the season concluded with the currents; red, white and black. After St. Swithun's Day, 15th July, we were looking to pick the first apples of the season. There was an early variety of cooking apples; the name escapes me now, as well as an early desert apple by the name of 'Beauty of Bath.' That was followed by an early variety of plum by the name of 'Early River.' Other crops of apples, pears and plums followed. There was little spare time to think or do anything else. After picking the fruit it had to be graded, packed and taken to market. Some varieties of apples and pears were stored for a week or two for ripening. The main crop however went into store to be sold later in the season. Yes it was an interesting life and I kept on learning and learning fast not only about the work on the holding but life in the south of England in general.

Culture for instance. I learned that English culture can and does differ from other countries in the U.K. and even then there can be regional differences. As time went by I learned a lot about these variations and the difference between German and English cultures:

Christian festivals for a start. In my youth much greater emphasis was given to the spiritual side of the festival and in Germany we had more of them too. Whilst in Britain more emphasis is given to the Monday following as a holiday rather than the significance of the festival. The New Year and birthdays too are celebrated differently. Difference of culture there may have been at the outset; I soon became used to them and made them my own.

On days when we did not pick fruit we either gave the henhouses a good cleanout or cut the grass in the orchard which Glad's chicken had no access to, or, we had a go at the hedges. The front hedge was cut by the two ladies of the house and always looked neat and tidy, whilst Bill and I tackled the hedge marking the boundary at the far end of the property which was much taller and wider. When we finished fruit picking, about mid- November, we started pruning again and tidying the place in general. That brought us nearly to the season when I came first to Le Nid. What a year and what an experience it was for me. When I had arrived, I was a novice in speaking or reading English as well as in any agricultural work, and now nearly a year later my life was so enriched. Helping Glad with her chicken made me realise how much care and attention livestock requires keeping animals fit and free from disease. Double summertime was a great problem to farmers during the war but it was accepted to be a sacrifice on behalf of the nation. With double summertime, not getting dark until after midnight, the hens would not go to roost until then and we could not shut up the houses. Then it was up again by six in the morning or even earlier to start the milking and other essential work on a farm. These were eighteen hour days and were very tiring and very demanding. Let no misguided politician persuade you double summertime is good for Britain, it is not.

Something else happened in my first year at Le Nid. During the months living, working and being near Glad every day and all day, as I frequently accompanied her to the wholesalers or Durley Mills for feeding stuff or maybe to neighbouring farmers for straw or during harvest time screenings from the thresher. Whatever, we got to know one another very well and romance blossomed and one September afternoon I proposed marriage to Glad. To my surprise she accepted my proposal without hesitation. Where and how you want to know? It was on a lovely, warm sunny evening after we had finished loading the van with apples to be taken to the wholesalers in the morning. Sitting side by side on a banana box holding her hands in the packing shed I asked her to marry me. That was the way it was.

That news was received with great joy by all who knew Glad, and many who had known her from childhood, except one person, her Mother. Not that she had any objection of me being of German birth, or my proposing to her daughter. Her problem was she thought her daughter never would get married. Well, she was wrong, she wanted to. On the day I asked Glad's parents for the hand of their daughter in marriage, her Father's face shone with delight, whilst her Mother's face looked grim. She kept a grudge against Glad for a long, long time before she realised she had not lost a daughter, but gained a son. After that she could not do enough for me to the point that Glad began to wonder what she had done to be out of favour. I learned as time went by that she had her moments and that one could not always please her.

My first Christmas at Le Nid

Chapter 20

Integrating into the British way of life

It did not take long to pick a date and time for our wedding. The most suitable season for us was during the winter months. So we chose the 24th February, the Feast Day of St. Matthias. I left it to Glad to let the friends of the family know about her forthcoming Nuptial event. As for me, there was just one letter to write to let the family in Germany know about my decision. When I wrote to my parents and told them of my experiences here in England, how I felt about it all, and how happy I was, and the reason for my decision to stay in England and get married to Glad, they were happy to hear about it and in fact encouraged me to stay, as they did for my brother, Werner, who found himself in Frankfurt/Main at the end of the war. As a matter of fact our parents told us to stay where we were as there was nothing to come home for. Not unexpectedly, we had plenty of advice about the possible pitfalls not least because of the difference in our ages. But Glad was sure and so was I.

On my next monthly visit to Ganger Camp in Romsey, which was always the last Sunday of the month, these visits were one of the conditions for billeted P.O.Ws. The purpose being:

  a) That you were still around,

b) To collect your pay and mail,

c) To spend your money in the canteen on toiletries etc. so as to keep it in the British economy,

d) To have my hair cut.

Heaven knows where the camp barber had learnt his trade, if he had learnt it at all, more often than not, it looked awful. After my first visit to the camp at the end of June, Glad was convinced she could make a much better job of it and she certainly did. In any case she had been cutting her father's hair for many years by then and now she took on mine as well. When my parents came over for an extended holiday in the nineteen fifties, she cut my father's hair three or four times during their stay with us. She continued to cut my hair for the next 55 years until her failing eyesight no longer allowed her to do close work.

But I transgress, on that monthly visit to the camp at the end of September, when I told the office and the lads, no one was surprised. Those who had been to Le Nid, for a Sunday lunch and tea, had expected it. All were jubilant about the news. As movement restrictions were eased further it became a routine to bring back to Botley one of my friends in the camp to spend a day with the Gannaway family. That meant Glad had to make one more round trip to Romsey on the Sunday evening, quite a sacrifice as petrol for private cars was strictly rationed. The first friend that came for the day was Joe. He was very pleased with his return visit as he could see the fruit of his hard labour earlier in the year. Alfred came the following month, he was a great character, witty and full of fun and always ready for a laugh.

Earlier that year he had the little finger on his left hand amputated because of a festering war wound received at Monte Casino. He spent a week in Cambridge Hospital, Aldershot, and had a great time there by all accounts. Anyway he made light of it and was always good company. He came again later in the year and at Christmas when he applied for 72 hours leave, to spend it with us at Le Nid.

On the Sundays when I did not have to go back to camp, the four of us, father, mother Glad and I, went on a rural rides in the afternoon, but always back in time to feed the flock. Throughout that summer we covered practically the whole of Hampshire from the Sussex/Hants boarder in the east to the New Forest and Bournemouth in the west; Andover in the north as well as the north-west of Hampshire and on into Wiltshire to Salisbury. The first Sunday outing was over the Hampshire Downs around Bishops Waltham, a small, pretty country town, which at that time had the only privately owned and family run Bank in the country. I still visit the place whenever I am in that area. Little has changed over the years, but how much longer will it remain to be seen. It was not long before Glad took the risk, to go beyond the seven mile limit, to show me Winchester, the old Capital of Wessex, some twelve miles from Botley. On that occasion I wore unmarked P.O.W. clothes! The area round Winchester was well known to me as I had worked in that part of the county the previous summer and autumn, but I must say it was quite exciting to walk the streets of this ancient city. After that, most Sundays, we went well beyond the seven mile limit. That was the maximum distance P.O.W.s were allowed to go from the place of residence, unless we had obtained a special pass, but that was a lengthy process and time consuming, so we did not bother. One Sunday Glad and I made an early start and went to Cheddar Gorge in Somerset. We called on her friend Ruth, who lived in the Cathedral City of Wells and whom she had not seen for a while. They had met early in the war when, when Ruth was in the A.T.S. and stationed for a while in the camp at the end of Shamblehurst Lane. That was quite a day for us both and a great experience for me.

All the while we made plans for our wedding, where to live and how to expand after feeding stuff restrictions were lifted. When Mother got used to the fact that Glad would not change her mind, she became more approachable and offered us two rooms in the bungalow and cooking facilities, which we readily and happily accepted and Glad's father was delighted to hear. We were not too sure about the Honeymoon. It would be mid-winter and whatever the weather, the hens, although not very many, still needed to be fed and watered and Glad did not think it right to burden her parents with the task. At that point I was officially still a prisoner of war and practically still penniless. All I could do was to assure and reassure Glad, that whatever she decided was fine by me.

And so we came to my first Christmas at Le Nid. Glad managed to scrounge extra feed from farmer friends and our miller, to fatten a number of cock birds for the Christmas market. With red meat rationed and even then in short supply, poultry, which was not rationed, sold as the proverbial saying has it, 'like hot cakes'. Most of the birds went to private buyers, and the few Glad had left, she took to the local butcher who at that time bought anything he could lay his hand on that could be sold as meat or meat product. The week in the run up to Christmas brought back memories of the times I spent in Bergen on the Isle of Ruegen with my uncle who was a butcher there, when every minute was given over to getting ready for market day.

On Christmas Eve, after having fed the birds, we left the shutting up to Glad's father and Glad and I made our way to the camp to collect Alfred who was to spend three days over the holidays with us. As Mother and Father had met Alfred before, the evening was very relaxed and we had some fun playing a number of board games after supper. As bed time approached Glad mentioned that she would be going to church early in the morning and asked if we would like to go along with her. Not knowing anything about Alfred's religious background, we talked about it for a moment and although I was a Lutheran, I learnt he was of the Roman Catholic persuasion. Even so we decided to accompany her in the morning, which pleased her very much. After saying good night we got ready for bed and as we got into bed, we discovered Glad and her mother had had some fun with us by making apple-pie beds! When making our beds, they had concealed brushes between blankets and in the pillows which made us wonder, just as we were stretching out and our heads were touching the pillows, what on earth had got into bed with us. It caused quite a bit of amusement and laughter for the ladies as they were standing outside in the hall by our bedroom door, but we had taken it all in good fun!

Soon after 6 a.m. the next morning, Christmas Day, Glad called us and said there would be a cup of tea before we set out for church and we would leaving in about half an hour's time. Half an hour was plenty of time for us. We left for church in good time and received a warm welcome from the verger, a Mr King, who went straight to the clergy vestry to inform the Rector, the Reverend Fred Hadfield that Miss Glad Gannaway was in church with two German prisoners of war. To have Holy Communion services so early in the morning was quite common in rural areas at the main Christian Festivals, simply because the farming communities have to carry on with their daily routine regardless whatever the day. It must also be noted that midnight services at Christmas were unknown at that time. The congregation therefore on this morning were farmers and stockmen. Milking and feeding the animals on those days started half an hour late. The attendance was very good considering the time and I recognised one or two familiar faces. Surprising as it may seem, the service itself was not all that difficult to follow, even so it was for the first time I had seen it in print and heard it spoken. At the end of the service the Rector said a prayer in German which really lifted our hearts, and made us feel more welcome and our visit to the church much more meaningful. On leaving the church the Rector wished us a happy Christmas in German and hoped we would have a nice holiday. Christmas Day 1947 was the first time that I entered All Saints Botley not knowing it would become my spiritual home one day.

Back home, Glad and I attended to the chickens whilst her mother laid the table for breakfast which was a full

English one. After breakfast the ladies got on with the dinner, Bill went and collected the eggs and made sure the fowls had enough water in the troughs, and brought enough fuel into the house to see us through the day, whilst Alfred and I just whiled the morning away. In due course Christmas dinner was served which was a sumptuous affair. After the meal and before the washing up, for which Alfred and I volunteered, we opened our presents. With no pay as yet and the money, I did have, which could only be spent in the camp canteen, I had bought Glad a fountain pen. Alfred gave her a box of note paper. Alfred and I between us gave her Mother a bouquet of flowers and Bill an ounce of tobacco, for which Glad had given us the money. Neither Alfred nor I had any idea what was in our parcels. So it came as a great surprise that Alfred found a shirt in his, for which the clothing coupons were donated by Bill, as a gift from the three Gannaways. I was given two parcels, of which one also contained a shirt, this time the clothing coupons were sacrificed by dear Glad. The other box was a little packet which after opening revealed a pair of gold cuff links which I still have and wear when I have the opportunity. After that, Glad slipped out to give the chickens their afternoon feed whilst Alfred and I got on with chores. When all was done, we settled around the wireless set and listened to the family's favourite entertainers e.g. singers, comedians, musicians until it was time to shut the hens into their houses. Later that evening we had another meal and spent the rest of the time amusing ourselves playing cards and board games until it was time for another cup of tea and bed time.

So Boxing Day dawned and the only work scheduled, apart from feeding ourselves, was to attend to the chickens. After breakfast Glad got on her bike and went up to Hedge End to buy a daily paper for her parents. Her Father liked to keep up with world affairs and Mother liked the politics and gossip. Alfred and I helped Bill to get the fuel for the day indoors, had a look at the paper, but we could not make much sense of it, and before long it was lunch time. After clearing up after lunch and washing up, Glad, Alfred and I went for an afternoon stroll across the fields and Glad showed us where she had spent her childhood and called upon an old friend, for a cup of tea, before making our way back home. Bill had fed the chickens while we were out and as it was nearly shutting up time Alfred and I said we would go and shut the chickens up for the night. That evening we either listened to the radio or played cards and more board games until it was time for bed.

Next day was really a working day, but as Glad and her Mother had some shopping to do they invited us to go along, which we were only too pleased to do. The first call was at the butchers in Woolston and then to the baker in West End and then back to Botley to the grocers. Why all this running about? These were the shops the frequented before they needed to register with various traders. As they had good service over the years they remained with them after rationing and registering was introduced. Well, it made a nice morning out and Alfred saw some more of England.

After lunch Alfred packed his overnight bag and after the hens had their afternoon feed, we took Alfred back to camp and left Bill to shut in the chickens as it would be dark before we got back from Romsey. All in all everyone thought our time together went extremely well and we wondered what the New Year would bring.

Who would have thought at the beginning of the year that, by the end of it, I would be on the brink of getting married!

Chapter 21

A New Beginning

Once Christmas was over and we had seen in the New Year, we seriously began to make plans for our wedding. Glad dearly would have loved to have been married at All Saints, Botley. That was her parish church when she lived in Boorley Green and the church she continued to attend after the family moved to Shamblehurst Lane. To make it possible for us to get married at All Saints, it was suggested she might rent a room from one of her many friends in Botley for three weeks, pay a nominal amount for rent, place a suitcase containing some of her clothes in that room and that would make her legally a parishioner. She did not fancy that at all. In her opinion it would be cheating and dishonest. In the end all that mattered was that we were married in a church. The Reverend Hatfield totally agreed with her and he suggested that we went to see the Vicar of St. John's, Hedge End, our parish church, and see the Reverend Evan Jones, to make arrangements for our wedding, and we might ask him if the Rector of Botley could assist. Mr Hatfield was sure his colleague in Hedge End would raise no objections and so it turned out to be. In fact Mr Jones was delighted to learn Glad was getting married and he would not miss that day for anything.

The first people we told about the date and time of our marriage were Frank and Maggy Cozens, the wholesalers we dealt in Woolston, who were good friends of the family. They were with us right from the start. As there would be nobody from my family coming over from Germany to the wedding, I would have like to have asked Alfred to be my 'Best Man'. However, that was not to be. At the beginning of January it was announced that the repatriation of German P.O.W.s was to commence later that month. Alfred was to be among the first group from the Ganger Camp to be repatriated. So I asked Frank Cozens to do me the honour and be my 'Best Man'; he was delighted to do so. I was invited to stay with the Cozens the night before the wedding so as to uphold the tradition for the bride and groom not to sleep under the same roof on the night before their wedding. Where are you going for your Honeymoon, they asked? We told them that we would not go immediately but thought perhaps sometime in May before we started fruit picking. 'Nonsense', said Frank, 'you cannot do that. If you don't go now you'll never go!' 'But there are Mum and Dad to think of', answered Glad. 'They can manage two or three days without you', Frank replied. With that he picked up the phone, asked for telephone enquiries and for the number of the Strand Palace Hotel in London, and requested to be connected. He booked two nights, 24th and 25th of February, and that was it! They told us that was where they had spent their honeymoon.

Next we thought about was the guest list. Food of course was rationed and at that time it was all self-catering. The Wedding Breakfasts were held in public halls, e.g. either Village or Church halls, or British Legion and Free Mason halls, or other places like these. Facilities were limited then and all you could offer and serve on these occasions were simple and basic dishes. One could engage outside caterers but you had to supply the food.

If there were more than twelve guests at the Wedding Breakfast one could apply for extra ration coupons. The maximum you could apply for was for twenty-four people. If you had more guests than that, you either had to make do or scrounge extra food from somewhere. These regulations did not bother us for the following two reasons. . Firstly, we were advised by our clergy friends, to keep our forth coming marriage out of the public domain: the reason being that no P.O.W., as far as was known, had married a British girl in Hampshire and there was no knowing how the general public would react. Secondly, they suggested we got married by Common Licence, as this would do away with publishing the Banns of Marriage. We took their advice and all went well in the run-up to the big day.

There were one or two other things to be taken care of before the wedding day. One was to notify the appropriate Government Department, in my case the Ministry of Agriculture in Winchester, of my forthcoming change of status and at the same time to apply for a work permit, which was readily granted. With that permit came my ration book as well as clothing coupons and points to buy furniture and other restricted items. With leaving the camp the military authorities handed over my file and other papers to the Home Office and the Agricultural Department to the Ministry of Works. Being an alien now, I now had to report to the local police station in Eastleigh every three month. Never in all my days had I been in a police station before and I wondered what it would be like. The only image I had was from movie pictures. I need not have worried, I received courteous attention and the officer interviewing me was polite throughout the interview. He wished me well on my forthcoming marriage as I left the station. Somewhat different to Glad's experience from the clergyman she had to call on to obtain the licence for us to get married. He queried the wisdom of it all to get married to foreigners in general and P.O.W.s, in particular, as she knew nothing about my past and background and I could have told her any old yarn. Glad did not care, she came away with what she went for and that was all she cared about.

With only eight weeks to our wedding day, we had no time to waste. Loads of things needed to be done and to be arranged. There were our wedding clothes to buy. Glad struck it very lucky here. As she liked Winchester best, the first shopping spree was to that city. As luck would have it, we found a suitable suit for her, something she was looking for, on our first visit. The Spring Selection was just arriving and among the first to be unpacked happened to be that suit. It was in a classic style and in a suitable colour. It fitted perfectly. I was nowhere near as lucky! Having only just received my first clothing coupons, a day or two ago, I had not yet replaced any of civilian clothes, I currently wore, as they were second hand bought for me by Glad and that included shoes. So for the next three weeks, whenever we could spare a few hours to go shopping, we were off to Southampton, Fareham, Salisbury, and Eastleigh. We visited every Gentleman's outfitter in these towns but could not find a suit off the peg to fit me. Enquiring about having a suit made to measure, we were told every time, that it would take at least three months, sometimes even longer. Eventually we found a suit, in the Fifty Shilling Tailor in Above Bar at Southampton, for £4. It was brown, pin striped and double breasted.

We also found a shirt for twelve Shillings and a tie for Half a Crown to go with it. What a relief! The new pair of shoes we were looking for presented no problem. We were now ready for the big day.

Being the end of February and officially still winter there was just one thing that might spoil it all, SNOW! So far we had been spared the hard weather we experienced the previous year. We had some snow since Christmas, but it fell in small amounts and in each case it did not last for long; nor were the temperatures nearly as low as last year either. Not surprisingly then, when it did snow the Friday before the wedding it was not unexpected, but with four days to go, most of it might well be gone, as daytime temperatures were above freezing and the white stuff was melting quite quickly. By Monday we could see the ground and the roads were clear as well. Monday was also the final day of getting ready. We did as much as possible, both outside and inside the house to leave as little as possible for Glad's parents to do. Glad also completed the final touches for our Wedding Breakfast as it was self-catering, which she could easily manage, with only seven people sitting down for the meal. My tasks were all outside. Cleaning out the chicken houses and making sure there was enough firewood in the shed opposite the back door.

Having done all we could, we had our tea and I got ready to catch the 17.30 bus to Woolston at the end of the lane. The closer we got to Southampton the less evidence of the snow, we had a few days ago, but the forecast was of a frosty night. I arrived at our friends, the Couzens an hour later and was made most welcome.

They both tried to assure me all would be alright in the morning and Maggie went a couple of times through the marriage service with me, just to ensure I had an idea of the order of things. Later on in the evening we had a light meal and soon after went to bed. That was my Stag Night that was.

After a good night of sleep, I joined my hosts for breakfast; Frank had already been down to his store to see all was well. With the wedding at 10.00 in the morning there was no time to linger. Not knowing what the road conditions like, after the frost during the night, we needed to allow at least half an hour to get to the Church in Hedge End. Frank had ordered a taxi. With their house facing north, as well as being on a slope and with an icy road surface, the taxi driver had stopped just a fraction too far down the hill, and was unable to get started again. Before we could get going, the three of us pushed the car up the hill to some level ground and there we got into the car. With the sun shining on to the road, the ice had gone and we were off.

Yes, we arrived at the Church on time. The two clergy were waiting and gave us a warm welcome. Glad had hired the local taxi man from Hedge End to bring her parents, her friend Ami and herself to church. Maggie, Frank and I were the only ones inside. Glad arrived on time and all seemed well, for which we were all grateful, as the day before the wedding Polly still thought she might change Glad's mind about going through with the marriage. The service went well. The two clergy were excellent. Slowly they went through the service and in next to no time I was a happily married man with an equally happy bride beside me. Happy on two counts:

firstly that we were married now, and secondly that her mother had, at long last, accepted that fact.

As we came out of church the sun greeted us very warmly. Although there was still quite a bit of snow about it was a pleasant morning. With no official photographer in sight, Ami and Maggie took a few pictures and off we went home were we found the table laid to have our Wedding Breakfast, which Glad prepared before she left for church. Ami, she told me later, was absolutely useless. She was more of a hindrance than help, and her mother was in one of her moods, which did not help. The only help she had had that morning was from her father. As before long we needed a taxi to take us to the station, and with only six sitting at the table, we asked the driver if he could take us and, if it was alright, would he like to join us. With petrol rationing very strict and not having another fare booked until evening, he accepted our offer. With the meal and speeches over we got ready and left for our Honeymoon.

We left from Eastleigh station and dropped off Ami on the way not far from her home. It was nearly two years since I had been on the train, but this time round it was a different feeling with no soldiers to keep an eye on me. On the way to Waterloo Station in London, I wondered what I would think of London and would the city compare with Berlin? We would just have to wait and see. Anyway, the train arrived on time and we transferred to a taxi which took us to the Strand Palace Hotel where after booking in we went to our room, freshened up, had a light tea and then went to the Palace Theatre for the first house to see the Crazy Gang which was very funny and most enjoyable. After the show we went back to the hotel had our supper and thanked God for a lovely day and a happy time.

The next morning, Wednesday, we went to the West End for a shopping spree, Oxford Street to be precise. We bought a number of things for our home which we started more or less from scratch. Among them a writing case made from leather, which is still in my possession today. We had lunch out and then took a taxi back to the hotel and got ready to attend a Matinee performance of Oklahoma, which was then the rage of the town. I was looking forward to seeing the show as I was familiar with its musical score from my days in the U.S.A where the show had been running for quite a while. Since its opening night in November 1948 at the Drury Lane theatre it had performed to 'sold out' houses. It is a musical I never tire of seeing. Back at the hotel we had our evening meal and got ready for the journey home. How was London comparing with Berlin? Shall we say it felt good to walk the streets of a big city again!

Glad was quite anxious to get home to see how the old folk coped. As we took an early train home, we arrived back in the early afternoon and found all was well. The news that we were married had spread round like wildfire! On the way back to Botley from marrying us, the chain came off the Rector's bicycle which made him late for the meeting with the young wives. He apologised and gave the reason why. That was enough to set the bush telegraph beating and in next to no time everybody knew of us being married. Hence cards of congratulations and good wishes were awaiting us on our return.

As always in farming, there was no time to rest; jobs were waiting to be done, so a new chapter in my life had begun.

GEORGE GEBAUER

Our Wedding Photograph

Chapter 22

Farmer George

Yes, that is what I turned into with the help of my many friends who lived in the neighbourhood. Why they should have been so kind and helpful to me, I shall never know. That was one of the reasons I decided to stay in Britain because of the truly warm welcome I had received from all the people in and around Botley, as well as the kind heartedness shown to me by all the people I met both in business and social life. They were all strangers to me at that time and one needs to remember that I was also a stranger to them. More than that, not only was I a stranger, but I was also still a Prisoner of War. That warm welcome came from people that had suffered so much in recent years, because of the war, and were still experiencing rationing, as well as shortages of all kinds. They were also facing austerity in the near future. Here I was being shown all this kindness and being given all that help. Being surrounded by so many friends, and experiencing so much goodwill, made me feel very humble. So it was not very difficult for me to decide to stay in Britain, to settle down and strike roots.

This was really all due to the Gannaway family who were highly respected by all in the community. Bill for his integrity and honesty, Polly for her strong character and generous heart, and Glad, not only as she was their daughter, but also for her being courteous and polite as well as showing consideration to other people. Since arriving at Le Nid, a year earlier, I had learned a great deal about living in the countryside and working on the land but very little about farming and market gardening. I soon discovered there is more to growing crops than just putting in the seed and hoping for the best. Bill was a gardener by profession of course and a very good one at that, but a bad teacher. One learned best from him by working alongside him and observing what he did and how he did it. Even then it took a year or two to get it right as weather conditions vary from season to season. The introduction of how to care for livestock came from Glad. She knew all about breeding, hatching and rearing chicks. Before, during and immediately after the war she carefully selected eggs for hatching looking for good shape, sound and firm shells from hens that had a cock bird running with them. When the hens became broody in the spring, she picked the hens she knew would make good mothers and then set them in batches of four with a cluster of thirteen eggs under each hen. She was very good at this as most of the time a minimum of eleven eggs hatched out. As for the ratio of sexes, she could only trust to luck. In any case the cock birds were reared for the table and gave quite a good income as meat was still rationed but poultry and game were excluded.

This changed when feeding stuff becoming more plentiful. The big hatcheries came into their own then. In the early years the chicks came by overnight train and were delivered early in the morning by the railway company. The rearing shed had been prepared well in advance and heated for 48 hours before their arrival. Glad made sure the shed was warm enough to receive the baby chicks on arrival. To start with we had them in batches of 100, partly because of limited food supply and also shortage of accommodation. As time went by we had them in batches of 200 three times a year, January, May and September. Delivered either by van from the hatchery or we went and collected them the day they were hatched. For a while we also reared a batch of capons for the Christmas Market but found it too much to cope with and we gave them up after three or four years.

Poultry was not the only expansion we made. There were two pig pens from pre-war days which had not been used for some years except for storing fruit for short periods. Bill in his younger days had had a licence to slaughter pigs on private premises. With laws on hygiene as well as on health and safety being tightened, slaughtering pigs on farms and other premises became almost impossible just before the Second World War, so Bill did not renew his licence, and keeping a few pigs at home fell by the wayside. One day, in my eagerness and enthusiasm, I suggested why should we not have a few pigs again! Yes the sties needed repairing, but for a little outlay they could be used again for the purpose they were built for. After talking and thinking it over, the family said I could have a go at it. Being friendly with the foreman of the local saw mill, I went and talked to him about it and what I might need. He soon fixed me up with what I required for the job, as large amounts of timber could only be obtained by licence, at that time, so home I went as pleased as Punch.

Whilst Bill and I repaired one of the pens, Glad in the meantime went to one or two farmer friends who bred and fattened pigs, to see what the chance was of having a couple of piglets from a large litter in the near future.

Fred Taplin, as always, met our request. A few days later he brought round two healthy, strong and lively piglets. As with everything new in life, we all wasted a lot of time watching the playful piglets and their antics. It was not long before I repaired the other pig pen, purchased two more piglets and planned to build a third pen adjacent to the existing ones. This time the plan was to buy a whole litter and then select two gilts and keep them for breeding. We bought a litter of eight! As so many times before, with this venture came the steep learning curve in pig husbandry. To start with there was little trouble, but as time went by the vet needed to be called to cure minor ailments. That is how I became a farmer and pig breeder.

When the gilts were old enough for breeding, again it was Fred Taplin who supplied what was needed, this time the boar. When the time of farrowing came near, I did not know what to expect as I was totally ignorant of any female giving birth. I just had to watch and learn by experience. When the first gilt started delivering her litter I just stood watching in amazement how this little might just brought into the world found its way to the teat and with it life and survival. If it had strayed from its mother it would certainly have died of hyperthermia and starvation. There usually are one or two newly born piglets in a litter which move away from their mother and need to be directed to the teat to obtain the life giving milk and warmth of the sow. Fortunately this did not happen to any of the piglets of our first two litters but in later years this was often not the case.

For the next nine weeks we frantically went on with building yet another sty to accommodate the two litters.

It was not long before we kept back two more gilts for breeding, built more sties, and then we needed a boar of our own. Again it was Fred Taplin whose help we sought in selecting the right one for us. We eventually finished up by having on average 200 pigs on the holding. Whenever we found ourselves short of room to house all the pigs, which occasionally happened when we had a number of large litters (with twelve or more piglets in a litter) in close succession, we sold a litter or two. This of course works fine as long as all goes well. Life was always so rosy. When in the 1960s an outbreak of 'Foot and Mouth Disease' happened on our neighbouring farm, we were almost at breaking point. With no movement of livestock on or off the farms in a five mile radius, we were hard pressed to find room for the newly weaned litters. Any shed that could be converted to hold pigs went through a make-over and in the end this proved quite costly. The problem with these notifiable diseases, one never knows how long they will last, and with a daily count and inspection of your life stock by a veterinary surgeon, you dare not take any chances. But we survived and I am still alive to tell the tale.

Going in for pig keeping and breeding was not the only line I started. In 1950 with milk and butter still rationed, I suggested to the family why not keep a 'House Cow' to supply the milk and butter for us. There was plenty of grass and space between the rows of trees in the orchard to keep a cow. She needed to be tethered of course but it could be done. It would also save us cutting the grass twice a year. Mother-in-Law was delighted with the suggestion as she always dreamed of having a dairy herd and making butter and cheese. Bill had not been too keen on the idea simply because he was just not interested in livestock of any kind. Hence the line of work that was more to his liking, the orchard and the market garden. However there was one condition, I had to learn how to milk first, before Polly would buy a cow for me.

Now where could I go and learn to milk a cow by hand? By now all the dairy farmers had machines to milk their cows. Well, there was only one person to approach with the request to teach me how to milk a cow, Fred Taplin. He had a herd of pedigree Guernsey cows, all good natured and quiet. Fred was a general farmer with some arable farming as well as livestock. He also had a milk round in Hedge End and supplied the Botley Grange Hotel with cream, milk and eggs. He also undertook some haulage work in the winter. Glad and I went to see him and told him of my proposal. For whatever reason he did not seem surprised and agreed with Polly, which he rarely did (he being a Liberal and Polly a staunch Conservative) of the importance of me knowing something of how to handle a cow and how to milk. So we agreed from now on I would report at 6 am every morning to learn how to milk a cow. The men working for Fred had got to know me quite well by now and teased me mercilessly for the first two or three days, but when they realised I took it seriously and would not give up, they became most helpful.

Fred selected a quiet animal for me to practice on. He tied her up away from the others, so that I could have a go away from the other work that was going on in the milking parlour all round me. Step by step he patiently showed me how to approach the cow, wash her udder, and sit down on a three legged milk stool and the hand movement of how to milk. So I did as instructed, but what I was not told was that cows can and do kick. Approaching the whole procedure rather timidly and uncertainly and the poor cow unfamiliar with what was going on, she kicked so as to get me away from her udder and her foot ended up in the milk bucket! So that was not much of a start. Once more I was shown how to approach a cow to milk her this time stressing the importance of keeping your left shoulder and arm firmly against the cows leg and thereby getting a warning when she is about to lift her leg to lash out. So I made another attempt to get some milk from her, this time I was more successful and managed to get about half a pint. Fred thought I did quite well for the first time and at least I had got some milk. He then sat down and milked the cow and took as much milk as she would give. When cows get upset they don't let down milk easily. As there was no reason to bother the poor creature any further, he let her go and would milk her dry at the afternoon's milking. Now how many farmers would go to that length for a complete stranger? Only people with a generous heart like Fred, because he would help anyone if he could.

For the next two months or so I turned up at six in the morning to practise on this poor cow. In the end she became quite used to me and me to her. During those weeks I learned much about the behaviour of these animals, how they become quite trusting to the voice that attends them, providing it is in a quiet manner with a kind voice. Early in September Fred told us the cow he had looked out for us had calved and all was well and, as soon as her calf was weaned, he would bring her over.

With the expected addition of a cow to our livestock, we prepared the stall were she would be tied up and also made the grass we had cut in the orchard into hay. Straw for bedding in the winter we had plenty of, because of the pigs. We had also begun to grow fodder beet for our sows, so there was nothing to worry about on this score. As for greens, up to Christmas there was the cabbage that was not good enough for market and after Christmas there were the brussel sprout stumps. When the day of her arrival came, we all were very excited and all wondered how I could cope on my own. For this time I could not look for help from Glad, as she had no knowledge of how to handle or to milk a cow. But I managed and became very good at it. We called her Jennifer - a character in the then current radio comedy show "Ray's a Laugh!"

You may have guessed it! We did not stop at one cow. Ten weeks after her coming to Le Nid I took her back to Fred to mate with his bull. I walked her to end of the lane and then just around the corner was Fred's farm. We made arrangements that after the morning's milking I would take her over and she could stay till the afternoon and I would go back and collect her, which I did. The next anxious moment now would now when Jennifer was due to calf next summer. In the meantime we enjoyed the rich milk and cream and all the by-products you get from the milk. The following summer when it was time for Jennifer to deliver there was yet more to learn about livestock husbandry. As so many times before, everyone was most helpful telling me the signs to look for when the time of calving approaches, the behaviour of the animal and so forth. All well-meant of course and helpful to a degree but in the end it comes down to one's own experience. Jennifer delivered her calf, a heifer, without trouble and thankfully all went well and to plan and we were very grateful for that. We named her June.

As the time came to wean the calf, a decision had to be made what to do with this pretty, big eyed little thing. Well it did not take too long to come to a decision. During the eight to nine weeks before calving we did not have our own milk and butter and oh how we missed that. It is truly amazing how one gets used to having plenty and here we were having it to buy again. So we decided to keep the calf and have two house cows. The reason we were able to do this was we had just taken on an extra five acres of land and that enabled us to keep this extra cow. Another reason was the two ladies of the house just could not bear to see little June go. As before with the pig enterprise, eventually we increased the number of cows on the holding to four using any surplus milk to fatten our calves for the meat market. We were able to do this because another farmer friend, Will Oakley, with a large dairy herd always gave us first option to buy any of his bull calves before they were sent to market.

What next you may wonder, well, let me tell you - BEES! It happened like this. One day in 1961 on a sultry, thundery day in May, a swarm of bees settled in one of our apple trees. I suppose I could have left them there to rest as they would have taken off before too long to be on their way again. But no, I phoned George Dangerfield to find out what to do. What George did not know about country ways and country living was not worth knowing. As he was tied up at the time, he was unable to come to help me but he told me what to do! Get a ladder, put it securely on a branch close to swarm, take a strong cardboard box large enough to hold the swarm, give the branch the bees had settled on a good, strong, quick shake hoping the majority of bees will drop into the box. When back on the ground, turn the box carefully upside down and place a thin piece of wood under one side only for the bees to have access to it. If you caught the queen bee, and she is in the box, the bees that are buzzing around will join her. I followed instructions to the letter, gave the branch a good, strong, short shake, managed to catch most of the bees including the queen and carefully turned the box and placed it on the ground as I was told to do. How many times was I stung? I just don't know. Glad gave up counting after she pulled out the fiftieth sting.

What to do next was the big question. Earlier in the year an old school friend of Glad's, Alf Knight, had offered us all his bee equipment. Now that he kept a grocer's shop, he had neither the opportunity nor the time to look after bees any longer. Glad phoned him asking whether or not the equipment was still available. Yes it was, thank goodness, and we were welcome to collect it and he would happily give it to us. Off she went to Hedge End and returned with two Supers and a Queen Excluder, a Honey Extractor and Ripener, all in very good condition and worth quite a lot of money. Whilst Glad was gone I went on with the routine work until her return, then assembled the hive, placed it in an open space, facing south, away from places of work and pathways frequently used by us. George Dangerfield turned up about 6 pm., assessed the situation and approved of what he saw. He placed a board up to the entrance of the hive, making it act as a ramp so to speak, then fetched the box with the bees in, turned it upside down at the bottom of the board, directed the bees up the ramp, and hey presto into the hive they went. This was yet another first and very exciting it was too. George taught me how to spot the queen bee, which can prove difficult at times; the little blighters are very quick and not always easy to spot. The advice I received from George was most helpful. As we were about to start a new colony, we needed the queen. Future swarms which came from our own hive needed the queen removed as there was already one queen left in the hive and two queens in one hive won't work! Yes that was quite a day and a memorable one too, as so many others had been before. It was not long before we increased the number of hives to three and so I became a beekeeper as well.

Fred Taplin and George Dangerfield were not the only two that helped us in time of need and crisis. Jack Hack, another farmer, as well as Harold Yeats were friends we could call upon. Also Charlie Watts, who was a market gardener and a local Councillor, would always send us help, as would Jack Barker. Jack Candy was the one to send for whenever any machinery broke down. Anything mechanical needing attention, Jack was the one! Honestly, he got any machine going again. I learnt a lot from Ernie and Mary Crawford, our nearest neighbours, often by just talking to them, which over the years proved valuable and very helpful. They had four delightful children, two girls, Ann and Jenifer, as well as two boys, John and Keith, known as Dickie. They were with us as much as they were at home, especially at holiday times. In fact, they were regular customers for eggs, fruit and honey and we thought they were ours. Not having children of our own, we always made them very welcome.

Among other friends who helped us was Maggie Cozins's brother Ted, a shipwright by trade, especially when we were extending our farm buildings. Les Parker, physically very strong was the man to help when heavy work was involved, and there is plenty of it on a farm!

Chapter 23

All Work and no Play makes Jack a dull Boy!

In the late summer of 1947 we started going to dances in the British Legion Hall in Botley on Saturday nights. A three piece band played for dancing, a violinist, a piano player and a drummer. Sometimes a trumpet player augmented the band to four. They were not a bad little group, keeping in tune anyway and to the right beat. Again everyone there made me welcome, young and old alike. We were well aware that "All Work and no Play makes Jack a dull Boy," so we continued this pattern for a long time after we were married.

Then there were the annual events. Polly being a staunch supporter of the Conservative Party made sure that we represented her at the annual dinner of the local branch. Most people there came across to us and chatted for a while and said they were pleased to see me. Another annual Dinner and Dance we attended was that of the Swanwick and District Basket Factory of which Bill was a founder member. Two or three times a year we went to dances at the Guild Hall or Royal Pier in Southampton organised by the local branches of national institutions, listening and dancing to big and well known bands or orchestras of the time.

There were trips to the theatre in the autumn and winter. We both enjoyed Ballet and Musicals. In November of 1948 we made another visit to London.

With food rationing easing, we could now stay four nights in a hotel without surrendering our ration books, so for four nights we stayed. On this trip we went to see 'Annie get your Gun' and 'Bless the Bride,' as well as a Variety Show at the Palladium. In fact for many years, we went to London on or about the time of my birthday in November and again on our Wedding anniversary in February to see a show. We also went to church on the day of our Wedding anniversary every year. Being the feast of St. Mathias, we were fortunate to have an eight o'clock celebration of Holy Communion at All Saints', Botley. Also, at the weekend nearest to our anniversary, we usually invited a few friends and neighbours for a drink and a chat. As you might guess friends reciprocated, so many evenings during the winter months were taken up one way or another.

Frank and Maggie Cozens were very anxious that I would not think too badly of the English, as if I would! Right from the beginning, they invited us to family events such as weddings, anniversaries, twenty-first birthday parties and so on. Maggie (formerly Hall) had all her family involved as well. Most of their children were about my age so we had a few twenty first birthdays to go to as well Weddings and Silver Weddings too. The kindness and friendship shown to me by these good people in these early days, after the war, remains unbelievable to me, considering they were bombed out of their houses not all that long ago, some even more than once.

All this helped me to experience and get to know the British way of life and the people. To make their way my way, and to settle down and live the life I had chosen.

With no other Germans in or around Botley and district, it made the changeover from one culture to the other much easier, as there was nothing of my old ways to hang on to. Fred Hatfield, the Rector of Botley at the time, came to call on us once a month and with it kept my interest in the church alive as did his successor Michael Carey. He too was a great Pastor and parish Priest. Michael introduced a few changes which were not always liked nor well received. He also brought to Botley the "Sung Eucharist," which was well received by most regular worshippers, which was not surprising as All Saints' had a good and long choral tradition and with it they were able to enrich the service of Holy Communion. The other reason for accepting this without too much opposition was because Michael Carey kept the service of Matins at the traditional time. So no one was denied their familiar pattern of regular Sunday worship at their Parish Church. Michael was most helpful to us, especially to Glad, during the years when we cared for and nursed Glad's parents, offering prayers and a service of Holy Communion at a time that suited us. He also did so at the time of their deaths and burials and kept us in touch with church and parish life.

The year of 1948, from the beginning to the end, was indeed a year that would set the course my life to follow, a life among country people, with country ways and a rural background. At the beginning of the year I was officially still a Prisoner of War out on parole. The Ministry of Agriculture and Fisheries was still responsible for my whereabouts and wellbeing. Just before Christmas that year, I received a notice to report to the regional office of the Hampshire County Council Agriculture Committee's Regional Office in Fareham in the forenoon on December the 31st to receive my Discharge Papers. I must have been one of the last, if not THE last, to be released as a P.O.W. in Britain. I did not have to be told twice!! Having recently obtained my full driving licence, I made my own way to Fareham and reported to the office where I was expected. All the papers needing my signature were there ready to be signed. It took less than ten minutes to complete all the formalities and I walked out of the office a free man and with it began the countdown to become a British Subject. In those days one needed to have been a resident in the country for at least five years. So in March of 1953, Coronation Year, I applied to the Home Office in Whitehall for the necessary application forms and after completing them I returned the questionnaire and other forms to London with a two pound registration fee. A few days later I received a reply informing me that so far the Home Secretary had not considered applications for naturalisation from persons of former enemy countries. As soon as Parliament authorised it, he would do so. In the meantime they would file my application and credit the two pounds to my name for the future.

Sometime in late June in Coronation Year, I received a large envelope from the Home Office containing all the forms needed when applying for British Citizenship. Five sponsors were needed as well as audited accounts for the last five years. Obviously Frank Cozins was one of them and Jack Scivier, our miller, was another. Les Parker, being a Special Constable, made an ideal sponsor as well as did Doctor Pern, the family doctor, who brought Glad into the world. Finally, Jack Henry a member of the Hall family made the fifth. The

Accountant was a Mr Bond the senior member of the Firm of Accountants Whittaker, Bailey & Co. in Southampton. He was quite a fatherly figure to me, very kind and courteous. After completing the forms I send them off to London with all the names and addresses of the sponsors and accountant. All one could do now was to sit back and wait. The wait turned out not to be too long. In November of 1953 I had a letter from the Home Office informing me that my application had been granted and on receiving the £50 fee, the final forms would be forwarded to complete the process. The cheque went off by return of post and just before Christmas I had the final papers requiring my swearing an Oath of Allegiance to Queen and Country before a Justice of the Peace. No problem here, as I knew two, Harold Yeates and Charlie Watts. I chose Charlie Watts who was delighted to act for me at this big moment in my life. So on December 26th 1953 (Boxing Day) before a Justice of the Peace, with my right hand raised and my left hand on the Bible, I swore my allegiance to Queen and Country and became a British Subject.

GEORGE GEBAUER

My Certificate of Discharge (obverse)

CONTROL FORM D.2
Kontrollblatt D.2

CERTIFICATE OF DISCHARGE
Entlassungschein

| ALL ENTRIES WILL BE MADE IN BLOCK LATIN CAPITALS AND WILL BE MADE IN INK OR TYPE-SCRIPT. | I PERSONAL PARTICULARS Personalbeschreibung | Dieses Blatt muss in folgender weise ausgefüllt werden: 1. In lateinischer Druckschrift und in grossen Buchstaben 2. Mit Tinte oder mit Schreibmaschine. |

SURNAME OF HOLDER _GEBAUER_
Familienname des Inhabers

CHRISTIAN NAMES _GERHART_
Vornamen des Inhabers

CIVIL OCCUPATION _ELEKTRO,SCHLOSSER_
Beruf oder Beschäftigung

HOME ADDRESS Strasse _RUPPRECHT.STR. 32_
Heimatanschrift Ort _BERLIN -LICHTENBERG_
Kreis
Regierungsbezirk/Land

DATE OF BIRTH _25. NOV. 1925_
Geburtsdatum (DAY/MONTH/YEAR)
Tag/Monat/Jahr)

PLACE OF BIRTH _BERLIN_
Geburtsort

FAMILY STATUS ~~SINGLE~~ ~~Ledig~~
Familienstand MARRIED Verheiratet
~~WIDOWED~~ ~~Verwitwet~~
~~DIVORCED~~ ~~Geschieden~~

NUMBER OF CHILDREN WHO ARE MINORS
Zahl der minderjährigen Kinder

I HEREBY CERTIFY THAT TO THE BEST OF MY KNOWLEDGE AND BELIEF THE PARTI-CULARS GIVEN ABOVE ARE TRUE. I ALSO CERTIFY THAT I HAVE READ AND UNDERSTOOD THE " INSTRUCTIONS TO PERSONNEL ON DISCHARGE " (CONTROL FORM D.1)
SIGNATURE OF HOLDER _Gerhart Gebauer_
Unterschrift des Inhabers

Ich erkläre hiermit, nach bestem Wissen und Gewissen, dass die obigen Angaben wahr sind. Ich bestätige ausserdem dass ich die " Anweisung für Soldaten und Angehörige Militär-ähnlicher Organisationen u.s.w. (Kontrollblatt D.1) gelesen und verstanden habe.

II MEDICAL CERTIFICATE
Ärztlicher Befund

DISTINGUISHING MARKS
Besondere Kennzeichen

DISABILITY, WITH DESCRIPTION
Dienstunfähigkeit, mit Beschreibung

MEDICAL CATEGORY
Tauglichkeitsgrad

I CERTIFY THAT TO THE BEST OF MY KNOW-LEDGE AND BELIEF THE ABOVE PARTICU-LARS RELATING TO THE HOLDER ARE TRUE AND THAT HE IS NOT VERMINOUS OR SUFFERING FROM ANY INFECTIOUS OR CONTAGIOUS DISEASE.

SIGNATURE OF MEDICAL OFFICER
Unterschrift des Sanitätsoffiziers

NAME AND RANK OF MEDICAL OFFICER IN BLOCK LATIN CAPITALS
Zuname/Vorname/Dienstgrad des Sanitätsoffiziers (In lateinischer Druckschrift und in grossen Buchstaben)

Ich erkläre hiermit, nach bestem Wissen und Gewissen, dass die obigen Angaben wahr sind, dass der Inhaber ungezieferfrei ist und dass er keinerlei ansteckende oder übertragbar Krankheit hat.

P.T.O.
Bitte wenden

† DELETE THAT WHICH IS INAPPLICABLE
Nichtzutreffendes durchstreichen

PSS 2242 5 45 2000~

298

My Certificate of Discharge (reverse)

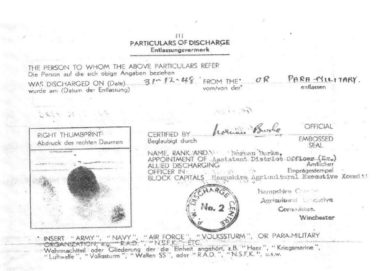

GEORGE GEBAUER

My Certificate of Naturalisation (obverse)

Certificate No. **BNA** 29543 Home Office No. G.43150.

BRITISH NATIONALITY ACT, 1948.

CERTIFICATE OF NATURALISATION

Whereas Gerhart Gebauer

has applied to one of Her Majesty's Principal Secretaries of State for a certificate of naturalisation, alleging with respect to him self the particulars set out below, and has satisfied the Secretary of State that the conditions laid down in the British Nationality Act, 1948, for the grant of a certificate of naturalisation are fulfilled :

Now, therefore, the Secretary of State, in pursuance of the powers conferred upon him by the said Act, grants to the said

Gerhart Gebauer

this Certificate of Naturalisation, and declares that upon taking the Oath of Allegiance within the time and in the manner required by the regulations made in that behalf he shall be a citizen of the United Kingdom and Colonies as from the date of this certificate.

In witness whereof I have hereto subscribed my name this 14. day of December, 19 53.

HOME OFFICE.
LONDON.

J. anderson

UNDER SECRETARY OF STATE.

PARTICULARS RELATING TO APPLICANT.

Full Name	Gerhart GEBAUER.
Address	"Le Nid", Shamblehurst Lane, Botley, near Southampton, Hampshire.
Profession or Occupation	Pig Breeder and Poultry Keeper.
Place and date of birth	Berlin, Germany. 25th November, 1925.
Nationality	German.
Single, married, etc.	Married.
Name of wife or husband	Gladys Violet.
Names and nationalities of parents	Otto and Margarete GEBAUER (German).

(For Oath
see overleaf.)

My Certificate of Naturalisation (reverse)

Oath of Allegiance

I, *GERHART GEBAUER*

swear by Almighty God that I will be faithful and bear true allegiance to Her Majesty, Queen Elizabeth the Second, Her Heirs and Successors, according to law.

(Signature) *Gerhart Gebauer*

Sworn and subscribed this 26th day of *December* 1953, before me,

(Signature) *C. Watts*

Justice of the Peace for *Hampshire*
A Commissioner for Oaths.

Name and Address
(in Block Capitals) *CHARLES WATTS.*
GRANADA ROAD, HEDGEEND SOUTHAMPTON

Unless otherwise indicated hereon, if the Oath of Allegiance is not taken within one calendar month of the date of this Certificate, the Certificate shall have no effect.

HOME OFFICE
−2 JAN 1954
REGISTERED

Chapter 24

Road to Holy Orders:
The first step

For a while in the late nineteen fifties our social life was somewhat curtailed. Glad's parents had reached the stage when not only were they unable to work but they also needed to be looked after and eventually nursed as well. Friends continued inviting us out for an evening and we accepted it once or twice but Glad felt uneasy throughout the evening and did not enjoy it one little bit. So I suggested we forget all about going out and make the most of the evenings at home, for the time would come, when we could go out again. So we concentrated on the task in hand and looked after the old folks. Doctor Pern suggested for them to go into a Care Home, but Glad would not hear of it. She did not have too good an opinion of Care Homes anyway. They are different now to what they were in the nineteen fifty's. Bill died on December 22nd 1958, when he was ninety, and we buried him on Christmas Eve. Polly died two years later on the December 6th 1960 aged eighty eight.

Thanks to our many friends it did not take us too long to pick up the social life again. We made even more friends! As we no longer had the responsibility of looking after Glad's parents, we were able to get more involved in church activities. Elizabeth Salwey, the widow of a former Rector of Botley, Geoff Salwey, having moved back to Botley, invited us for an evening meal soon after Polly's funeral. For the evening, she had invited a number of newcomers to Botley as well as some friends of hers she wanted us to meet. Here again was a person, who had suffered great personal loss during the war, showing me warmth and friendship. The Salwey's had two sons, both killed in the war in the space of two years and I was told Geoff was near breaking point in the pulpit when preaching the Sunday after the death of his second son. I had met Geoff briefly a number of times; he was a gentle person, a pastor of the old mould. Liz Salwey as she preferred to be called had known the Gannaway family ever since they came to Botley in 1921 and was very fond of Glad. Michael Carey too was pleased to see us more frequently knowing how difficult it had been for us to attend church. Kitty Fox, another family friend who visited us frequently, insisted we came to see her now and meet some of her friends. And so the circle widened.

Early in 1963 Michael Carey was appointed Archdeacon of Ely and we were sad to see him leave as he was such a good friend and help to us. But life has to go on and in due course we would have a new incumbent. In the meantime there was the interregnum to get through. I offered my help to the Churchwardens, Alfred Pern, who was our doctor of course and Bertie West who was the village chemist. It would not be much as I knew very little about the everyday running of a parish. They called on me once or twice during July and August, when the entire world seemed to be on holiday, to ring the bell for Evensong on a Sunday night. That was my first involvement with church life. The next came later in the year on the evening of the induction of the new

Rector. As always on these occasions the church was expected to be filled to overflowing and extra sidesmen were needed. One afternoon a few days before the induction, Dr. Pern called on us asking if I could help on the night to be assistant sidesmen. The answer was yes of course. The evening of the rehearsal I duly reported to the wardens to be instructed what to do. This was the first time I saw all the officers of the parish together in one place - Wardens, Secretary, Treasurer, P.C.C. members, sidesmen and a few other helpers as well. This was quite an experience for me. I also met our new Rector, Canon Philip Duke-Baker, a happy man he appeared to be. We exchanged a few words, had a laugh and I wished him well. As it turned out, he would become my mentor. During his time as Rector we became very good friends. The nineteen sixties saw a lot of changes in the Church of England and he introduced them very successfully taking most of the congregations with him. Again the musical tradition of All Saints' played a vital part in the changeover. Philip, being a very good musician, helped and being excellent organ player, as well, helped even more.

The following spring at his first Annual Church Meeting he persuaded me, and a few others of my age group, to stand for the P.C.C. as he wanted the views of younger people when proposing changes in future. So it was that the new P.C.C. had four new faces, mine among them. My election onto the council was entirely due to the Misses Maffey, there were four of them, and they were highly respected in the village, and they went around canvassing for me, especially Gladys and Ethel. It was not long after, that I was invited to read the lesson and put on the reading roster.

Whilst most former Rectors of the Parish were on their own, Philip Duke-Baker had some help in his time. On his arrival we had a Reader, Lloyd Fielder, who was very enthusiastic about playing his part in parish life. With some developments taking place in the village, there were new families arriving and with many of them joining our congregation, he felt a Men's Fellowship might be the answer for the men to get to know one another better. The women who were new to the parish had the Mothers Union or could join the flower arrangers or met outside the school gates. For men there was nothing. With the Rector's permission Lloyd first talked to us individually, and then put a notice in the Magazine about the time and place of the first meeting. A good number turned up and as always with these gatherings, we learned a lot from and about each other. I certainly learned a great deal from my friends in the group who came from totally different backgrounds to mine and they were refreshing to meet. Lloyd led us until he was ordained and moved to Emsworth in Hampshire. Philip also had a curate for a time, Kenneth Parkinson. He came to us for health reason and stayed with us for two years until he was better. After Lloyd Fielder left, the Group asked me to carry on the good work begun by Lloyd. I consulted the Rector and he thought it might be a good idea if I did.

Glad, who was always given to hospitality, started entertaining many of our friends for lunch. Not in great numbers but a few at a time so that we had the opportunity to speak with them and to learn something about them too. There was a lot to learn about the church and church affairs. One thing we started was to have a Rogation Tide Service on our holding, the time of year when the church prays for favourable weather for the crops. The first two years we had them in the afternoon and invited old friends to pray with us such as the Cozens and the Henry's or as in the second year Amy and her husband, yes she too got married, and friends from Bitterne, Southampton, the Sutton family. After the service Glad provided quite a sumptuous tea. It was during the time that Kenneth Parkinson was our curate. The Rector and Kenneth talked to villagers about the service and people asked us if they could come the next year. With so many of them at work in the afternoon in the middle of the week, we transferred the service to the evening. As Glad continued to provide refreshments after the service we had to limit the numbers attending which resulted having a waiting list. At these evenings we had happy fellowship and good companionship resulting in a greater witness of the church in Botley.

Being able now to attend some of the meetings of the church, such as prayer groups or bible study as well as Advent and Lent courses, my faith deepened and I felt I had something to offer to the church, thus the call to be a Reader. I talked to the Rector about it and for some reason he did not seem surprised. His response to my feeling was very positive, he would write to the Warden of Readers in the Diocese in the next day or two to set the process of selection in motion. A few days later I had a letter asking me to make an appointment to see a senior Reader for a talk about my calling to this ministry of the church. Two weeks after that I was invited to meet the warden, Canon Heritage, Residentiary Canon of Portsmouth Cathedral and part time teacher at the Portsmouth Grammar School for Boys. A very kind man, easy to talk to, who told me at the end of our time together that what the church was looking for in an applicant to be a Reader was someone who was keen and able to help and assist the Incumbent. He was sure I met the criteria and accepted me for training. He assigned Canon Norman Miller, who was the Vicar of Titchfield at the time, to be my tutor and I would hear from him in due course. Again, he was a very kindly man who understood my situation of having only limited time to set aside for study. He told me not to worry and submit the work when it was completed.

So it was then that on 1st November 1968, All Saints Day, I was licenced as a Reader by Canon Heritage at All Saints', Botley. Being our Patronal Festival, Philip Duke-Baker had invited the Vicar and people of Curdridge, (many of them came to Botley to do their shopping or see the doctor), as well as the Vicar and people of the Parish of Hedge End, which at one time had been part of the parish of Botley, to this very special occasion for me and the parish. Among the personal friends of ours who made the effort to attend were the Cozens's, the Henry's and Sutton's from Southampton (Edwin Sutton came down from Birmingham to join his family), Dorothy and Horace Rodgers from Salisbury, Dorothy a childhood friend of Glad's, Amy and George Quantrell from Eastleigh and more local friends, Kitty Fox, Rhona and Len Lyon plus the regular friends and congregation of All Saints. The church was packed, the licencing part of a Sung Eucharist service had well-chosen hymns and the choir rendered a suitable anthem. An inspiring sermon by Canon Heritage made it a most impressive and meaningful service, so much so, that Len Lyon went to his Vicar after the service with the request to be confirmed, which he was a few months later, and then became an ardent and regular worshipper at St. John's in Hedge End. I felt very humble that evening, with all the people making the effort to come to church on such a dreadful day, weather-wise. It had rained all day and in the evening the heavens opened even wider and it was chucking it down. There was local flooding that evening, but thank God, all went well.

Chapter 25

Road to Holy Orders:
The next step

The next step came during the time I was studying for my Reader's licence. As I got deeper into my studies I had an urge to make a greater commitment to the Lord and felt the call to the priesthood. With livestock farming one could never be sure whether or not the animals needed you at a time when you were expected at church, especially when rostered to preach. The animals would take priority then, they were after all ones responsibility. Self-interest would come first and the Lord's service second. I felt, if accepted for training, we would have to give up the farm as a non-stipendiary position could not be an option for me if I made this greater commitment. I spoke to Glad about it who understood how I felt having supported me and still did in my studies and writings to become a Reader. She would be sad to leave Le Nid which had been her home for the last fifty years, but if I was called she would go with me wherever the Lord sent me. Once more I went to the Rector and spoke to him about it. He fully understood my feeling of being called to the ordained ministry at this stage not having completed my studies. He suggested I obtained my Reader's licence first; get some experience of Parish work and pastoral care, as well as church work in general, before he would set in motion the selection process for ordination. In the meantime he would train me as if I were his Curate and not his Reader.

After I was licenced as a Reader a year went by, nothing happened and I was anxious to make a start at least to be interviewed and to find out whether or not I would be accepted for training. Another year went by and still nothing happened. I began to think the Rector had forgotten all about me. All the time I endeavoured to learn as much as I could and I took note of what Philip did and how he did it, and tried to be of as much help to him as possible. Then the day came. One Thursday morning, when I was in church to assist him with the morning Communion service, he told me he had written to the Bishop recommending me to be selected for ordination and that he had also sent a letter to the same effect to the Diocesan Director of Ordination. The reason he had now done so, he told me, was that he was about to retire and he could not see himself carrying on without me. He tendered his letter of resignation to the Bishop saying he was retiring for health reasons, which was perfectly true, as we all knew he was not in the best of health. He hid it well, it must be said, and was seldom absent from church unless otherwise engaged or on holiday.

In due course the Director of Ordination in the diocese contacted me and a similar course of interviews, as to that of Readers, took place only this time an additional step in the process was to attend a residential selection conference as the result of it was also taken into account in the overall selection process. The question then, would the Diocesan Selectors think I was suitable to go before the selection board? Apparently I was, as my name was forwarded to the head office in London. My being recommended for further consideration was entirely due to the way Philip Duke-Baker trained me when I was his Reader. One of the jobs the secretaries that served on the selection board, ACCM as it was known then, had to do was to find a suitable time and venue for the candidate to attend. There were a number of them throughout the year in all parts of the country. In my case the secretary that acted as chairman at my selection conference bent just about all the rules to make it possible for me to attend a conference at all. These selection conferences were held mostly in retreat houses, or similar venues, were residential and lasted from Monday evening until Friday morning. With my commitment at home, I could not be away for four consecutive nights, so I was booked in for a conference at Old Alresford Place near Winchester in the last week in November 1970. The arrangements were that I would have to be in Alresford by 09.00 and stay until all the day's programme was complete, usually 21.00. So I spent 12 hours with my fellow candidates to get to know them and to be known. For me that meant an early start milking the cows and feeding the pigs and off I sped across country in the dark with little traffic about. I was greeted warmly, especially on my birthday, and in the evening I raced home to see if there was anything needing to be done which Glad could not cope with during the day. From mid-morning onwards until after the pigs were fed in the late afternoon friends came, including one of my sponsor's Charles Bowers, to help Glad with the heavier work. My other sponsors were Dr.Pern and Gladys Maffey. As for the evening milking, guess who, good old Fred Taplin. On the last day at the end of the evening session we all went into Alresford and had a drink. I said my good byes and thanked the secretary for guiding us through the interviews, because I was not returning the following morning , as after breakfast the candidates made their way home whilst the selectors stayed behind until they had decided each candidates future. On Saturday morning I had a letter from John Phillips, our Diocesan Bishop, congratulating me on my being recommended for training.

Where to apply for a place was the next thing to sort out. Not every college allowed their married students to live out. The nearest and most suitable one for us was Salisbury Theological College. There married students could live out from the beginning of their training. Chichester was another possibility, this was the Bishop's choice, but there the married students had to be fulltime residents for the first term or two. Glad was not at all happy about this as she would be in a strange place with new surroundings, no friends, and no husband. Chichester was not a happy prospect. After some discussion about all this it was agreed I that I should make Salisbury my first choice. Without hesitation I sent a letter requesting to become a student at the college. To support me in my application, I had a number of friends who knew the Principal, Canon Harold Wilson. They had either worked with him in the past on some church initiative, or were fellow students with him when they studied for ordination in Salisbury. All of them wrote to the Principal giving the reasons for their support. Glad and I had an invitation for an interview early in February when we talked to the Principal in a very relaxed manner for an hour or so. He felt we would fit in well at the college and could make a valuable contribution.

He then took us to see the bursar to talk about financial matters and living accommodation. As we proposed to buy our own house, we were not making demands on the already overstretched housing pool for married students, especially the newlyweds such as Kenneth and Sarah Stevenson. Kenneth later became my Bishop when he was appointed to the See of Portsmouth. By the time we had finished talking to the bursar it was lunch time. We were taken to the dining room and joined the Principal for the mid-day meal. Before he said prayers he introduced us as future members of the college starting with the Autumn Term. After lunch we were taken on a quick tour of the college by two of the students, one single and one married, who also talked about the social life in the college. Before we left for home we visited Castle Street where most of the Estate Agents have their offices to pick up some information on the houses that were on the market in Salisbury and nearby villages. On the way home I was extremely happy that at least the near future for us was taken care of. Glad on the other hand was rather quiet and subdued as she had to leave the place that was her home for the last fifty years. For me to go to Salisbury on my own and for Glad to stay on at Le Nid was not an option as I needed her with me for practical and moral support. As she said, she could always go to see Dorothy and Horace Rodgers who might cheer her up when she was low in spirit.

The news that I was to be training in Salisbury was received with great joy by all our friends inside as well as outside the church. We now made definite moves to sell up. First we chose an Estate Agent and put the holding on the market. Then we started the sale of the livestock. They mostly went for slaughter. There was no great hurry to do so, as we had till the end of July before we would leave. Over the next few weeks we loaded the trailer with all the old iron that had accumulated over fifty years which could then be towed away on it if so desired. We had no problem with that as the chap that bought our tractor also bought the trailer and old iron. The bees we gave away to one of the local beekeepers who had been very helpful to me over the years. As for the property, there were plenty of potential buyers and the highest offer was accepted. Finding a house to buy took a little while. We had to make several trips to Salisbury before we found the one that suited us. Eventually we did, it was 49 Lower Road, Bemerton. Just across the road from us was the river Wylye with the water meadows beyond and the river Nadder could be seen in the distance. It was a desirable part of the city to live in. On the third of August we moved to Salisbury. That gave us enough time to settle in and find our way around the City before commencement of the term on 13th August 1971 and another phase in life for both of us.

Chapter 26

The Road to Holy Orders: The Final Leg

Starting my training and looking ahead to the future was quite exciting in many ways, breaking with the past was not. Le Nid without any livestock was dull and dreary, almost dead. Turning our backs on it was almost a relief, leaving our friends behind, people who made me welcome and helped me no end over the years, was not. On the last Sunday at All saints, after Evensong, the congregation was invited to stay on and say good bye to Glad and myself. Most of them surprisingly did, augmented by many folks from the morning congregations. It was the evening congregation that suffered most of all my 'firsts.' Leading them in prayer, my first sermon, and my first time officiating at Evensong without the Rector being present. I did my first bereavement call in Botley as well as visiting the sick. Here they were, sending us out into the world on a new mission with their blessing and good wishes. Yes, it was an emotional time saying good bye to the people of Botley who did so much, indeed went out of their way, to make me feel at home among them.

But the decision was made, the property sold, a house in Salisbury purchased, life had to go on, and it did. Yet there were moments when Glad, or Gladys as she wished to be known as from now on, felt a little homesick, which was not surprising. She felt like a fish out of water. Life on the land was a busy one and here, apart from looking after me, life was rather dull and with little purpose. As for her wish to be called Gladys from now on, it was simply because she loathed being called Glad. When as a child she requested to be called Gladys no one took any notice of her, least of all her mother. So the name stuck all these years. The move to Salisbury and the start of a new life and meeting new people, gave her the opportunity from now on to be introduced as Gladys which made her very happy. As for her, the feeling of not being part of college life did not last long. With a caring community in the college, there was a large wives' group, they soon made her part of it. The Principal too invited her to help with binding and re-covering books in the library. All this helped to make her part of the college community. As for myself, not having had any connections with academic establishments for thirty years or so, it felt very strange to be a student at my age, now approaching 46. Thankfully I was not alone nor the oldest of the Freshmen that term. There were 51 students all together starting in August that year. Twelve were in their twenties, as for the other 39, our ages ranged from 38 to 54 coming from a variety of backgrounds. There was a diplomat; an insurance agent who had worked for many years in East Africa and the Far East, mainly Japan; a factory manager; a civil servant who had worked in the Foreign and Commonwealth Office and had been stationed in many parts of the world. Quite a number of our geriatric group were ex-members of the armed forces. We had also teachers among us with one or two having taught abroad, and there was I, a Pig and Poultry Farmer! I was not the only student with a farming background though, there were two more. One whose family farmed in Dorset and the other had been a farm manager on a large estate in Wiltshire. We all got on well together and were very supportive of each other whatever our background. All but two of the mature students that started at the same time as myself were married, so over the next four months we got to know wives and children as well.

The families living in Salisbury got to know each other very quickly as they were part of college life. Certainly, Friday evenings at the College/Family Sung Eucharist, when all members of staff and students were expected to be present. Wives and children living in Salisbury also attended, because after the service we shared the evening meal together. Wives who stayed at home for family reason and lived away also joined us on special occasions such as Easter or Christmas or at the end of term when those of us, who lived in Salisbury, provided accommodation for the families of our fellow students.

Once settled into college and the new way of life, the time seemed to fly by as every term brought new experiences. The final term of our first year, between Easter and Trinity, was spent in a South London Parish near the Elephant and Castle. Our accommodation there was in a large Victorian Vicarage. The aim was to experience and share life with people who care for others and do their best to improve life of the less fortunate among us. The students were placed in hospitals or hospices. Some with Social Services or Charities. I was placed with Social Services who had their offices in the Old Kent Road. In the first week I sat in reception and observed what was going on. How people were received, how the social worker dealt with the homeless, the hungry, the destitute and emergency cases. It was quite an eye-opener to me how these workers set about solving each individual case. I also realised what an isolated life I had lived among the farming community in Hampshire in the last twenty five years. In the second week, and indeed for the rest of my time in London, I called on people who were long overdue for a visit by a social worker. Back at the office I made my report to the manager and brought the clients' files up to date, a job I very much enjoyed and found worthwhile. The experience was invaluable for my future work as a shepherd of souls among God's people and a minister in the Church of God.

The final year at college simply flew by. With final exams starting early in 1973, study and revision was a priority for me. With Gladys typing all my hand written work, no easy task it must be said as my writing was more of a scribble and always had been even in my school days which often got me into trouble. It also gave me more time for study and research of the subject I was writing about. Looking for a parish in which I might serve my Title began in earnest as well. My mentor, and dear friend, Philip Duke-Baker kept an eye on me all the while making sure I went to a parish in which I could happily exercise my ministry. Fortunately, it took up not too much of our time. I looked at only two parishes. The first one, apart from the Churchmanship, was not at all suitable for me. I would have felt like a fish out of water. I would have been the junior among eleven clergy, yet the oldest of them all. Not that the younger colleagues of the team could teach me a thing or two about parish life and being a priest in the Church of England, but I felt uneasy about it all and told the Bishop so. He fully understood and the next parish he invited me to look at seemed just right not only for myself, but Gladys as well.

By Easter 1973 exams were over, a parish in which I could serve my Title secured, so the pressure was off. Most of the time in college now was spent in the library reading at leisure, making final notes for future use. All members of staff, Principal, Tutors and Office Staff alike, were anxious to help us to be ready for whatever the future might bring. In fact all the staff had been most helpful to me and anxious for me to feel at home and make my time in Salisbury a happy experience. The tutors of the Old and New Testaments as well as Geno Tellini, who lectured in Doctrine, offered to obtain textbooks printed in German to help me with my studies, for which I thanked them but declined, as apart from studying the subjects in the curriculum, what I needed more than anything else was to increase my English vocabulary and studying subjects in German, I felt, would only complicate matters. As it turned out I made the right decision as I kept up well with the rest of my group. In fact when it came to doctrine and liturgy I was top of the class, my Lutheran upbringing no doubt! The two years in college gave me a new outlook on life and broadened my horizon, it had filled in lots of gaps in my education, and I would not have missed it for anything in the world.

Our time in Salisbury had shown us again the kindness and warm-heartedness of the British people. Not only by the staff and members of the college but also by our neighbours in Bemerton who were most welcoming, none of them church goers, it must be said, yet all anxious to make us feel at home and one of them. All of them offered help whenever needed. It was all very touching, specially so when only after two years among them on the day of our moving to our new parish, all of them came with gifts, some monetary, to say goodbye and wish us well for the future.

Next stop was Portsdown Hill, on the northern outskirts of Portsmouth. The Curates house there was owned and maintained by the Parish. So it was in good order and everything was functioning. Our move from Salisbury to Portsmouth went very smoothly and the Vicar was there to welcome us. The neighbours too, bid us welcome and hoped we would be happy in 157 The Dale, Widley, our new address. We had just one week to settle in before I went into my Ordination Retreat, being the final chapter on the road to ordination. On the Thursday before Ordination, which was set for Sunday 1st July 1973. All the 12 ordinands, 6 of us to be made Deacon, 6 to be priested, gathered at the Diocesan Retreat House in Catherington. It was the first time that I had met any of the other candidates. We used the time before the official start of the retreat to get to know each other and learn a bit of what was going to happen from the six brethren that been through the same procedure twelve months ago.

There to welcome us was the Warden of the house, the Bishop of Bedford, who was the retreat conductor, and one of our Archdeacons. The two and a half days before our ordination were very relaxing as everything was done in a quiet and unhurried manner with plenty of time for prayers and meditation. After Supper on the eve of our ordination the Bishop came to visit us with the Diocesan Registrar to complete the legal side that goes with ordination in the Church of England. Sunday morning arrived and we were all up and about before the rising bell sounded. After getting dressed and saying Morning Prayer we had breakfast, packed our few belongings and made our way to Southsea where the ordination service was to take place. It was in the Church of St. Jude a very large church and as always, on these occasions, filled to capacity. We went straight into a committee room and robed, neither having seen a member of the family or any friends on our way in. When all was set and ready, the rather lengthy service began.

The service went well as expected. Those to be made Deacons were presented first to the Bishop, the Right Reverend John Phillips, by the Venerable Ronald Scruby, the Archdeacon of the Isle of Wight. We made our vows and pledges and then individually, in alphabetical order, knelt before the Bishop who laid his hands upon us and pronounced us Deacon in the Church of God. The Archdeacon then invested us with the stole of office. Mine was given to me by our dear friend Elizabeth Salwey. The cassock and surplice I wore was a farewell present from the congregation of All Saints, Botley on our last Sunday before leaving, which also included the preaching scarf. The Misses Maffey presented me with my academic hood. After all six candidates had received their authority of office from the Bishop, we returned to our places in the chancel.

This was followed by a similar ceremony for those who were made Deacons the year before. This time it was the

Archdeacon of Portsmouth, the Venerable Christopher Prior, who made the presentation to the Bishop, requesting the Deacons to be priested. The Bishop then laid his hands upon each of them in turn, this time joined by all the priests in the congregation, giving them the authority of a Priest.

The service took about two hours but it was worth it after all the hard work that went before and the sacrifices made by the families of the candidates, not least by Gladys, who had found it very hard, never having ventured far from Botley, until we had moved to Salisbury two years earlier. But today the goal had been achieved and all the friends, that made the effort to come to the ordination to pray and to support us, were outside the church to greet us and wish us well in the new phase of our lives that had now begun. It took quite a while to speak to everyone, but I did. After all the people had departed for home, Len and Rhoda Lyons, more good friends, took us for a celebratory lunch at the Bear Hotel in Havant. Reflecting upon it, even now it seemed a very emotional and joyous day.

The real work began the next morning with a staff meeting at the vicarage. Here again, Vernon Herbert who was my Vicar, as well as Wardens, Choir Master and members of the congregation at Christ Church, Portsdown, showed me kindness and were most helpful and anxious for Gladys and myself to be happy in our ministry among them. My fellow clergy in the Havant Deanery too made us most welcome. Their wives certainly saw that Gladys needed help and support to adjust to that new life we had now entered, especially Angela Beaumont. They became life-long friends. We experienced that kindness and support and warm friendship in Purbrook as well as in Warsash and all the parishes we served.

It is this warmth and kindness, as well as the genuine welcome the British people show to strangers that made me love them. Long may it remain part of the British Character.

God bless you all.

The Author

EPILOGUE

After my Ordination on Sunday 1st July 1973, I served in the following Parishes:

Christ Church, Portsdown   1/7/1973 – 8/10/1978

St John's, Purbrook   9/10/1978 – 31/1/1991

I also held the post of and served as:

Havant Deanery Secretary for St. Luke's Hospital for Clergy in London 1979 – 1989

Chaplain to the Mayor of Havant   February 1981 – May 1982

Havant Deanery Chapter Clerk   1982 – 1987

Since I retired I have the Bishop's permission to officiate in the Diocese of Portsmouth. I help to provide cover wherever and whenever requested to do so, which is mainly in the Fareham Deanery or in the Botley Group of Parishes. Since the death of my dear wife Gladys in February 2007, I have confined my work to St. Mary's Hook-with-Warsash or All Saints Botley.